The Common Good Economy

The Common Good Economy

A New Compass

MARIANA MAZZUCATO

ALLEN LANE
an imprint of
PENGUIN BOOKS

ALLEN LANE

UK | USA | Canada | Ireland | Australia
India | New Zealand | South Africa

Allen Lane is part of the Penguin Random House group of companies
whose addresses can be found at global.penguinrandomhouse.com

Penguin Random House UK
One Embassy Gardens, 8 Viaduct Gardens, London SW11 7BW

penguin.co.uk

Penguin Random House UK

First published 2026
002

Set in 12/14.75pt Dante MT Std
Typeset by Six Red Marbles UK, Thetford, Norfolk
Printed and bound in Great Britain by Clays Ltd, Elcograf S.p.A.

The authorized representative in the EEA is Penguin Random House Ireland,
Morrison Chambers, 32 Nassau Street, Dublin D02 YH68

A CIP catalogue record for this book is available from the British Library

ISBN: 978-0-241-72224-4

Penguin Random House is committed to a sustainable future
for our business, our readers and our planet. This book is made from
Forest Stewardship Council® certified paper.

FSC www.fsc.org MIX Paper FSC® C018179

To my mother, Alessandra, whose spirit will
be with us for ever. Her kindness,
creativity and dedication to community building
taught me more than any book ever will.

Contents

Acknowledgements

I sometimes feel envious of people who can step away entirely to write a book. In theory, I took a year's sabbatical and even a wonderful month-long writing residency at the Rockefeller Villa in Bellagio. But in practice, over those two years I continued to work intensely, away from the book, with my wonderful colleagues at the UCL Institute for Innovation and Public Purpose on projects around the world. At times I worried that this meant I was not giving the book the undivided attention it deserved, and yet, without that practical work, this book would have had little meaning. It is precisely those experiences, working closely with governments and communities in Brazil, Barbados, Camden, Scotland, British Columbia and beyond, where I learned and which made writing this book necessary for me in the first place.

I worked with MP Georgia Gould, when she was leader of Camden Council in London, on ensuring that Camden's missions genuinely reflected citizen engagement; collaborated with Esther Dweck, Brazil's Minister for Public Administration, on public sector reform – from procurement to digital public infrastructure; and learned from Edel Moraes, Brazil's Secretary for Traditional Peoples, on why the Amazon Fund must be governed by the traditional communities it is meant to serve. I learned from the Prime Minister of Barbados, Mia Mottley, about the centrality of social partnership between government, business and labour to decision making in Barbados, particularly in agreeing on national missions and placing culture and Bajan identity at the heart of the process. In a visit to Mexico City's *UTOPÍAS* with the mayor's team I learned about pathbreaking ways to put art, beauty and design at the centre of community wellbeing, and through a walk around Barrio Siloé in Cali, Colombia, I learned from local youths on their battle against discrimination, crime and poverty, rebuilding a community from the ground up; and I worked with the artist Alvaro Barrington on mapping the extraordinary value that carnivals bring to the world, from Notting Hill in London to Salvador, Bahia in Brazil: if only we knew how to value and fund them properly. All of these experiences shaped the arguments in these pages.

Along the way, I also came to better understand the deep distrust many people feel towards governments and businesses after decades of being left behind – invited into change through new slogans, but rarely through genuine participation and transformation. I felt the impatience of younger generations with our collective inaction, particularly on climate change and global injustice. This book is mainly for the youth of tomorrow, who deserve a better world and one that is full of hope and economic tools that can deliver.

I am deeply grateful to the many people who helped bring this book to life. First and foremost, my three research assistants – Carla Rainer, Anna Hope Emerson and Camila Idrovo – who, over two years, passed the baton between them with extraordinary care. Their attention to detail, thoughtful conversations and willingness to challenge the structure of the book were invaluable. I am especially thankful to my colleagues Rainer Kattel and Carlota Perez, who read the manuscript and, as always, offered incisive comments grounded in their deep thinking about the state and future of capitalism. Thanks also to Ted Clayton, De'Sean Weber, Dan Chandler and Michael Prest, and to my wonderful fellow writers at the Rockefeller Foundation's Bellagio residency for their suggestions and contributions.

My son, Leon Cresto-Dina, has been an inspiration for his commitment to making the criminal justice system less prejudiced and unfair. His conviction that crime amongst youth can only be fought by investing in their social and economic wellbeing is an example of how the common good must begin with dignity, care and creation of places where people truly feel valued.

Stuart Proffitt, my editor at Allen Lane, once again provided not only guidance but meticulous edits – always measured, never overwhelming. I am thankful to his entire team and equally thankful to my agent, Sarah Chalfant, and her team at Wylie, who accompany a book along its global journey with such care.

Finally, I deeply thank my children, Leon, Micol, Luce and Sofia – and husband Carlo – for making my life so fun and full of love even when it all feels too much. Also my father, who showed me the excitement of being a questioning academic, and my very dear mother, Alessandra, to whom the book is dedicated, who incorporated all the attributes of empathy and learning that the common good requires.

And to my students at the UCL Institute for Innovation and Public Purpose, who inspire me every day, for their passion, curiosity and impatience for a better way to govern this planet we all inhabit.

As always, any errors, exaggerations, rants or awkwardness that remain are entirely of my own making.

Figures and tables

Figures

Tables

PART I

From Corrections to Objectives

Practical men, who believe themselves to be quite exempt from any intellectual influences, are usually the slaves of some defunct economist. Madmen in authority, who hear voices in the air, are distilling their frenzy from some academic scribbler of a few years back.

– John Maynard Keynes (1883–1946),
The General Theory of Employment, Interest and Money

1.

Why we need a common good economy

We live in a world in which climate change is projected to cause 83 million excess deaths by the end of the century due to rising temperatures, with the most vulnerable people being hit the hardest. A world in which 4.5 billion people lack essential health services, and where 2 billion people do not have access to safe drinking water. All this while the scale of wealth amassed by tech billionaires and financial sector executives has reached levels that eclipse entire nations, exposing the deepening inequality driven by financial markets and rapid technological progress, in the face of which governments seem increasingly powerless.

In such a world many understandably no longer believe in our ability to collaborate and solve problems together. Indeed, the multilateral system is under threat, with a surge of nationalism and *make my own country great again* rhetoric, intensifying geopolitical tensions to levels we have not seen since the Second World War. In this world, the idea that 'empathy is for wimps' takes hold, going back to the age-old dogma that it is through self-interested actions that society becomes more productive.

And yet it does not have to be this way. The problems we face today have as much to do with what we believe about ourselves (*are we self-interested or are we collaborative?*) and the way we value each other (*is value created by one lone genius or is it collectively created?*) as with the resulting decisions we make every day on how to structure our economies (*are we only intervening when things go wrong or are we collectively setting goals to where we want to go?*).

Much of my work has focused on challenging the outdated economic paradigms that have led us to believe that we are purely self-interested, that value is created by only a few individuals and that the best a government can do is fix market failures. A big part of this has been helping governments develop their capacity and capabilities to solve problems by setting ambitious goals and tackling them in a collaborative way, with attention to how all policy levers can be redesigned in an outcomes and mission-oriented way. My previous books reflect much of this thinking.

In *The Entrepreneurial State* (2013), I argued that value is not solely created by the private sector but is co-created with the state and other actors, and how the myths that arise when we do not admit this are used to lobby for wealth to be shared inequitably. In *The Value of Everything* (2018), I sought to expand the notion of collective value creation into a different way to understand value, and especially to create a more rigorous understanding of the difference between value creation and value extraction – or what the classical political economists called profits versus rent. In *Mission Economy* (2021), I advanced the idea that the only way for an economy to have direction and purpose is with mission-oriented policy tools, helping to steer the cooperation between public and private actors around the biggest problems of our time, from protecting biodiversity, to reaching net zero, to reducing the digital divide. If done right, this can help achieve good growth: public and private investments that catalyse innovation towards a more sustainable and inclusive economy. And in *The Big Con* (2023), my co-author and I looked at the capacity and capabilities required inside our governments to work in an outcomes-oriented way with others, and the decimation of that capacity over the last decades due to privatization, outsourcing and the over-use of consultancies inside government institutions.

In trying to put the ideas in my previous books into practice, it has become more and more clear to me that to successfully address the big problems we face today – such as health for all and combating climate change – we need not only an *entrepreneurial state* and *mission-oriented policies* but also a new economics of collective action around *the common good*. This is because all the problems we face require collaboration between different actors and collective intelligence between them. If we do not know how to work together, with collective value creation at the centre, then we cannot reach 'good' outcomes. And critically, that notion of 'good' cannot be just filling the gaps for what the private sector does not do. It must be an objective we reach together – not a correction for something that is missing. As Keynes's quote at the start of Part I reminds us, this means moving beyond the traditional economic theory wedded to market failures or government failures. So long as 'public goods' (such as public roads, national defence and basic research) are just correcting for the absence of private sector investment in these areas, then it is not a theory of the public good but a theory of what the private sector is missing. And so long as the 'commons' (such as community-managed lakes and forests) are correcting for weak governance of both businesses and state actors, structuring ambitious and proactive collaboration around shared objectives will remain difficult. A framework based on failures of different kinds is – by definition – negative and reactive and will ultimately fail.

Throughout the book I develop the concept of a common good economy as an economy that is outcomes driven, with participation, learning, transparency, reciprocity and sharing rewards at the heart of how collaboration towards those outcomes occurs. It means getting economic relationships and structures right from the start, instead of correcting and picking up the pieces afterwards. This perspective shifts the question from 'What should the state (or business) do?' to 'How can we – governments, businesses, communities, individuals – work together to solve challenges that affect us all? And how do we value each other as part of that process?'

The common good cannot be an afterthought but must be placed at the centre of all economic relationships. For example, during a health pandemic, if the goal is to allow all people across the world to have access to vaccines (the outcome), it is not enough to simply produce the vaccines (the output). *How* they are produced matters. Similarly, if a fund is set up to help improve the lives of people living in Brazil's Amazon forest, then the degree to which the people of the Amazon participate in the fund's governance matters. Putting the goal at the centre of innovation collaborations and the structure of financing mechanisms, so that knowledge and power are shared, is critical for the common good. This is what it means to care about *pre-distribution* as much as redistribution.

I have long argued, in my books and other writings, that the problem in capitalism is not growth per se, but how we have gone about it. We have the wrong metrics, which confuse price with value – so that polluting actually increases GDP when someone is paid to clean it up. We have the wrong valuation: not taking into account that the cost of inaction (on areas like climate change) is greater than the cost of action. We have the wrong evaluation: prioritizing short-term wins, instead of long-term economy-wide transformation. And in the end, we have the wrong debate: those who argue for de-growth, or those who argue growth has to come at the expense of solving problems like global warming. By focusing on economy-wide goals that determine the structure of public–private contracts, like decarbonizing transport through investments in sustainable mobility; by focusing on long-term impacts so as not to get caught up in narrow discussions of (false) budget constraints; and by making sure that we value and reward all those who contribute to the health, wellbeing and productivity of our economies, we can achieve good growth. What the book does is give much more attention to how the relationships between all actors are critical to our ability to achieve good growth: the relationships between business and government (e.g. water rights, property rights), between capital and labour (e.g. sharing rewards), and citizens and the state (e.g. having a voice and real deliberation in local governance). What is the point of talking about a new greener economy, if the relationships along the way replicate the key problems in the old economy?

To focus on these relationships I draw on the philosophical tradition of the common good, from the ancient Greeks who worried about 'the good life' through modern communitarian thinkers who have placed emphasis on relationships and community building, as well as holistic approaches from non-Western philosophy that emphasize the interdependence of individuals and a closer relationship with nature. Critically, this means paying as much attention to *how* all economic actors relate to each other as to *what* we aim to achieve. Aristotle linked the *telos* (the goal) to the *polis* (locus of political participation). To meet today's existential challenges, we must do the same. We must become intentional about creating better economic relationships that enable us to work together in pursuit of the common good. Just as in an orchestra, where the way musicians play together is as important as what they play, so too must our economies be evaluated not only on what they produce but also on how different participants collaborate and are valued in the process.

In this, we can also learn from biologists, who devote far more attention than economists to studying ecosystems and the ways in which different organisms relate to one another. The common good depends on partnerships and relationships designed so that the ecosystem of actors is *symbiotic* and *mutualistic*, rather than on the parasitic and extractive dynamics that are so prevalent today.

Structure of the book

This book is structured in three parts: Part I considers theory, Part II practice and Part III the places where people meet and relationships are built.

Part I begins by exploring broader understandings of the common good, drawing on insights from philosophy, biology and Indigenous knowledge. The exploration is focused on how these different perspectives have looked at the way that actors in a system interact, through relationships that embody the objectives being sought. It then examines how the idea of the 'good' has been narrowly represented within economics and considers how we might reimagine economic thinking by learning from the common good tradition in other fields to rethink how relationships and structures can be shaped around collective action. The section concludes with key elements that need to underlie the common good compass: market shaping, symbiotic ecosystems and collective value creation. These are used to rethink the governance of all actors in the economy and their relationships: government, business, finance and labour.

Part II uses the theoretical insights in Part I to build a common good 'compass' designed to guide economic actors to work together towards the common good, holding the concept to account so there is less 'common good washing'. The compass addresses both the definition of collective goals (the what) and the means of achieving them (the how). Its five elements focus on setting direction and ensuring that co-creation, knowledge sharing, benefit sharing and transparency occur throughout the process. The rest of Part II explores the five elements of the common good compass, drawing on examples from around the world where seeds of the common good have already taken root – for instance, in health innovation, where collaborations are designed to share both knowledge and rewards, or in Camden and Barbados, where genuine citizen participation has shaped goals on the ground. These seeds provide hope and valuable lessons, combating the idea that this is about utopias. Yet without a holistic framework for the common good, such efforts do not scale and remain isolated examples of progress within a wider system still shaped by reactive measures and extractive dynamics. By providing a more rigorous and practical framework for the common good, the compass can help these initiatives grow and scale into a more systemic way of structuring relationships, bringing the common good from the periphery to the centre of how we organize our economies. Each chapter examines one element of the compass in detail, but it is the interaction among all five that matters most. Neglecting any one of them leaves the framework open to capture by special interests, resulting in 'common good washing', where actors in the public or private sector claim to serve the common good or the public interest, or vague notions of 'purpose', even though their actions fail to deliver it.

Part III moves the gaze from policies and activities to actual places, both local and global, as this is where relationships are formed. If a place is designed to promote genuine participation it can make people feel valued and part of a community and enable them to flourish in the process. Such places – for example, youth centres, public libraries and community organizations – should not be seen as 'extras' to fund with spare money, but as core to our ability to value relationships and form community. The lessons from local places can help shape the global places where different countries meet to discuss common problems, whether related to global finance or 'pandemic preparedness'. If those places render the voice of some countries louder than others – as they do today – it is very hard to build trust and work together. Indeed, without global solidarity and learning from experiences across the world, we end up with nationalistic policies around 'good' that only increase inequality, worsen geopolitical tensions and make it harder to find collective solutions to our common problems.

The message of this book is one of hope: we *can* structure our relationships to collectively pursue the common good. But working collectively does not happen by chance – it must be built into the structure of the system itself. This can sound daunting. In many parts of the world, the prevailing mood is cautious at best and pessimistic at worst. A system that embraces and practises the common good can appear distant or even unattainable. That is precisely why it matters. Together, we can radically redesign our economic system around principles of the common good. This is not a trade-off for economic growth, as is often claimed. Since growth depends on public and private sector investment, if we can direct that investment towards solving problems, we can achieve 'directed' growth that steers the economy towards goals such as those around climate change, while making sure that the processes along the way create more inclusion and equity for all.

This book is for everyone who believes in building a fairer and more sustainable world: government, business leaders, educators, activists and citizens alike. Without the social movements that fought for justice and equality, we would still have children working in factories and women without the right to vote. But progress cannot rely solely on activism; equity must ultimately be embedded in the way our systems function at their core. How governments govern, how businesses make profits, and how partnerships are structured. As a mother of four teenagers, I also write this book for young people impatient with the 'blah blah blah' of previous generations – those who have talked about the politics of missions or the purpose of business while the climate continues to burn and inequality fuels global tensions. They rightly demand action now on the most pressing challenges of our time. To meet this call, we must structure our economies around the common good. There is no time to waste.

2.
The wider good outside economics

The problems we face require an immense amount of collaboration, collective intelligence and investment. If we are failing to achieve this, it is because we have chosen not to work together in an outcomes-oriented way. Why? Too often, our problems are not recognized as collective ones, leading to individualistic and nationalistic solutions. Even when they *are* recognized as collective, solutions are rarely designed to incentivize coordinated action and true collaboration, between public and private actors, and between citizens and states – whether due to distrust or to poorly designed contracts that allow one side to benefit more than the other. There also persists a false narrative that solving societal problems such as inequality or climate change is not compatible with achieving economic growth. This means that actions to resolve these problems end up happening on the periphery rather than at the centre of how we design our economies, leading to a lack of both scale and seriousness in the endeavour. It also means that attempts to improve the system happen in a reactive rather than a proactive way – correcting for failures in the economy, rather than shaping the economy to deliver on goals.

In trying to galvanize cooperation and collective action to solve global problems both within countries and between them, some leaders have appealed to the 'common good'. Pope Francis, for example, called for a common good approach to put 'community' at the heart of all socio-economic development. In his second encyclical, *Laudato si'* (2015), he defined the common good as 'the sum of those conditions of social life which allow social groups and their individual members relatively thorough and ready access to their own fulfilment' (Pope Francis, 2015, par. 156). He identified two principles from

Catholic Social Teaching to guide the pursuit of the common good: *subsidiarity*, the belief that the authority closest to a local need is best placed to address it, and the *preferential option for the poor*, which calls for the world to be seen through the eyes of the most vulnerable and to care for them. Decision making for the common good, in this view, means defending the dignity of the socially, politically and economically marginalized – not just with words but with policies and new forms of collaboration. It requires building a network of solidarity through which the unheard can participate in critical decision making.

Another world leader who has referred to the common good is UN Secretary-General António Guterres. He has called for a UN *Common Agenda* (UN, 2023b) which promotes the idea that there are global public goods such as health, water and decent housing which are essential to humanity's future and that we need a collective response to ensure universal access. In the Common Agenda report, he said: 'We must recognize that humanity's very future depends on solidarity, trust and our ability to work together as a global family to achieve common goals.' Guterres has argued that a *common agenda* must underpin the United Nations' 17 Sustainable Development Goals (SDGs). These ambitious goals represent high-level responses to global challenges, from zero poverty (SDG 1) to zero hunger (SDG 2), to health and wellbeing for all (SDG 3), gender parity (SDG 5), climate action (SDG 13) and the health of life below water (SDG 14). Yet the latest data shows we are unlikely to achieve the SDGs by the target year of 2030, and on many of them we are actually going backwards. For example, the global hunger rate rose to an estimated 9.1 per cent of the population in 2023 (between 713 and 757 million people), up from 7.5 per cent in 2019 (Sachs et al., 2025). Thus, if there was ever a time for the common good to come back to the global agenda, it is surely now.

The concept of the common good has also gained renewed attention in academic research over recent decades. A search of scholarly databases for articles and book chapters explicitly addressing the common good in their titles, abstracts or keywords shows a marked increase in its usage (Figure 1), particularly in the social sciences and

Figure 1 Academic work on the common good by year (1995–2024)

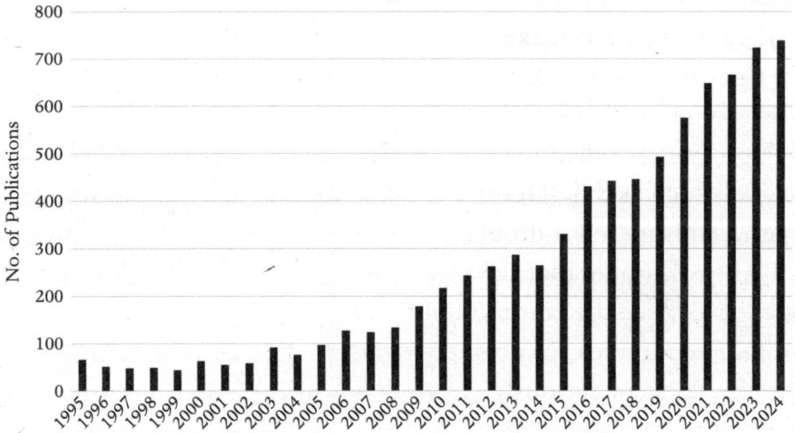

Source: Scopus

Figure 2 Academic work on the common good by subject (1995–2024)

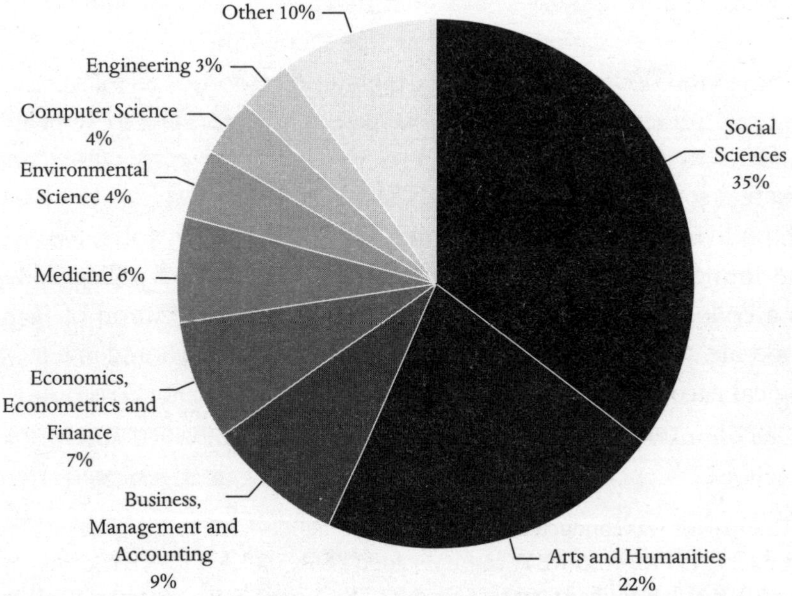

Source: Scopus

humanities, but also across a wide range of other fields, such as medicine and computer science (Figure 2).*

But how can we make sure the concept of the common good is a rigorous one that is not used lightly, but holds all to account? What does it really mean to revive the notion of the common good, as Pope Francis called for, and to use it as a foundation for collective goals such as the SDGs, as Secretary-General António Guterres urges? Is this merely a utopian idea, or is it achievable?

This book argues that achieving these goals is indeed possible, but only if we place the common good at the centre of how we structure our economies. To do so, we must first recall what it means to take the concept seriously, drawing on its long and rich tradition beyond the boundaries of traditional economics. This is important because, as we will see throughout the book, the common good is often conflated with weaker notions such as *public good*, *social value* or *public interest*, limiting its potential to serve as a guiding principle for how societies organize and pursue collective goals. As such, we begin with an exploration of its philosophical roots.

2.1 *The philosophical origins of the common good*

In Ancient Greece, the pursuit of the common good aimed to create a society that enabled individuals and communities to flourish by living in accordance with virtue. Plato and Aristotle, two of the foundational thinkers of philosophy, understood political life as a collective endeavour oriented towards the realization of 'the good life'. Their visions of the common good were rooted in teleological accounts of human nature and civic virtue. For Aristotle in particular, the *polis* (city state) was not merely an instrument for

* The analysis was conducted on the Scopus academic database using the following query: TITLE-ABS-KEY('common good') OR TITLE-ABS-KEY('common goods'), which identified texts that contained the exact phrase 'common good' or 'common goods' within their title, abstract and/or keywords.

maintaining order or facilitating economic exchange, but a moral community in which *eudaimonia* (human flourishing) was realized through active participation in public life. Plato and Aristotle, though both committed to the idea that politics should serve this higher collective purpose, diverged sharply in how they conceptualized and sought to achieve it.

In *The Republic*, Plato (*c*.428–348 BCE) envisioned a highly centralized and hierarchical system of governance, leaning toward authoritarianism. Authority, he argued, should reside in the hands of philosopher-kings, whose knowledge and virtue qualified them to rule for the benefit of the entire population. In this model, the majority of citizens should be guided by elites rather than active participation, reflecting Plato's scepticism about the capacity of most people to govern.

By contrast, in *Politics* and *Nicomachean Ethics*, Aristotle (*c*.384–322 BCE) proposed a more pluralistic and participatory model. He was the first to use the idea of the common good to distinguish between just and corrupt institutions, writing that true forms of government 'are those in which the one, or the few, or the many, govern with a view to the common interest; but governments which rule with a view to the private interest, whether of the one, or of the few, or of the many, are perversions' (Aristotle, 1984, p. 2030). In other words, for him, the *telos* (goal) of government was to serve the common good.

Unlike Plato, Aristotle rejected the idea that only a small elite could govern wisely. He viewed participation in the *polis* as a vital practice through which individuals, as 'political animals', developed moral and civic virtues, including justice, temperance, courage and wisdom. These virtues, he maintained, could be fully exercised and perfected only through deliberation and active civic engagement. For Aristotle, participation in the *polis* and the pursuit of the common good were inseparable, since the *polis* provided the setting in which citizens cultivated the virtues necessary to fulfil their mutual obligations of care and responsibility. He rejected the notion of monarchy as 'contrary to nature', arguing that disproportionate rule by one person undermined the quality on which political life depends. Genuine governance, he insisted, is defined by rule among equals rather than by relations of mastery and servitude. As such, for Aristotle, the *polis* could only exist through the active participation of its citizens. Of course, Aristotle's *polis* was deeply limited by the social norms of his time, with women, slaves and many others excluded from political participation – a reality that sharply contrasts with the inclusive vision of the common good we must seek today.

For both Plato and Aristotle, the moral and civic dimensions of political life took precedence over economic ones. By subordinating the economy to the pursuit of the common good, they largely overlooked how economic forces can shape society and influence what the common good requires. Xenophon (430–354 BCE), in contrast, was among the first thinkers to address the economy more substantively. In works such as *Oeconomicus*, he highlighted the interconnectedness of ethics and economic management, emphasizing that effective household and agricultural administration require both moral virtue and practical skill. His writings suggest that economics is not merely a technical matter but an essential component of promoting human flourishing and public welfare.

The Roman statesman and philosopher Cicero (106–43 BCE) later built upon this classical foundation, adapting the Aristotelian idea of the *polis* to the context of the Roman Republic. Cicero used the common good to distinguish true political communities from other forms of human association. He referred to the common good as *salus populi* and *utilitatis communion*, which translate as the 'safety of the people' and 'an assemblage of people in large numbers in agreement with respect to justice and a partnership for the common good'. For Cicero, a republic was not merely a collective of self-interested individuals, but a moral community 'united by their agreement on principles of justice that govern their mutual relations' (Jaede, 2017, p. 3). The welfare of people, he argued, is the highest priority and must be secured.

The medieval Italian theologian Thomas Aquinas (1225–74) later developed a Christian conception of the common good that profoundly shaped Western political thought. Aquinas integrated

Aristotle's understanding of the common good as essential to the cultivation of virtue with Christian theology, arguing that the ultimate purpose of society is to guide people towards holiness and union with God (Yuengert, 2001). He further argued that the common good is not only a particular goal, but also the way in which groups are organized. For example, a market or a political system might itself constitute a common good if its structures enable individuals to pursue higher moral and communal goals. By emphasizing that 'the forces of private interest are driven by objectives incompatible with the laws of God and nature' (Mastromatteo and Solari, 2014, p. 88), Aquinas also highlighted the necessity of public authority to ensure that private pursuits do not undermine collective welfare.

For these early thinkers, the common good was a deeply normative ideal. It defined not only what society *is* but what it *ought* to be, and the kinds of virtues, relationships and institutions necessary to sustain it. Their visions of the common good combined ethical, political and economic considerations, grounding the legitimacy of governance in its capacity to cultivate human flourishing.

2.2 *Classical political economy and liberal theory*

Intellectual and social changes in early modern Europe, particularly during the Enlightenment, produced a gradual shift in political thought, increasingly emphasizing individual freedoms and interests over moral virtue or communal goals. Thomas Hobbes (1588–1679) argued that the state's primary role was to protect individuals' ability to pursue their personal interests. Writing in the aftermath of the English Civil War, he believed that an absolute authority – the Leviathan – was necessary to avoid chaos and war, which he called 'the state of nature'. Achieving this stability required individuals to give up certain natural freedoms by entering into a social contract, through which they gained the protection, order and civil rights provided and enforced by the state. This is a very different idea from that of Jean-Jacques Rousseau (1712–78), who believed humans were naturally good, compassionate and peaceful, but are corrupted by society and its institutions. He argued that in the 'state of nature', people lived freely and harmoniously, guided by their innate sense of empathy and reason. While Hobbes saw a central authority as necessary to control chaos, Rousseau believed it was the source of inequality and moral decline.

Like Hobbes, John Locke (1632–1704) also emphasized the need to protect individual rights, but with a more optimistic view of human nature. He argued that the state's primary role was to safeguard the rights to life, liberty and private property, rather than impose absolute authority. But unlike Hobbes, Locke envisioned a government based on the consent of the governed, where political power is limited and accountable. Through this social contract, individuals retain fundamental freedoms while enjoying the protection of their rights, bridging the concerns of stability with those of personal liberty.

Building on these ideas, later Enlightenment thinkers such as Jeremy Bentham (1748–1832) developed a theory of utility as the guiding principle for law and public policy.* He argued that all human actions are motivated by the pursuit of pleasure and the avoidance of pain, and that the role of government is to organize society so as to achieve 'the greatest happiness for the greatest number'. His utilitarian framework treated every individual's happiness as equal in value, seeking to aggregate these individual interests to produce the greatest overall benefit for society as a whole.

This focus on individual preferences and their aggregation also influenced economic thought. David Hume (1711–76) and Adam Smith (1723–90) examined how social stability and prosperity could arise from the cumulative effects of individual actions. Hume argued that government is founded on utility and mutual interest, rather than

* Jeremy Bentham's theory that 'it is the greatest happiness of the greatest number that is the measure of right and wrong' (1776, p. 93) was an influential axiom and precursor to the idea of optimality or efficiency in economics. For Bentham, the utility of an act (or whether it could be considered good or bad) was determined solely by the benefits and/or costs that arise as a result (Crimmins, 2024).

on a social contract or divine right. For Hume, political authority is legitimate only insofar as it maintains order, peace and justice, conditions essential for society to thrive. Smith, building on and extending these insights, emphasized that economic order and growth often arise naturally as individuals pursue their own interests, and self-interested behaviour could generate broader social benefits. These thinkers demonstrated how political and economic thought could be linked through the analysis of incentives and behaviour.

At the same time, the German ethical economy, rooted in Hegelian philosophy, offered a counterpoint to the rising focus on individualism. Georg Wilhelm Friedrich Hegel (1770–1831) and later thinkers emphasized the need for ethical institutions and an ethical state (Mastromatteo and Solari, 2014). For them, the state was not merely a 'servant of markets' tasked with securing property rights and fixing market failures, but had a broader mandate to define and pursue the common good. Some scholars argue that Hegel's concept of the common good 'consists of rationally determined social values that bring different individuals' interests into coherence with one another' (Murphy and Parkey, 2016, p. 829). By structuring political and social institutions this way, the state can provide a framework in which the common good can be actively determined and pursued by the community.

Karl Marx (1818–83) and Friedrich Engels (1820–95) critiqued the concept of the common good, arguing that it often served to protect the interests of the ruling classes while restricting subordinate groups from pursuing their own. This perspective was later echoed by some feminist scholars, such as Martha Nussbaum (1997), regarding the perpetuation of inequitable gender relations.

By the late nineteenth and early twentieth centuries, the emphasis on individual freedoms had consolidated into a dominant liberal framework, placing individual autonomy and self-interest at the centre of political thought. John Stuart Mill (1806–73) and, later, John Rawls (1921–2002) argued that individuals are best placed to judge their own welfare and should not be subject to external restraints. Mill (1859) championed individual autonomy, resisting the authority of moral or religious communities that sought to impose goals on others. Similarly,

Rawls (1971; 1993) maintained that the state should remain neutral among competing conceptions of the good life, focusing instead on securing the freedoms and opportunities necessary for individuals to pursue their own wellbeing without coercion.

2.3 The communitarian challenge

Rawls's *A Theory of Justice* (1971) redefined political philosophy in the latter half of the twentieth century, providing a moral foundation for liberal democracy and articulating a conception of justice capable of commanding agreement among free and equal citizens. Central to his approach was the 'original position', a thought experiment in which rational individuals choose the basic principles of justice from behind a 'veil of ignorance', unaware of their class, gender, talents, religion or personal goals. This veil was used to ensure impartiality: since no one knows where they will end up in society, they are incentivized to select principles that are fair to all.

From this thought experiment, Rawls derived two principles of justice. The first guarantees equal basic liberties for all citizens, including freedom of speech, conscience and the rule of law. The second, known as the *difference principle*, permits social and economic inequalities only if they benefit the least advantaged and arise within a context of equality of opportunity. These principles prioritize freedom and equality over utilitarian calculations of aggregate welfare, shaping political and economic institutions so they promote justice and fairness for all. Yet even behind the veil of ignorance, individuals can still be assumed to be driven by their own self-interest, selecting principles that protect them should they end up in the worst-off position – effectively hedging their bets while producing rules that are fair to everyone.

Rawls has been subject to significant criticism. A key critic has been Amartya Sen, who, in *The Idea of Justice* (2009), contends that Rawls's theory of justice is overly idealized and detached from practical concerns. He critiques what he terms Rawls's 'transcendental institutionalism', the notion that we must first identify the perfectly just society before we can act to reduce injustice. For Sen, justice is not about constructing an ideal world but about comparing real world arrangements to determine which is better or worse. In this view, justice is an ongoing process of public reasoning and practical improvement, not a fixed destination reached through conceptual design alone.

Sen also challenges Rawls's focus on the distribution of 'primary goods' – freedoms and resources, like income and wealth, assumed to be universally valuable. Instead, he insists that what matters is what people are actually able to do with those goods, giving rise to his influential 'capability' approach (discussed below). Justice, according to Sen, should be measured by individuals' real freedoms to pursue the lives they value, not merely by the formal allocation of resources. While sharing Rawls's commitment to equality and fairness, Sen advocates a more flexible, empirically grounded and pluralistic approach that centres on people's actual agency in the real world rather than hypothetical choices made behind a veil of ignorance.

Communitarian philosophers have been fierce challengers of Rawls and the broader liberal tradition for portraying individuals as isolated, autonomous agents, rather than as members of broader social, cultural and political communities. Emerging largely in the late twentieth century, communitarianism emphasizes the importance of social bonds, shared values and collective responsibilities. At its core, this vision holds that human beings cannot be separated from the communities to which they belong, as individual identities are fundamentally shaped by relationships with others. This perspective does not deny individual agency; rather, it insists that agency is always shaped within a social context. From this point of view, the liberal conception of the individual is seen as deeply flawed as it overlooks the interdependence that defines human life.

Michael Sandel, a leading communitarian philosopher, develops this critique in *Liberalism and the Limits of Justice* (1982). He introduces the concept of the 'unencumbered self' to describe Rawls's model of the individual, imagined in the 'original position' as capable of selecting principles of justice independently of specific values, attachments or communal identities. Sandel argues that this is an unrealistic and morally empty view of personhood as people are not abstract choosers but socially embedded beings, shaped by histories, relationships and shared moral traditions. He further criticizes Rawls for prioritizing justice over a substantive notion of the common good. According to him, relying solely on justice and equal rights overlooks the socially constructed nature of individual identities. He suggests that a good life is only achievable when people recognize themselves as integral members of a community. A just society must therefore engage in public reasoning about the common good, rather than simply mediating between private interests.

Other communitarian thinkers reinforce and expand these critiques. Charles Taylor (1989) emphasizes the role of 'recognition' in identity formation, arguing that our sense of self is deeply dependent on how we are perceived within our community. Alasdair MacIntyre (1981) highlights how the fragmentation of modern society has eroded coherent moral language, advocating a return to virtue ethics rooted in tradition and community practices. Amitai Etzioni (2004) blends communitarian ideals with modern democracy, emphasizing the need to balance individual rights with social responsibilities and arguing that strong communities are essential for a healthy society. While their approaches differ, communitarians share the central concern of rebuilding the social fabric in increasingly individualistic societies. Drawing on Aristotle, they emphasize that living a good life depends not only on what we want to achieve (*telos*) but also on the communal relationships and places (*polis*) through which those goals are pursued.

Some scholars argue that the gap between Rawls and his communitarian critics may be narrower than it appears. While the 'original position' seems to encapsulate the atomistic individualism that communitarians rightly criticize, some argue that Rawls's thought experiment is meant to capture the moral ideal of citizens as members of an ongoing political community, who want to live with their fellow citizens on terms of fairness and reciprocity. Moreover, Rawls explicitly says that 'the values of community are not only essential but realizable' within his framework and readily acknowledges that our values are shaped by our social context. Recognizing these points, we can draw on both traditions. While Rawls provides principled grounds for securing fundamental freedoms and a fair distribution of resources, communitarians remind us that markets and institutions must be designed to nurture the relationships and shared purposes that make human flourishing possible (Chandler, 2024).

Still, communitarian philosophy is particularly important for a common good economy because it stresses the relational obligation of care and collective responsibility that members of a community share (Dupré, 1993; Hussain, 2018). From this perspective, the common good is not simply the sum of individual interests but also encompasses common interests and mutual concern. It is understood as 'the promotion of the good that is common to all members of society by virtue of their common humanity: human authenticity, the growth of personality, or of a personhood that transcends both individual and society' (Lutz, 2002, p. 37). These 'goods' can include what we think of as public goods and common-pool resources in economics (developed in Chapter 4), as well as the overall social wellbeing of the community. Some scholars expand this understanding to also include self-determination, equality of status, opportunity and treatment, and sharing in the growth of productivity (Wilber, 1987).

For communitarians, achieving the common good requires political institutions that prioritize collective goals over individual interests (Mastromatteo and Solari, 2014). Sandel, advocating a 'politics of the common good', argues that 'when politics goes well, we can know a good that we cannot know alone' (Sandel, 1982, p. 183). Communitarian philosophy thus emphasizes that political life should cultivate civic engagement, strengthen community bonds, and shape citizens' values and identities, making the common good central to governance. This has implications for the way communitarians view the economy.

In *What Money Can't Buy*, Sandel (2012) explores the moral limits of markets, challenging the expansion of market thinking into spheres of life where moral and civic values should take precedence. He argues that certain goods are diminished or even corrupted when they are bought and sold. As he puts it, 'markets are not mere mechanisms; they embody certain values. And sometimes market values crowd out nonmarket norms worth caring about' (Sandel, 2012, p. 113). Drawing on Aristotle, Sandel conceives of the common good as the cultivation of virtue and civic responsibility, qualities he believes market logic erodes. For this reason, he contends that an economy oriented towards the common good should rely heavily on non-market mechanisms to preserve and promote moral and civic norms. He develops this further in *The Tyranny of Merit: What's Become of the Common Good?* (2020), where he argues that modern meritocracy has weakened the common good by framing success as a personal achievement rather than a collective effort. This mindset, he suggests, fosters division and moral disconnection, as those who fall behind are seen as deserving their fate while the successful claim undue moral credit. Sandel instead envisions the common good as a shared civic project grounded in humility, solidarity and mutual recognition of our dependence on one another.

While Sandel's critique rightly highlights the moral limits of markets, the risk is that his analysis creates a markets-in versus markets-out mentality, leaving certain spheres outside the domain of market exchange, rather than showing how markets can be redesigned to incorporate moral and civic values. In building a new economics of the common good, I argue we should not accept that good can only be achieved outside market processes, or inside by simply fixing market failures. That leaves problematic notions of the market untouched. As will be argued in Chapter 4, to do so we must develop a theory and practice of 'market shaping', not fixing, with the goal of aligning economic activity with shared societal objectives, and taking care to embody principles of the common good inside structured economic relationships.

2.4 Lessons on collective intelligence from biology

Beyond political philosophy, disciplines such as biology and the social sciences can deepen our understanding of the common good, offering valuable lessons on cooperation, collaboration, collective intelligence and mechanisms for sharing rewards fairly. Insights from evolutionary biology and behavioural economics show that humans have developed sophisticated mechanisms for cooperation based on reciprocity and fairness. Contrary to traditional economic theory, which assumes humans act solely out of self-interest and competition, experiments across diverse cultures show that people consistently reject unfair distributions even at a personal cost, suggesting that our sense of reciprocity extends beyond rational calculation (Bowles and Gintis, 2013). This instinct for fairness is likely as fundamental to our success as our capacity for reason or language and should inform the way we design our economic institutions.

Given the importance of reciprocity, it is also key to understand what it is not. While economists often use the concept of partnerships and ecosystems to look at public–private relationships, they often treat them as 'neutral' and thus are not as rigorous as biologists are when using such words.

Figure 3 Parasitic vs. mutualistic ecosystems

Two types of ecosystems

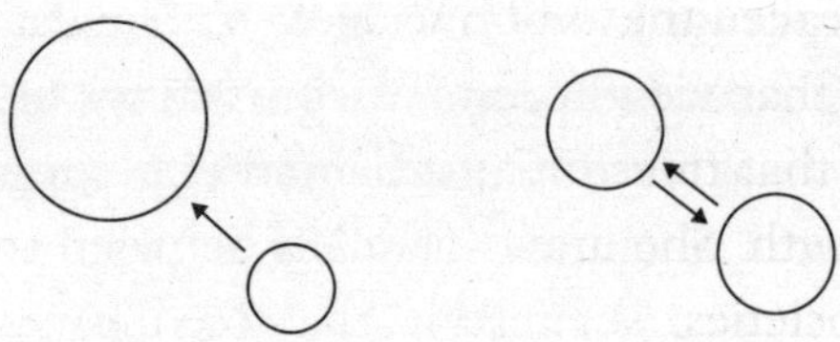

Parasitic
A harmful relationship in which one group (the parasite) benefits while others are harmed

Mutualistic
A symbiotic relationship in which all groups benefit

Source: Author's construction based on Mazzucato (2022b)

Biologists recognize that relationships between organisms are never neutral and that the outcome of different types of ecosystems depends on the way in which these relationships are shaped (Thrall et al., 2007; Gowdy and Ferrer-i-Carbonell, 1999). Parasitic ecosystems benefit one organism at the expense of others, whereas symbiotic or mutualistic ecosystems allow all organisms to benefit while keeping each other in check. When balance in the ecosystem is disrupted, by one organism becoming disproportionately powerful, the ecosystem is threatened with collapse. Figure 3 illustrates the difference. The human gut provides a clear example. Too many harmful bacteria lead to a loss of microbial diversity, which can bring on serious health issues, highlighting the importance of maintaining microbial diversity and balance for overall system health.

Another important insight from biology relates to how organisms communicate, collaborate and organize to achieve collective intelligence. Biologist Stefano Mancuso (2021) emphasizes that plants distribute their sensory and decision-making capabilities throughout their entire organism, with each part of the plant independently sensing, responding and adapting to environmental changes. Mancuso suggests that humans can learn from plant resilience by designing organizations, technologies and societies that are decentralized and adaptive, making them more dynamic and better equipped to handle uncertainty and change.

Similarly, forest ecologist Suzanne Simard (2022) has studied how trees communicate via underground mycorrhizal fungal networks, which she has called the 'wood wide web'. She challenges previous work on trees that view forests as competitive environments and argues instead that trees often collaborate to support each other's health and growth. She draws parallels between tree communities and human societies, suggesting that communication and nurturing relationships are essential for the health of both forests and humans. Both Mancuso and Simard offer valuable insights into how humans can learn from plant ecosystems to address complex societal challenges, such as climate change, and promote the common good by valuing all actors in a system.

These ecological lessons are not new to economic thought. Indeed, back in the 1700s, the Physiocrats (early French economists trying to formalize economics) used biological metaphors to describe a system's ability to reproduce itself (Quesnay, 1766; Mazzucato, 2018c). They were particularly concerned about the parasitic relationships between farmers and landlords, where the wealth produced by the former was extracted by the latter rather than reinvested back into the system. The Physiocrats therefore labelled the merchants and the landlords as the 'sterile' class, highlighting the risk that such value extraction could render the system unproductive. The Physiocrats' use of biological metaphors is different from modern economics' use of Newtonian physics (and the related mathematics of calculus), with its emphasis on equilibrium, centres of gravity and averages (Mazzucato, 2000; Beinhocker, 2007).

Various disciplines have considered how to better understand the dynamics of collaboration and collective intelligence. Scholars of the 'collaborative economy' study the conditions that allow communities to flourish, emphasizing community building, inclusivity and sustainability (Gomez-Alvarez and Morales-Sánchez, 2021). Relatedly, work on 'collective intelligence', emerging from fields such as sociology and psychology, captures the idea that people working together can solve problems better than they can individually, resulting in continuous experimentation and innovation (Malone and Bernstein, 2015). Moreover, this intelligence is even greater when there is social diversity, as a growing body of research has shown that diverse groups make better decisions (Phillips, 2014). However, these discussions are generally about grassroots participation, and less about structuring economic relationships. We explore how these insights can be used to put the common good at the centre of our economies in Part II.

2.5 Insights from Indigenous knowledge and nature

In many academic fields there is a Eurocentric bias that has long marginalized other intellectual traditions and reinforced colonial hierarchies of knowledge. In philosophy, this narrow view obscures the fact that profound philosophical traditions around the common good have long existed outside the West, including Confucianism in East Asia, Islamic philosophy across the Middle East, Ubuntu in sub-Saharan Africa, Buddhist and Hindu thought in South Asia, and the diverse worldviews of Indigenous peoples across the Americas, Oceania and beyond.* Each of these offers rich and distinctive perspectives on ethics, politics, the common good, self and community. A full exploration of all these non-Western traditions would require an entire book of its own (see an attempt in Baggini, 2018). In this section, I explore Indigenous philosophies because they offer a holistic understanding of self that is inseparable from both community and the natural world. This ecological dimension speaks directly to a central concern of the common good: that human flourishing depends not only on community but also on the health of our planet.

Many Indigenous worldviews understand the self as emerging from relationships with community, the land and the spiritual world, rather than as something defined in isolation. This stands in contrast to conventional Western liberal thought, which prioritizes individual preferences and tends to interpret collective claims as reducible to their sum. By rejecting this separation, Indigenous communities view the individual and the collective as mutually sustaining, reflecting a more holistic understanding of the interdependence of the social, ecological and spiritual dimensions that sustain life. Hilary N. Weaver (2001), a scholar from the Native

* The term Indigenous is used in this book in alignment with international definitions, including the United Nations Declaration on the Rights of Indigenous Peoples (UNDRIP), to respectfully refer to communities with historical continuity and cultural distinctiveness who self-identify as Indigenous. While widely accepted in legal and development contexts, some communities prefer to be identified by their specific nation or language group, and others may regard the term as externally imposed or overly broad (see Peters and Mika, 2017). Its use here is intended to recognize collective rights and identities, not to diminish the diversity or sovereignty of individual Indigenous peoples.

American Lakota people, articulates this interdependence clearly: 'Indigenous identity is connected to a sense of peoplehood inseparably linked to sacred traditions, traditional homelands and shared history as Indigenous people. A person must be integrated into a society, not simply stand alone as an individual, in order to be fully human' (p. 245).

This relational view of identity also extends to how many Indigenous communities understand and enact wellbeing. For example, in Ecuador, the Quechua concept of *sumak kawsay* – translated into Spanish as *buen vivir* (literally 'good living') – reflects a worldview (*cosmovision*) in which the good life is not achieved through individual accumulation or consumption, but through harmony with nature and collective coexistence. Ecuador formally updated its Constitution in 2008 to incorporate *buen vivir* as a foundational principle of national development and governance. This constitutional recognition marked a significant departure from Western development models, embedding Indigenous understandings of interdependence, reciprocity and environmental stewardship into the legal and political fabric of the state. As the Constitution declares: 'We . . . hereby decide to build a new form of public coexistence, in diversity and in harmony with nature, to achieve the good way of living'. Importantly, *buen vivir* resists translation into familiar Western terms such as 'wellbeing' or 'welfare', terms which remain rooted in individualism and economic growth. *Buen vivir*, by contrast, is about the individual-in-community, embedded in a unique environmental and cultural context. It demands a shift not just in policy but in worldview, away from exploitation and towards interdependence (Gudynas, 2011; Balch, 2013).

This relational perspective – seeing humans as part of a larger web of life rather than separate from it – is central to Robin Wall Kimmerer's *Braiding Sweet Grass: Indigenous Wisdom, Scientific Knowledge, and the Teachings of Plants* (2013). Kimmerer, a member of the Citizen Potawatomi Nation in the US, explores the relational way in which Indigenous knowledge and scientific knowledge can complement each other through 'two-eyed seeing'. She also examines reciprocity in the relationship between people and nature – don't just take but give back – and the value that these relationships create so that we can understand plants as teachers, with sweetgrass as a gift and symbol of that interconnection: 'One thing I've learned in the woods is that there is no such thing as random. Everything is steeped in meaning, coloured by relationships, one thing with another.' (Kimmerer, 2013, p. 298).

Expanding on these ideas from Indigenous knowledge, in his recent book *Is a River Alive?*, British nature writer Robert Macfarlane (2025) argues that we must rethink how we define 'life' when we consider rivers. A firm supporter of the Rights of Nature movement, in his work he builds on the concept of the 'natural contract' by French philosopher Michel Serres (1995), who argued that natural resources should be understood as living entities with which humans hold an ethical relationship (or contract). Both Macfarlane and Serres emphasize the mutual reciprocity that must underlie these relationships for the rights of nature to be respected and sustained.

Building on this ethical framework, this idea of granting legal personhood to natural resources, once considered marginal, is now central to an emerging legal and political discourse around the rights of nature and environmental personhood. At its core, this movement challenges the long-held legal assumption that nature exists primarily as property to be managed or exploited for human benefit. Instead, it asserts that natural entities possess intrinsic rights. Over the past several decades, activists, Indigenous communities and legal scholars have made significant progress pushing for ecosystems to be recognized as legal subjects. Ecuador's 2008 Constitution, mentioned above, was one of the first in the world to formally recognize the rights of nature, reflecting the country's strong Indigenous movements. New Zealand followed with the recognition of the Whanganui River as a legal person, acknowledging Māori cosmology and legal traditions that view the river as an ancestor. Similar steps have been taken in Bolivia and Colombia, building a growing body of legal precedent that redefines the relationship between humans and nature (Łaszewska-Hellriegel, 2022; Reeves and Peters, 2022). Central to this transformation in how we view nature is a renewed understanding of the common good, one that transcends human interests to encompass the well-being of all life forms and ecosystems. Recognizing nature's rights requires moving away from exploitation and individual ownership towards symbiotic relationships that foster an inclusive and sustainable future.*

2.6 Philosophical foundations of social economics

This chapter closes by examining how social economics has tried to reorient economic analysis around ethical questions, human dignity and the common good – heavily influenced by the philosophical questions examined in this chapter. Unlike neoclassical economics, which we will see treats individuals as isolated utility-maximizing agents, social economics emphasizes the social embeddedness of economic life and the responsibility of institutions to support human flourishing. At its core, social economics adopts a humanistic perspective that stresses the common qualities of people, inspired more

* These ideas on the relationship between humans and nature were explored in the *Future Assembly*, a 2021 exhibition at the Venice Biennale to commemorate the seventy-fifth anniversary of the United Nations. The exhibition questioned what representation, governance and value mean for the UN in an era of planetary crisis. The exhibition proposed expanding multilateralism by imagining a forum where more-than-human entities – such as rivers, forests and glaciers – are not merely protected objects but are recognized as political subjects in their own right with seats at the UN General Assembly (Studio Other Spaces, 2021). The multidisciplinary group that curated this project, led by artist Olafur Eliasson, former president of Ireland Mary Robinson, Kumi Naidoo, Paola Antonelli, myself and others. The exhibition featured a living timeline paralleling the seventy-five-year history of the UN Charter, highlighting both the victories and setbacks of the rights-of-nature movement. For more information, visit: https://studiootherspaces.net/futureassembly.

by Rousseau than Hobbes. Social economists argue that current economic systems undermine the common good in three fundamental ways: (1) producing involuntary poverty; (2) sustaining unemployment and reinforcing structural inequalities; and (3) violating equal rights through class and gender divisions and inequitable global trading systems (Lutz, 2002). Instead of centring economic analysis on utility maximization of individuals or on incentive-based frameworks, social economics prioritizes the promotion of the 'good' within all humans and our universal need for connection. It views people as relational and moral agents whose wellbeing depends on cooperation, care and mutual respect, rather than as self-interested actors responding to engineered incentives. From this perspective, economic systems should cultivate the social and ethical capacities that enable collective flourishing and the pursuit of the common good.

This tradition has deep historical roots. Swiss historian and economist Jean Charles Léonard de Sismondi (1773–1842) is often regarded as an early proponent. In *New Principles of Political Economy* (1819), de Sismondi challenged orthodox economics by insisting that economic systems should be judged not only by efficiency or output but also by their capacity to reduce inequality and support society's most vulnerable members.

A major advance in social economics came with Amartya Sen's capability approach (1979). This framework shifts the focus from utility-based welfare to what individuals are actually able to do and be – what Sen calls 'functionings'. Functionings encompass basic conditions such as nutrition and health as well as more complex aspects like self-respect and meaningful participation in community life. An individual's 'capability set' – the range of functionings they can achieve – reflects their freedom to pursue a life they value, shaped by both personal characteristics and broader social, economic and institutional conditions.

Martha Nussbaum (2000) extended this approach by proposing ten central capabilities that any just society should secure, including: life, bodily health, bodily integrity; senses, imagination and thought; emotions; practical reason; affiliation; concern for other species; play; and control over one's environment (both political and material). While Sen deliberately avoided prescribing a definitive list, Nussbaum's framework is explicitly normative, asserting that these capabilities represent essential conditions for a dignified life. Despite their differences, both Sen and Nussbaum underscore that economics must move beyond market metrics to engage seriously with moral dimensions of wellbeing, human development and social justice.

Social economics also aligns closely with the Catholic social tradition, particularly with Pope Leo XIII's encyclical *Rerum Novarum* (1891), Pope Pius XI's *Quadragesimo Anno* (1931) and the teachings of Pope John XXIII. Catholic social thought has historically emphasized the just distribution of income, wealth and material wellbeing, arguing that economic structures must serve the common good. This perspective resonates with Pope Francis's *Laudato si'* (2015), mentioned above, which highlights the need to address poverty, hunger and poor health as central to promoting the common good.

Several scholars have sought to explicitly integrate the common good into economic thought. Lutz (1999), for example, calls for a moral reorientation of economics, arguing that human needs and dignity should take precedence over capital and that the economy must be fully integrated into society rather than treated as autonomous. His work provides a strong foundation for an economics centred on the common good, though it focuses more on individual needs than collective challenges. Other thinkers, such as Dolderer, Felber and Teitscheid (2021), envision the common good economy as both an extension and a transcendence of neoclassical economics. Their approach incorporates neoclassical insights like market failure while also integrating disciplines beyond economics – including ecology, psychology and sociology – to frame the economy as a living system governed by democratic and ecological principles.

Philosophical reasoning has also inspired approaches to deliberative action, which emphasize reason giving, discourse and mutual understanding as foundations for cooperation. Emerging from political philosophy and democratic theory – particularly Habermas

(1984) and deliberative democracy theorists (Dryzek, 2000) – these approaches suggest that preferences are not fixed but shaped through public reasoning. Participatory mechanisms such as citizens' assemblies and participatory budgeting provide procedural legitimacy, as collective decisions gain moral justification through inclusive debate. Sen's conception of democracy similarly builds on 'public reasoning', highlighting the role of participatory deliberation in fostering legitimacy, trust and reduced polarization.

While social economics reorients economic thought towards meeting basic needs and safeguarding human dignity, it generally continues to operate within a conventional understanding of markets. As in communitarian thinking, the discussions of the 'good' often take place outside the core mechanisms of market exchange. This ironically leaves the traditional view of the market untouched, and then not surprisingly remains wedded to market failure theory. It does, however, expand on market failure theory by incorporating additional goods essential to human wellbeing – including public goods such as parks, roads, public buildings and the legal system, global public goods like air and water; and the higher needs and social web necessary for 'human flourishing and self-realization' (Lutz, 2002, p. 37). But ultimately, social economics has not overturned traditional theory of markets and thus can at best mitigate the harmful effects of markets – such as inequality and exclusion – rather than reimagining or redesigning markets to actively promote the common good.

Conclusion

While philosophical accounts of the common good have often begun from a normative and teleological perspective (i.e. Aristotle's conception of *eudaimonia*), this book adopts a different starting point. It assumes that what counts as 'good', and how this translates into economics, should be determined collectively. The central question, then, is how the process of determining the common good can be made explicit, co-created, and grounded in local contexts, and what kind of economic framework can support such a process. In a time marked by distrust, what is needed is not an elitist, top-down account of human flourishing, but a shared compass that enables societies to negotiate and pursue it together, in ways that serve the majority rather than those invested in maintaining the status quo. This is the task of this book. The first step, however, is to draw on insights from outside economics and to challenge how economics currently understands the notion of 'good'.

Communitarian, biological and Indigenous perspectives reveal that individuals do not exist in isolation, but within interdependent social and ecological networks. Identity, wellbeing and even the generation of value in the economy are inseparable from these relationships. This challenges the idea of value as something produced only by individuals and instead points to collective value creation, in which markets are shaped by shared institutions and common objectives.

The distinction biologists draw between symbiotic and parasitic ecosystems provides a useful analogy for rethinking economics. A symbiotic economy requires attention to the quality of relationships, which are shaped and governed through a wide range of mechanisms such as property rights, water rights, intellectual property and data flows. These underlying arrangements determine whether economic systems foster cooperation or enable exploitation.

Much of mainstream economic thought has ignored such interdependence, treating humans as isolated agents and markets as neutral mechanisms. This perspective leaves little room for the social and ecological dimensions of value creation and confines collective action to addressing failures after they happen. By focusing on the way relationships are structured from the start, both within communities and with nature, we open the possibility of shaping our economy to actively advance the common good.

3.

The narrow good in economics

Mainstream economic theory begins from a very different starting point than political philosophy. Its focus is on individuals, with the role of the state largely reactive, only intervening to fix the economy after it goes wrong. In this sense, it resembles a Hobbesian lens, where humans' self-interested behaviours guide society and the state imposes rules to maintain harmony and progress. Unlike the ecosystem perspective in biology, relationships are treated in purely transactional terms rather than as interdependent networks.

This individualistic focus has deep historical roots. From the time of Adam Smith, markets have been studied through the outcomes of individuals pursuing their self-interest. In *The Wealth of Nations* (1776), Smith argued that when individuals follow their own self-interest, supply meets demand. He famously wrote: 'It is not from the benevolence of the butcher, the brewer or the baker that we expect our dinner, but from their regard to their own interest' (Smith, 1776, p. 19). In other words, it is not charity that ensures everyone has meat, but the butcher's self-interest in making a profit. If the meat is bad, consumers will not buy it, and the market self-regulates.

Yet Smith also wrote the book *A Theory of Moral Sentiments* (1759). Here he argued that a good economy must be one that inspires virtue from our moral judgements, and empathy from the capacity to understand and share the feeling of others. He believed that the development of our morals happens not in isolation but in connection with others. Justice in this process is key, but so is 'beneficence' (voluntary acts of kindness), which ultimately is what holds society together. And ironically his notion of the 'free market' was not free from the state, but free from rents whereby wealth created by society is extracted out to the few. How to reduce rents and stimulate innovation was critical to his analysis.

This division between Smith's two books is still the kind of schism we have in economics. On the one hand is the obsession with the market, and (only) fixing it when things go wrong. This leads to the 'market failure' role of the state. And on the other hand, is the talk about higher-level morals and principles (e.g. like solving the climate crisis today), which when viewed through the market failure lens end up creating only incremental steps that do not fundamentally re-steer our economy from not producing those bads in the first place. So while 'good' is discussed, it is not part of the core of economic analysis – it is seen as an add-on, through fixing of failures as they arise.

Three centuries later, mainstream economic theory continues to assume that society functions best when individuals and firms act in their own self-interest: firms maximize profits, consumers maximize utility and workers maximize their preference function of leisure versus work. Markets are studied through the interactions of these behaviours and the resulting equilibrium outcomes, such as consumer surplus – the difference between the maximum price a consumer is willing to pay and the actual market price – or producer surplus – the difference between the market price a producer receives and the minimum they would accept. Relationships between individuals and organizations are viewed transactionally, with economists weighing the costs and benefits of each exchange. Transaction cost economics extends this perspective by examining how 'frictions' arise, through information asymmetry, bounded rationality or opportunism, and how these frictions shape the efficiency and outcomes of market interactions (Williamson, 1981).

In contrast to political philosophers, who emphasize social bonds and shared objectives, economics treats rational calculation as the driver of behaviour. If frictions are removed, the system is assumed to reduce uncertainty and operate more efficiently. Within this framework, government intervention is limited to correcting market failures: if markets fail to produce enough of a good that is considered important, or too much of a good that is considered bad (e.g. goods that create pollution), the government must step in and either invest in the missing good or prevent the bad from happening. In both cases, the approach is reactive.

Economic theory has, of course, evolved beyond a strict view of rationality, with the development of behavioural economics. However, these insights do not fundamentally change the core assumptions of mainstream economics: that humans are self-interested actors and that the government's role is to correct market failures.

3.1 Aggregating self-interested maximizers

Mainstream economic theory today is known as 'neoclassical economics' because it comes after classical political economy, which includes the writings of Adam Smith (1723–90), David Ricardo (1772–1823) and Karl Marx (1818–83) (see Smith, 1776; Ricardo, 1817; and Marx, 1887). Classical political economy placed much emphasis on underlying theories of value and how these relate to the relationships between classes (between landlords, the capitalist class and workers). A revolution in economics occurred in the late nineteenth century when this emphasis on social classes and objective conditions of production was changed to a focus on individual preferences, and subjective decisions dependent on maximization exercises: firms maximizing profits, consumers maximizing their utility preferences, and workers maximizing their preferences for leisure versus work (Mazzucato, 2018c). Economics, in this view, largely studies how these individual choices interact through exchange to determine the distribution of work, the production of goods and consumption patterns. Value is 'revealed' after these processes play themselves out.

This framework also shapes how 'good' is generally conceptualized in economics, in terms of the goods that are produced, the price signals that emerge and any corrections to market failures that may be required. Market performance is evaluated after the fact to determine whether a good outcome has been achieved: for example, whether sufficient affordable housing has been provided by the market or whether the government needs to step in to provide it.

Central to this perspective is the idea that maximizing individual preferences and achieving so-called 'Pareto-efficient' outcomes is the primary goal of economic activity. Pareto efficiency – named after the Italian economist Vilfredo Pareto (1848–1923) and long emphasized by neoclassical economics – holds that individuals pursuing their own self-interest in competitive markets can give rise to the most efficient and welfare-maximizing outcomes (Samuelson, 1947). Efficiency is understood in a utilitarian sense, whereby an activity is efficient if it enhances someone's welfare without making anyone else worse off.

Thus while political philosophy has for a long time emphasized that a society should be driven by objectives (*telos*) and focus on the locus of interactions (*polis*) that make them possible, economics is more neutral on the objective, and examines if the 'good' is achieved after the fact, through welfare principles, derived from the aggregation of individual choices and behaviours that are presumed to reflect rational self-interest.

3.2 Public goods: fixing a market failure

It is precisely within this framework that collective action problems arise. Traditional economics views these problems as arising when a group must coordinate to provide a public good or manage a common resource, but everyone has an incentive to 'free ride', or benefit without contributing. If an individual's private cost of contributing exceeds their private benefit, the good will be under-provided. Free riders receive the benefits without bearing the costs, and as a result, collective goods are jeopardized because each agent prefers to withhold effort. For example, everyone may value cleaner air, but few have a strong personal incentive to pay for it if others don't bear the cost. Paul Samuelson (1954) formalized this as the *public goods* problem, showing that voluntary contributions generally fall short of the social optimum. He argued that public goods create market failures because each person's dominant strategy is to understate their willingness to pay, resulting in under-provision. Mancur Olson's *The Logic of Collective Action* (1965) reinforced this insight, emphasizing that in large groups no individual is likely to act as an entrepreneur to provide the group good, since the personal costs outweigh the personal gains.

The analysis of public goods in neoclassical economics arises precisely when maximizing decisions alone do not produce socially optimum outcomes. Thus, while the term public good is often confused in lay terms with the concept of the common good, they are in fact fundamentally different. Public goods are just corrections for something the private sector does not do. The common good is not a correction, but an objective that requires a very different type of analysis, which we return to in Chapter 4.

To understand this distinction more clearly, we can look more broadly at how goods are described in economics. Economists differentiate goods based on two fundamental attributes: rivalry, which refers to whether one person's consumption of the good reduces its availability for others; and excludability, which denotes whether people can be prevented from the consumption of the good (Hess and Ostrom, 2003). Based on these characteristics, different types of goods can be identified:

Figure 4 Types of economic goods

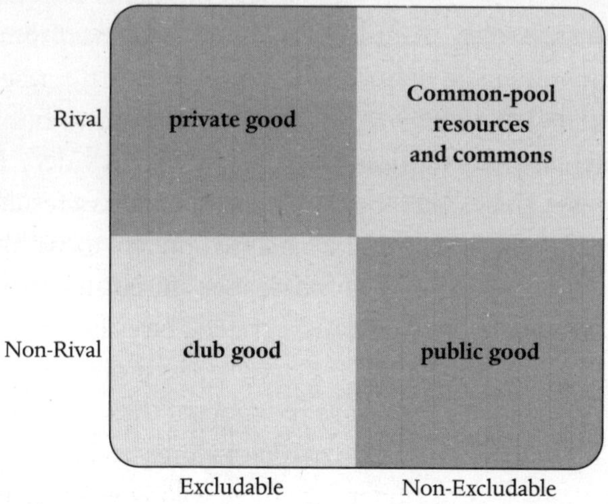

Source: Adapted from Hess and Ostrom (2003)

- **Private goods** are excludable and rival. They are goods that can only be consumed by a limited number of people at a time (Adams and McCormick, 1987). They are often created with the objective of commercialization or profit maximization. Examples are clothing or food.
- **Club goods** are those that are non-rival but excludable. One person consuming does not reduce the ability of another person to consume, so long as they pay (McNutt, 1999). Examples are subscription TV services and software.
- **Commons and common-pool resources** (CPRs) are the opposite of club goods: they are rivalrous but non-excludable, since preventing people from using them proves difficult, but their benefits are finite (Ostrom, 1990). Examples include water resources and forests. These goods are often subject to both government and market failure, and their sustainable management frequently depends on collective action by local communities or user groups, as further explored in Ostrom's work below.
- **Public goods** are non-excludable and non-rival. These are goods where the private sector has little incentive to invest as they cannot appropriate the profits, given that people cannot be excluded from using them and they are not limited (Samuelson, 1954). Examples are environmental protection, basic research and national defence. Recently this concept has been elaborated with an international dimension through the idea of **global public goods** (Kaul, 2016), which are public goods that require global cooperation, such as a stable climate that cannot be achieved by one country alone. They thus require international cooperation and/or global institutions to provide them.

Due to their non-excludable nature, public goods, global public goods, CPRs and commons have been particularly central to discussions of public policy and state governance, as the state is typically expected to provide or manage these goods because they are not provided by the private sector (e.g. Holcombe, 2000; Heikkila, 2004; Hazelkorn and Gibson, 2018). As a result, the concept of public good is clearly rooted in a theory of market failure which accepts public intervention in the economy only if it is geared towards fixing situations in which markets fail (Arrow, 1951).

This approach suggests that governments intervene to fix markets by investing in areas where there are positive or negative externalities. Public goods with positive externalities are characterized by under-investment as their high spillovers create difficulties for appropriating private returns. The opposite happens when there is too much investment in 'bads', such as areas that cause pollution or damage to health. Such negative externalities require public measures that prompt the private sector to internalize those costs: for example, a carbon tax to cut emissions or a tax on cigarette purchases. Market failures of this kind are said to arise in cases of information asymmetries, transaction costs and frictions to smooth exchange.

Market failure theory has been shown to be limited as a basis for policy intervention as optimal market conditions such as perfect information and no transaction costs have never been empirically demonstrated in practice (Coase, 1960; Stiglitz, 2010). In fact, the opposite conclusion should be reached: markets are always imperfect and incomplete and can thus never be characterized as 'Pareto-optimal'. As a result, a government always has the potential to improve a market outcome (Greenwald and Stiglitz, 1986). Indeed, if markets are always imperfect, and imperfect results are not externalities but rather functions of market design, this invites the question of whether it is markets that fail or the theory of how markets work that is failing! We will argue the latter in Chapter 4, when building a different understanding of markets as the foundation for the common good.

Key to the problems is that the market failure justification for policy implies that pure private markets and private goods can exist independently of public sector institutions or coordinated civil society action. While institutions are analysed in institutional economics (e.g. North, 1991), they are seen as correcting for market failures rather than being embedded in how markets work (Evans, 1995). Richard Nelson (1987, p.

556) notes that 'there is no satisfactory normative theory regarding the appropriate roles of government in a mixed economy' and no theory that captures the complex variety of institutional arrangements that people have developed to solve collective problems. Just as pure public goods are rare, so too are pure private goods. The 'market failure' dichotomy is therefore not particularly useful (Mazzucato, 2013; Collington and Mazzucato, 2024) and is why in Chapter 4 we begin with a different starting point: markets do not exist in a vacuum but are outcomes of how public, private and other institutions are governed and interact.

A limitation of public good scholarship is that it treats some systemic problems in capitalism (like climate change and inequality) as externalities and the results of failures of an otherwise perfect system, rather than questioning the structures underlying the system itself (Nelson, 2022). It frames tools like public investment as addressing the need to correct a gap in private finance. This view of the state as a market-fixer has led to the idea that government should not steer the economy but only regulate and facilitate it, which in turn affects the capabilities the state thinks it needs (Mazzucato, 2013; Collington and Mazzucato, 2024).

Global public goods

From an international perspective, the concept of Global Public Good (GPG) is one that draws attention to the international collaboration and investment that are required to solve problems of over-use and under-provision at the global scale (Barrett, 2007). This work focuses on situations in which national governments cannot guarantee the provision of a public good because of global linkages. 'Thus public goods often face a double jeopardy: market failure compounded by government failure' (Kaul, Grunberg and Stern, 1999, p. 8).

The global aspect means that no one nation can deal with the problem alone, thus requiring the involvement of inter-governmental organizations, such as the UN. A flood in one region of the world, for example, may have been caused by an emission-related change elsewhere, thus requiring global coordination (Global Commission on the Economics of Water, 2024). As a result, unlike traditional economic goods, GPGs cannot be defined by whether they are rivalrous or excludable. Instead, whether a good is considered private or public depends on political interest and capacity to make it part of the public and global domain (Kaul, 2016). This perspective explicitly considers power relationships and helps restore the more proactive role for the state in shaping and providing public goods at both national and global levels (Stiglitz, 2000).

However, most work on GPGs continues to draw heavily on the conceptual foundations and intellectual tradition of market failure theory and public goods, with a strong focus on remedying instances of overuse and under-provision (Boonen et al., 2019). In this framework, wellbeing is still defined in terms of individual welfare functions and state action remains relegated to the correction of externalities (e.g. Sandmo, 2007; Levaggi, 2010). This narrow interpretation treats collective welfare as the sum of individual benefits rather than as a shared objective. It is particularly evident in the work of scholars who describe institutions and international regimes as intermediary public goods – mechanisms that exist not as ends in themselves but as tools for enabling or coordinating the provision of GPGs (Kaul, Grunberg and Stern, 1999). In other words, cooperation and governance are seen as instrumental means to correct inefficiencies, rather than as collective expressions of the common good itself.

Insights from mechanism design

Mechanism design theory attempts to tweak the system to address collective action problems characterized as market failures by focusing on the way institutional arrangements can be engineered so that rational agents voluntarily choose cooperation even when individual incentives conflict with collective goals (Maskin and Tirole, 2001). Mechanism design treats collective action as a problem of institutional engineering: how to construct rules so that rational, self-interested agents produce cooperative outcomes (Hurwicz, 1972; Myerson, 1981). The main difference between standard market failure theory and mechanism design is that while the former considers the results of individual utility maximization, the latter considers how objectives can be embedded in institutional and contractual design to shape individual behaviour.

Game theory models inform mechanism design by studying cooperation dynamics. For example, Prisoner's Dilemma examines why two rational people might not cooperate even if it may be in their best interests to do so, and illustrates how individual incentives can produce suboptimal group outcomes (Dawes, 1980), a conclusion also supported by some public goods experiments (Ledyard, 1995). Different theoretical traditions diagnose this dilemma in various ways and prescribe different remedies, but the standard solution is state intervention – through taxes, subsidies or regulation – to align private incentives with collective interests.

In the context of public goods, mechanism design seeks to elicit true preferences and allocate costs accordingly. For example, if a community is funding a public park, people might understate how much they are willing to pay to avoid contributing more than others. Mechanism design would create a system of incentives that makes it in each person's best interest to reveal their true willingness to pay, ensuring the park is funded in a way that reflects actual preferences and shares the costs appropriately. While promising in theory, many mechanisms are complex, information intensive and vulnerable to collusion. Still, this approach has been applied to auctions, environmental regulation and public finance, offering a normative benchmark for institutional arrangements (Jehiel and Moldovanu, 2001). It can be understood as a reverse Prisoner's Dilemma: rather than taking rules as given and predicting suboptimal outcomes, it starts with the desired outcome and designs rules under which rational agents will voluntarily cooperate.

3.3 The commons: fixing a government failure

This focus on individuals and market fixing underlies most approaches in modern economics, including the theory of the 'commons'. Indeed, it is precisely due to the need for a more collective (less individualistic) and communal spirit that the literature on the 'commons' has become so popular. Eleanor Ostrom (1933–2012), who was the first woman to win the Nobel Prize in economics, in 2009, founded the economics of the commons by examining what happens when individualistic behaviour, combined with weak governments, undermines the ability of communities to sustain shared resources.

The commons emerged as a response to models such as Garrett Hardin's (1968) tragedy of the commons, the Prisoner's Dilemma, and Mancur Olson's (1965) logic of collective action, all of which predict that individuals exploiting shared resources will fail to cooperate for collective benefit. These frameworks portray people as trapped by structural constraints – 'prisoners' incapable of changing the rules that govern their behaviour. Ostrom challenged this view, arguing that the key question is not whether individuals are doomed to free-ride, but how they can build the capabilities to alter those constraints and achieve more cooperative outcomes (Ostrom, 2015).

Ostrom's theory demonstrates that communities can in fact often self-organize effectively without relying on either the state or the market. Successful commons and CPRs – sometimes referred to as *common goods* (plural) – are typically governed by clearly defined communities that establish collective rules and enforce sanctions for violations (Ostrom, 1990). Classic examples include environmental resources such as forests, fisheries and rivers. While some scholars have explored extending these insights to the global level, most work continues to focus on local governance, emphasizing negotiation, trust and deep knowledge of local conditions as central to the management and distribution of commons (Cogolati and Wouters, 2018).

To manage the commons effectively, Ostrom proposed eight design principles (see Figure 5), emphasizing that successful cooperation relies on local context, repeated interaction and mutual trust, conditions that enable communities to govern shared resources sustainably. While more theoretical and empirical work is needed to test how these principles hold in practice, this framework highlights the importance of linking economic analysis with political and institutional realities.

Figure 5 Ostrom's design principles

1. **Clearly defined boundaries**
   Individuals or households who have rights to withdraw resource units from the CPR must be clearly defined, as must the boundaries of the CPR itself.

2. **Congruence between appropriation and provision rules and local conditions**
   Appropriation rules restricting time, place, technology, and/or quantity of resource units are related to local conditions and to provision rules requiring labor, material, and/or money.

3. **Collective-choice arrangements**
   Most individuals affected by the operational rules can participate in modifying the operational rules.

4. **Monitoring**
   Monitors, who actively audit CPR conditions and appropriator behavior, are accountable to the appropriators or are the appropriators.

5. **Graduated sanctions**
   Appropriators who violate operational rules are likely to be assessed graduated sanctions (depending on the seriousness and context of the offense) by other appropriators, by officials accountable to these appropriators, or by both.

6. **Conflict-resolution mechanisms**
   Appropriators and their officials have rapid access to low-cost local arenas to resolve conflicts among appropriators or between appropriators and officials.

7. **Minimal recognition of rights to organize**
   The rights of appropriators to devise their own institutions are not challenged by external governmental authorities.

For CPRs that are parts of larger systems:

8. **Nested enterprises**
   Appropriation, provision, monitoring, enforcement, conflict resolution, and governance activities are organized in multiple layers of nested enterprises.

Source: Ostrom (2015, p. 90)

Despite its contributions, the commons literature retains a rigid dichotomy between the market and the state. Although Ostrom (2015) acknowledges that institutions are rarely purely public or private, the commons literature largely treats the two as separate spheres. Both market-based (private property rights) and state-led (central planning and regulation) solutions are seen as insufficient for managing CPRs. Consequently, the framework prioritizes bottom-up strategies, such as community monitoring of shared resources and local conflict resolution.

The commons literature has made an essential contribution by overturning the assumption that individuals who share resources are incapable of cooperation. It has demonstrated that communities can, under the right conditions, design institutions that foster trust, reciprocity and collective benefit. There is much to learn from this approach. Principles that govern how different stakeholders manage limited collective resources are crucial. However, what is missing is how to do this at the core of economic relationships and the implications for how we govern public institutions, the private sector and their relationships. The reliance on localized government limits the applicability of the theory to broader global challenges, especially ones that deal with complicated relationships with the corporate sector, e.g. how energy is created, how vaccines are produced or how digital public infrastructure is designed. And while the commons literature correctly rejects the idea that the 'tragedy of the commons' can be solved through privatization alone, the understanding of the state often remains confined to an old vision of centralized government planning, which is considered equally problematic. The only way to supersede this is to embed the commons in a new approach to how we understand the market, business and government – the objective of Chapter 4. Before doing so we look at how the attention of the commons on rules and institutions is linked to broader advances in institutional and evolutionary economics.

Link to behavioural economics

Ostrom's work reveals the important role of social norms, rules and governance structures in fostering collective action, demonstrating that communities often self-organize without state or market solutions. The commons principles reflect an understanding that cooperation is inextricable from local contexts, repeated interaction and mutual trust. This is where behavioural and evolutionary models pick up, with models that relax strict rationality and introduce social preferences, bounded cognition and cultural norms (Nelson and Winter, 1982). Experiments show that individuals often cooperate more than expected: in public goods games, people contribute significantly, especially when there is punishment for free-riding (Fehr and Gächter, 2000) and their cooperation is assessed through a framework of reciprocity in utility functions (Rabin, 1993). Evolutionary game theory explains how cooperative traits – like strong reciprocity – can evolve through repeated interaction, reputation or group selection (Nowak, 2006). Cultural evolution and gene–culture co-evolution theories suggest that norms promoting altruism can become stable (Henrich, 2004). Behavioural models also emphasize framing, emotions and heuristics (Kahneman, 2011), recognizing that individuals and organizations do not always maximize objective functions (profits, utility or costs) but often rely on routines and rules of thumb that create inertia and lead to different equilibrium outcomes (Simon et al., 2008; Tversky and Kahneman, 1992). Policy applications of this approach include the popular use of 'nudging' to influence behaviour, such as arranging cafeteria food to encourage children to make healthier choices (Thaler and Sunstein, 2008). Although lab experiments may have limited external validity, this framework enriches our understanding by integrating psychology and evolutionary dynamics into economics.

Notwithstanding the different assumptions about behaviours in commons scholarship, the role of the state remains rooted in neoclassical microeconomic theory and welfare economics. The need for government intervention is seen as critical for levelling the playing field and maintaining functional public infrastructure to provide a foundation for successful common resource management by other actors, but does not extend far beyond that (e.g. De Jongh, 2020). In this context, the state is seen as facilitating common resource management and not as being a fundamental driver of change itself. The concept of 'government failure' (Buchanan, 2003) risks leading to a self-fulfilling prophecy of 'weak' states and 'captured' states, for which communities often end up compensating. The commons literature generally sees decentralized capacity as a good model for coordinated action, but the state is excluded from the process.

It is not a coincidence that reasoning behind this approach has also led to the increasing use of NGOs and philanthropies in areas such as health (Zanotti, 2010; Nega and Schneider, 2014). While alternatives to state and market are critical (e.g. Ostrom, 2010; Brandtner, Douglas and Kornberger, 2023), it is essential to ask how capable states may nurture such alternatives while governing the economy to achieve collective goals.

The types of economic goods studied in this chapter, and summarized in Table 1, share one characteristic: they are all rooted in the same notion of either market failure or state failure. The dual characteristics of rivalry and excludability are the foundation for classifying goods and guide decisions about which entity – be it the market, communities or the state – should provide them. Thus,

Table 1 The limitations of traditional economic goods

	Scope	**Focus**	**Limitations**
Commons and common-pool resources	Local	Communities govern local resources.	Limited to the local level; implicitly assumes state is weak.
Public good	National	State fixes market failures and provides non-rival and non-excludable goods.	Oriented towards maximization of private rather than collective interests; state regarded as market fixing.
Global public goods	International	Global coordination between states based on over-exploitation and under-provision.	Top-down with risk of democratic deficit; rooted in market failure framework; ignores need for state capacity.

Source: Author's creation

within this framework the state's role is generally confined to public goods as responding to market failure and to common-pool resources where communities compensate for state failure. The question that arises is how the role of government can be envisioned in a way that moves beyond these attributes and proactively creates, with others, an economy aligned with collective goals (Mazzucato, 2021). This is particularly pertinent given how much attention the international community has devoted to shared goals without there being a comprehensive framework to underpin them.

3.4 Administering public interest and public value

Public choice theory, widely taught in public administration, extends the rational-choice framework underlying market failure theory to political decision making (Mueller, 2003). Developed by James M. Buchanan and Gordon Tullock in *The Calculus of Consent* (1962), it portrays voters, politicians and bureaucrats as self-interested agents. The theory highlights the risk of 'bureau-maximizing' behaviour, in which public sector employees seek to expand their department's budget and size, potentially leading to socially inefficient outcomes or 'government failure' (Buchanan, 1964).

By applying market logic to political and administrative behaviour, public choice theory reframed government as a collection of individuals pursuing their own interests rather than as a vehicle for advancing collective goals. This intellectual turn reflected and reinforced a broader historical shift in conceptions of the common good. As discussed in the previous chapter, in earlier traditions such as those of Ancient Greece and Rome, the common good was central to public discourse. Yet with the rise of the modern bureaucratic state and the expansion of capitalist markets, consensus on a shared vision of the good life became increasingly difficult to sustain. Political theory consequently moved towards procedural conceptions of the common good. Instead of prescribing a specific moral ideal, attention turned to designing institutions capable of mediating diverse interests, protecting individual rights and maintaining social stability within constitutional frameworks (Bahnisch, 2001).

Out of this procedural turn emerged the concept of the 'public interest', which gradually displaced the common good in political and administrative discourse. The public interest came to be understood as a neutral norm that aggregates and transcends individual preferences without defining substantive notions of good. For much of the twentieth century, traditional public administration was built around this ideal. It envisioned the pursuit of the public interest through institutional impartiality, bureaucratic professionalism and responsiveness to public opinion. Although it avoided prescribing what was 'good', it upheld key principles such as equal access to public services and the primacy of public over private interests.

Public choice theory directly challenged this procedural model. By extending market rationality to political decision making, it displaced even the residual focus on collective goals that had remained within the idea of the public interest, though already diluted compared to the richer notion of the common good. Government was no longer understood as an institution serving collective interests, but as a mechanism for individuals seeking to maximize their own utility. This logic paved the way for New Public Management (NPM), which translated the assumptions of public choice theory into administrative practice. The idea of government as 'administrator' comes out of the same period in history as the Thatcherite and Reaganite ideology of diminishing the state: not just in size but in its remit (Collington and Mazzucato, 2024).

NPM introduced the idea of 'market discipline' into the public sector and extended market rationality into the organization of government itself (Hood, 1991). It promoted management techniques drawn from the private sector, such as competition, performance measurement and efficiency incentives, as the means to improve public services. NPM scholars often denied the existence of a singular public interest, defining the public good instead as the 'liberty to pursue private interests' (Bahnisch, 2001, p. 3). Civil servants and elected officials were recast as self-interested agents seeking to maximize personal utility, while citizens were reframed as consumers.

Within this framework, private interests are normalized and institutionalized and the notions of common good or even public interest were largely sidelined or denied (Bahnisch, 2001).

In response to the limitations of NPM and as a counterpart to the theory of 'shareholder value', Mark Moore (1995) developed the concept of 'public value' as a strategic approach to public management. Moore argued that public managers should focus on creating public value – delivering outcomes that advance collective wellbeing and civic goals – rather than merely pursuing efficiency or cost cutting. Public value reframes the purpose of government action, emphasizing the role of institutions in addressing societal needs, reinforcing democratic legitimacy, and fostering cooperation between citizens and the state. To operationalize this, Moore developed the 'strategic-triangle' framework, helping public managers navigate three essential dimensions: defining public value, securing political legitimacy and support, and ensuring operational capacity (Moore, 1995).

Barry Bozeman (2002; 2007) expanded the concept further, framing public value as a tool to assess whether governments and markets effectively meet societal needs – or fail to do so. He defined public values as the principles that underpin a well-functioning democracy: the rights and benefits citizens should have, their responsibilities to one another and the state, and the ethical foundations that should guide governance. Crucially, Bozeman recognized that these values are not static, but continuously contested and reshaped through dynamic political and economic processes. Moreover, seeking to challenge the limiting framework of market failure, Bozeman introduced the concept of public value failure – where neither markets nor the state provide the essential goods and services required to uphold core public values. This concept sought to broaden the rationale for state intervention, moving beyond mere efficiency to address wider, often neglected, societal needs (Bozeman, 2002).

In practice, public value is often discussed alongside the related concepts of public good, public interest and social value – and sometimes even the common good – though each tradition carries distinct assumptions about collective goals (see Table 2). Understanding these differences highlights how historical, political, economic and philosophical contexts have shaped governance approaches. The common good is the oldest of these concepts but was gradually replaced by the concepts of public good, public interest, social value and public value in public discourse, reflecting the decline of more normative approaches to governance and the increasing emphasis on individual rights. For instance, as Bozeman (2007) explains, public interest is frequently invoked as a justification for government action, yet its meaning remains vague, inconsistent and often politically malleable. The same is true for words like public good and social value, which are often conflated with the common good but in fact refer to much narrower and more operational concepts that lack its substantive moral grounding.

Moore and Bozeman have each played an important role in

Table 2: Words often conflated with the common good

Term	***Definition***
Public Good	A good that is non-rivalrous (one person's use does not reduce availability for others) and non-excludable (people cannot be prevented from using it). (Samuelson, 1954; Goldin, 1977)
Public Interest	A procedural/neutral norm referring to outcomes that reflect the aggregated or reconciled preferences of citizens, without prescribing a substantive vision of the good (Bahnisch, 2001)
Social Value	Tangible or measurable social, economic or environmental benefits generated for individuals and communities by a policy, programme or activity (Mulgan, 2010; UK *Social Value Act*, 2012)
Public Value	The value generated by public institutions for society, encompassing outcomes that enhance collective wellbeing, democratic legitimacy and operational capacity. (Moore, 1995; Bozeman, 2002, 2007)

Source: Author's creation

shaping the public value literature and in encouraging governments to take a more proactive stance to reach collective goals. At the same time, the public value literature remains wedded to the theory of market failures, and thus focuses largely on policy design and managerial practice, without offering an economic foundation that explains how public value can be created or sustained, and how to embed this in a different theory of market processes. For instance, critics of Moore, such as Dahl and Soss (2014), argue that the language he adopts around public value can draw public value towards private sector notions of production and performance, narrowing the space for democratic engagement. Developing a more robust approach to public value therefore requires different notions of the state in economic policy (from market fixing to market shaping) and a different understanding of value itself, issues we take up in Chapter 4.

3.5 The common good: a mainstream view

Precisely because the concept of the common good is not strong in economics (unlike in philosophy, where it has benefited from a two-thousand-year debate), it is easy for words like the public good, public interest and social value to creep in. And when the phrase common good is introduced, it means little more than either correcting for bads, or doing some good on the sidelines. So, before finishing this chapter, it is useful to consider how neoclassical economics has *explicitly* approached the topic of the common good.

As discussed in Chapter 2, the idea of the common good is widely appealing but interpreted in multiple ways. For Aristotle, it meant cultivating virtue; for theologians, attaining salvation; and for communitarians, pursuing the good life within a community. Economics, however, has treated the concept in a less structured manner. Unlike 'public goods', which have a precise theoretical framework for non-excludable and non-rival goods, the common good remains conceptually messy, making it difficult to integrate into economic analysis.

In *Economics for the Common Good*, Nobel Prize-winning economist Jean Tirole (2017) distinguishes between the narrowly defined 'public good' and the broader, normative 'common good', which concerns what benefits society, including fairness, social cohesion, intergenerational equity and ethical responsibility. The common good, he argues, is not defined by consumption characteristics but by shared goals and values shaped through democratic debate and ethical reasoning. For him, it therefore requires balancing individual interests with collective welfare. Yet, despite this expansive conception, his approach too remains grounded in a market failure perspective.

Tirole's (2017) premise rests on the idea that individuals respond to incentives, and their behaviour, shaped by these incentives and preferences, may or may not align with the common good. Although he broadens standard analysis by drawing on psychology and behavioural economics, he treats deviations such as biases or procrastination as frictions to be managed through better-designed incentives, without questioning the fundamental conception of individuals as self-interested and preference maximizing. This individualistic view is defended as essential to understanding group behaviour, arguing that people respond to incentives embedded in the norms, expectations and networks of their social groups.

As a result, Tirole (2017) sees the economist's task as designing institutions that reconcile individual and collective goals by aligning incentives to guide society towards better outcomes. When markets fail to harmonize private behaviour with the general interest, the result is a market failure to be corrected. He categorizes such failures into three main types: (1) externalities (e.g. pollution affecting third parties); (2) internalities (e.g. individuals undermining their own long-term interests due to lack of self-control); and (3) information asymmetries (e.g. when buyers lack adequate knowledge about a product or service).

Although he affirms the complementarity between market and state, Tirole (2017) repeats the traditional view of the state as a regulator: establishing rules, correcting distortions, protecting competition, regulating monopolies, overseeing the financial system, promoting equal opportunity and redistributing resources through taxation.

This logic is especially clear in Tirole's (2017) discussion of industrial policy. He warns against government 'hubris' and opposes efforts by states to 'pick winners', advocating instead 'neutral' policies that avoid distorting competition. While he supports measures that improve investment conditions – such as regulatory clarity or targeted incentives – he remains sceptical of direct state involvement in shaping industrial or technological trajectories, preferring market-based tools like auctions for gathering information and allocating resources. The same pattern appears in his environmental policy proposals, where he favours carbon pricing – market-compatible instruments to internalize negative externalities – over command-and-control regulation, which he deems inefficient and prone to unintended consequences.

Moreover, although Tirole (2017) acknowledges power disparities and economic inequality, he frames them as technical challenges – arising from information asymmetries or misaligned incentives – rather than as expressions of deeper social or moral issues. Ethical and normative concerns are consistently reframed in terms of efficiency, with moral taboos understood as market failures, and public indignation over inequality or injustice seen as an unreliable foundation for policy. Conflicts of interest, in this view, reflect informational inadequacies rather than structural tensions. As Tirole puts it, 'moral criticisms of the market are simply reformulations of the concept of "market failure"' (Tirole, 2017, p. 8).

By contrast, former US Secretary of Labor Robert Reich (2018), in his book *The Common Good*, explores the idea of the common good in relation to what he perceives to be the erosion of shared values and mutual obligations in American society. He argues that the historic US commitment to the common good – stemming from the Declaration of Independence and the US Constitution, and expressed through ideals such as the rule of law, democratic institutions and a commitment to truth – began to erode in the late

1970s. He perceives three major structural breakdowns have driven this shift: the degradation of politics into partisan competition, the retreat of corporate responsibility in favour of shareholder primacy, and distortions within the market that encourage exploitation over fairness. Together, these dynamics have weakened public trust, accelerated economic inequality and shifted attention away from collective wellbeing towards private gain.

To restore the common good, Reich calls for a renewal of civic life grounded in trusteeship, where leaders see themselves as stewards of the common good. He emphasizes reclaiming the social use of honour and shame to condemn corruption and celebrate virtue, rebuilding a culture of truth telling in public life, and reviving civic education to instil responsibility and democratic values in future generations. In doing so, he envisions a society in which the common good once again guides the collective. Yet, like communitarians, Reich does not provide a framework for ensuring that the common good actively shapes how the economy operates at its very core: the role of business, the role of government policy beyond fixing markets, and how the two interrelate – topics we come to next.

Conclusion

From Adam Smith, economists have juggled between arguing that the free market will produce 'good' results and arguing that markets often fail and will thus need state intervention. The state is seen as needed to fill the gap of what the private sector will not provide – whether it is national security, rule of law or basic infrastructure. This gap-filling mode of thinking is linked to how 'good' has been understood, both in the sense of good market outcomes – seen as being created by maximizing agents – or by 'goods' that the market cannot provide due to market failure or government failure characteristics. The commons literature has moved beyond this approach by focusing not only on market failure but also on government failure – emphasizing the role of communities in managing shared resources.

The challenges we face today demand more than simply correcting for market and government failures. They call for a transformative approach that reshapes and repurposes markets themselves. Even progressive appeals to the common good have yet to fully clarify what this implies for how we structure and govern the way companies and the state function in modern capitalism. In doing so, the risk is that the analysis of the market remains intact, and the 'good' results are studied outside market processes, or at best as results of market fixing. In this context, the concept of the common good, public interest and public value are often conflated.

So how can we reimagine the common good at the centre of economics? Are we really all just self-interested? Are markets simply the outcome of individuals maximizing their own utility? And is the role of government merely to fix market failures after they occur? We examine these questions next.

4.
Rethinking good in economics

A common good economy requires embedding economic objectives within the fabric of social relationships and rethinking how all actors – individuals, public institutions and private firms – relate to one another. This demands removing it from a notion of market failures: it must instead be about how to shape markets and the economy, putting the common good at the centre of all economic relationships. And it also cannot be about non-market activities. It must go to the centre of how economies and markets work. A common good framework for the economy is about aligning goals, incentivizing collaboration, fostering collective intelligence, and ensuring that all participants share knowledge, risks and rewards. It moves beyond treating markets as neutral arenas for individual maximization, aiming instead to design systems that actively cultivate cooperation and shared wellbeing to make the common good possible.

To create a new economics of the common good, we must thus shift away from a focus on maximization exercises towards collective value creation, where interactions between business, government and other organizations are viewed not as mere transactions but as relationships to be guided through principles of reciprocity.

4.1 Rethinking markets: from fixing markets to shaping them

Market fixing assumes that markets function effectively when driven by business decisions and that, when they fail, the state should intervene to correct them. Market shaping starts from a different premise. It understands markets as outcomes of how economic activity is structured and governed. From this perspective, the role of the state lies in investing, coordinating and regulating, with close attention paid to how relationships between the state and the private sector are organized. Poor market outcomes may arise not from market failure but from these underlying structures, which need to be reconfigured rather than corrected. For example, if an economy is over-financialized, with shareholder value prioritization leading firms to reinvest too little of their profits into productive activity, the issue becomes how to reform corporate governance. Similarly, if markets are weak, because the state has been captured and laws are enacted that facilitate short-term profits, the question is how to reorient the state towards public purpose. This approach is not about fixing market failures but about shaping markets and, therefore, their outcomes. Markets as outcomes is therefore the first step in bringing the idea of the common good to the centre of the economy.

In his 1944 book *The Great Transformation*, Karl Polanyi helps debunk the notion of markets vs state. In his historical analysis he teaches us how markets were not natural developments, but were forced into existence by active state involvement: 'The road to the free market was opened and kept open by an enormous increase in continuous, centrally organized and controlled interventionism' (Polanyi, 1944, p. 162). By understanding the role the state played in forcing markets into existence, we understand that there are no deterministic market laws, but rather markets are outcomes of governance decisions. Similarly, Evans's (1995) concept of 'embedded autonomy' shows how states actively organize and stabilize markets through structured engagement with firms while retaining independence.

The fact that markets are shaped is not a normative point but a historical one. Market shaping can lead to more inequality, if the state is working for the interests of capital, as Marx argued. Or it can lead to more pollution, depending on the governance of companies, as well as the tax system. The question then becomes how to have the kind of government policy and governance structure that shape markets to create a more inclusive and sustainable capitalism. Outcomes orientation in this view means that instead of just viewing the bad things that arise in the economy as 'externalities', we can better understand how those bads are produced by the way markets work even in 'perfect' form, indeed through the very logic of the market.

The transition to a market-shaping view, driven by the common good, needs to thus start with an economy that has objectives, and markets are then shaped to achieve them. Through such a lens, relationships are no longer simply about cost benefit or supply–demand decisions and transaction cost economics, but rather are designed to achieve the objectives that markets are being shaped for. When we introduce the common good compass in Chapter 5, we will return to the question of who decides what the objectives are.

Critical for market shaping is not seeing 'bads' as externalities independent from how the market is shaped in the first place. Governments try to promote policies that internalize firms' externalities. For example, through carbon taxes, industrial relations reforms, sugar taxes and other mechanisms, governments can incentivize socially responsible corporate behaviour and increase the cost of social and environmental degradation. However, by seeing these problems as externalities in an otherwise perfect system rather than as their being deeply engrained in how markets work at their core, we end up only applying patches here and there, and little changes. Indeed, the investment firm Schroders has shown that if the externalities were truly addressed, 55 per cent of global profits (and hence a large chunk of global GDP) would be eliminated:

> The earnings listed companies generate for shareholders currently total US$4.1 trillion, which would fall by 55% to US$1.9 trillion if those social and environmental impacts crystalised as financial costs. One third of companies would become loss-making. The risk to profit pools and competitive positions is clear. (Schroders, 2019, p. 23)

In any case, what is the point of correcting after the fact? By the time these behaviours are recognized and dismantled, substantial financial and resource investments have already been made, and the social and environmental damage has already occurred. Ironically, when we clean up the effects of externalities like pollution, GDP actually *increases* because it requires payments to those doing the cleaning up.

Ecosystems vs transactions

If markets are outcomes of interactions between market actors, to develop a new economics for the common good we need to better understand how the relationship between the state, private institutions and civil society can be structured as a mutualistic 'partnership' or 'ecosystem.' In economics, public–private partnerships are discussed without a clear mechanism to ensure these partnerships are reciprocal and mutually beneficial.

Returning to the distinction made by biologists (in Chapter 2) between parasitic and symbiotic ecosystems, an economics of the common good must be built on symbiotic relationships between all actors: public and private, capital and labour, citizens and the state. At its core, this is about pre-distribution: preventing inequality by structuring relationships correctly from the outset, rather than relying solely on redistributive measures, which, while important, become less necessary if inequalities are prevented in the first place. Redirecting relationships to be more symbiotic requires attention to the social contract and how value is created. Since businesses cannot succeed without the involvement of multiple groups (labour, government, etc.), it follows that civil society, workers and governments should have the power to influence and benefit from business decisions (Mazzucato, 2018a).

Ecosystems are not just about policy design or behaviour but deep class and power relationships embedded in the law. In her book *The Code of Capital*, Katarina Pistor (2019) talks about how inequality is coded in the law. Without un-coding, inequality remains. Marx insisted that capital was a social relationship, based on capital exploiting labour. Pistor argues that capital isn't a natural or physical thing, but a legal construct crafted through what she calls 'legal coding': the selective deployment of legal tools (property rights, contracts, trusts and bankruptcy law) that give an asset priority, durability, universality and convertibility, enabling it to generate wealth and be enforced globally. Private lawyers act as the architects of this code, deliberately shaping financial instruments, corporate structures and even intangible assets to concentrate wealth among the legally sophisticated, perpetuating inequality across countries and generations.

Unless these legal frameworks are unravelled, it is nearly impossible to change the rules of the game that produce inequality and disempowerment. Attention to legal relationships must be matched by attention to all relationships at the interface between public and private sectors, from property rights to procurement contracts to bailout schemes. Only by redesigning these structures can we begin to foster the mutualistic ecosystems necessary for an economics of the common good.

Strengthening public value

Market shaping and symbiotic ecosystems must be connected to a renewed conception of public value. While Bozeman and Moore developed the idea of public value with a focus on government, in *The Value of Everything* (2018c) I argue that since value is not created exclusively inside or outside the private sector, but collectively by society as a whole, public value should capture the way value is created, not just the 'effect' it has on society. This means that government's role should be seen also as an investor, not just as a regulator or administrator. Under this perspective, public value must therefore address three questions: what value is created (for societal goals), how it is created (through fair and transparent relationships) and by whom (with genuine participation and co-creation) (Mazzucato, 2018c).

In recent years, terms such as 'public interest' or 'social value' have emerged as metrics that attempt to capture broader social, environmental and economic benefits that public actors might secure through tools like government purchasing (procurement). However, these approaches are often treated as add-ons rather than integrated into our understanding of collective value creation. Contractual commitments to social value are frequently ad hoc and lack alignment with broader organizational or societal objectives. This continues to reflect a market-fixing mindset that is primarily mitigatory (Mazzucato and Wainwright, 2024).

A dynamic view of public value, by contrast, recognizes the collective aspect of value creation. For instance, procurement policy can be designed not only *for* people but also *with* users in mind. Traditional procurement functions often focus narrowly on minimizing waste by weighing financial costs and benefits. While a public interest or social value lens might encourage additional considerations, such as green procurement initiatives, a public value lens will ensure that those designing procurement policies actively include the voices of the people who experience the service itself – an approach we return to in Chapter 7.

Table 3 highlights the difference between traditional notions of public interest/social value and dynamic public value, emphasizing distinctions such as the focus on outputs versus processes, technocratic versus participative methods and static versus dynamic market analysis.

In what follows, we examine the implications of market shaping, ecosystems and collective value creation for rethinking the roles of key actors in capitalist economies, including government, business, finance and labour, and for designing pre-distributive measures that foster a more symbiotic relationship between them.

Table 3 From public interest to public value

Public interest/social value	***Dynamic public value***
Value outputs and outcomes	Value outputs, outcomes, processes and relationships
Technocratic	Political and participative
Static market analysis	Dynamic market analysis
Understand value through the common lens of monetization	Weigh multiple and sometimes conflicting forms of value
Focused on what will be delivered	Focused on who will deliver it

Source: Based on Mazzucato and Wainwright (2024)

4.2 Rethinking government: from corrections to objectives

Market shaping requires rethinking the role of government beyond fixing markets. While traditional Keynesians think that the role of government is limited to counter-cyclical activity (more in the boom, less in the bust), strategic investments that spurred revolutions in IT, energy and health were not limited to a particular period in the business cycle. In fact, Keynes's view of government was much more radical. He argued that 'the important thing for government is not to do things which individuals are doing already, and to do them a little better or a little worse; but to do those things which at present are not done at all' (Keynes, 1926, pp. 46–7). What is not being done at all is not limited to doing what the private sector is not doing due to market failures. In the history of capitalist development, successful states have shaped markets and created new opportunities for business through investing in new technology, and also through challenge-oriented policies – from going to the moon to investing in the future of energy. As I argued in *The Entrepreneurial State*, without the US government investment, the history of ICT would have been very different. It was the US government that invested in the internet, but also the most radical changes in energy and health technologies. These were done with a purpose, often related to security interests. So, the real issue is how government investment can shape markets, or even create them, through a bold approach to outcomes orientation. Central to this is the redesign of policies that are less about outputs (simply counting activities) and more about concrete outcomes – such as going to the moon, reducing the digital divide,* achieving net zero and creating health for all.

Shaping markets is about steering with a clear direction: less about levelling the playing field and more about tilting it, rewarding and incentivizing projects that contribute to collective objectives. This means changing how we view government in the economy from a passive regulator to an active shaper of markets oriented around solving concrete problems. In my work I have called outcomes orientation *mission orientation* (Mazzucato, 2018a/b, 2021). Missions require government to set objectives and then to use all the levers to tilt the playing field in that direction (the mission being the *telos*). To act entrepreneurially, governments need to think in terms of being investors of first resort, not lenders of last resort, and apply all the levers at their disposal, from their purchasing agreements (e.g. procurement) to the loans and subsidies they provide to companies. Without a clear goal, these instruments are likely to just fund projects and activities here and there without the sum being bigger than the parts.

A *mission-oriented* approach also requires a holistic, all-of-government

* The 'digital divide' refers to the gap between those who have access to modern digital technologies like the internet, computers and smartphones and those who do not. It can include both access to physical technology and infrastructure as well as a skills gap. Permutations of this divide exist along the lines of income, geography (urban vs rural), age, education level, gender and so on. The concept captures not just access to tools and skills but also the ability to use technology meaningfully so as to benefit from its opportunities. One third of the global population – 2.6 billion people – remain offline as of 2024. In low-income countries, only 27 per cent of the population has internet access on average; in the Global North, the figure is 93 per cent (Poggi, 2025).

perspective. Departments must work together dynamically, combining top-down direction with bottom-up experimentation. This transforms the government–business relationship: rather than merely 'facilitating' or 'de-risking' private investment, the state should engage confidently and ambitiously with the private sector, setting reciprocal conditions and outcome-oriented contracts. Indeed, it is not a coincidence that NASA put 'no excess profits' into the procurement contracts for the Apollo mission. They were confident of their role and so did not want to be cheated by the private sector – they wanted to work well with them. And it was the same NASA head of procurement, Ernest Brackett, that set off an alarm bell when he warned that the excessive outsourcing to companies like McKinsey would weaken NASA's ability to work successfully with the private sector and would lead to NASA being 'captured by brochuremanship'. This is indeed why in addition to a new theory of government, we also need new practice which ensures that government has the capacity required to lead an outcomes-oriented approach (Mazzucato and Collington, 2023).

Market shaping, therefore, is not just about direction – it is also about capacity. It demands creative bureaucracies and new dynamic capabilities within the public sector.* Solving grand challenges – from the moon landing to climate change – requires governments to embrace uncertainty, welcome risk taking and encourage experimentation. If the state is to co-create value, it needs institutions that are experimental, adaptive, flexible, and capable of sensing

* In 2018, I founded the Institute for Innovation and Public Purpose (IIPP) at University College London precisely to help the public sector to develop the necessary capabilities to shape markets. At IIPP, we are currently building a Public Sector Capabilities Index, which I get into more in Chapter 10. This work aims to help cities move beyond static measures and build the institutional learning, trust and innovation capacity needed to address today's complex public challenges. The Index is designed to support city governments in assessing and improving their capabilities by identifying gaps, developing critical skills, learning from peer cities and attracting targeted investment. Ultimately, it seeks to enable governments to deliver services more efficiently and to evolve as more adaptive, legitimate and mission-driven institutions (Kattel et al., 2025b).

and seizing opportunities (Kattel and Mazzucato, 2018). This calls into question the bureaucratic and technocratic models of governance that dominate much of contemporary public administration, where risk aversion and rigid compliance undermine learning and innovation.

A growing body of work is rethinking the state not merely as a corrective force but as a *relational* one. Traditional models of public administration – rooted in hierarchical control, efficiency metrics and rule enforcement – have struggled to cope with today's complex and interdependent challenges. These models tend to treat the state as a provider of services or as a regulator that fixes market failures, prioritizing risk minimization and cost efficiency. Yet building a capable twenty-first-century state requires something different: a forward-looking, ambitious and human-centred model of governance that actively shapes relationships, fosters collaboration and co-creates public value.

This is where the idea of the relational state becomes central (Cooke and Muir, 2012). A relational state is one that recognizes that effective governance depends not only on the efficient delivery of services, but on the *quality of relationships* between citizens, public servants and institutions. It is adaptive, responsive and grounded in trust-based engagement rather than control. Instead of rigid accountability systems and standardized procedures, relational governance privileges discretion, local learning and collaborative problem solving – giving authority to those closest to the task. Empirical evidence from sectors such as education, health and community development shows that such decentralized and trust-based approaches can deliver better and more sustainable outcomes. For example, in *Radical Help*, Hilary Cottam (2018) discusses a project carried out in partnership with the UK's National Health Service (NHS) and local councils. Her team worked with people living with long-term conditions such as diabetes, depression and chronic pain. Instead of relying solely on doctors and formal appointments, the project created small, peer-based support networks that brought together patients, social workers, community nurses and local volunteers. The focus was on relationships and shared purpose: participants met regularly in informal settings, set their own goals, and supported one another in practical and emotional ways (for example, cooking healthy meals together or exercising as a group). Over time, this relational approach led to measurable improvements in wellbeing, reduced hospital visits and stronger community bonds, demonstrating that social connection and trust can be just as vital to health as medical care.

Conceptually, the relational state departs sharply from the assumptions of *transaction cost economics*, which frame public service delivery as a set of contractual transactions governed by metrics, incentives and performance targets. In contrast, relational approaches view the state–citizen interface as a co-productive endeavour where success emerges through dialogue, mutual understanding and the cultivation of shared goals over time. This shift redefines what state capability means. Rather than being about procedural compliance or technocratic optimization, it is about nurturing the dynamic capabilities that allow institutions to build trust and legitimacy, including listening, learning, empathizing and adapting.

This orientation aligns with broader traditions in public administration and political economy that emphasize embeddedness and discretion, from Lipsky's 'street level bureaucracy' to Elinor Ostrom's work on polycentric governance and collaborative problem solving. It also resonates with contemporary movements for democratic renewal that seek to bridge institutional and grassroots action. For instance, the inside/outside strategy pursued by progressive Democrats like Alexandria Ocasio-Cortez in the United States seeks to ensure the state reflects the will of the people by working inside formal institutions like Congress to draft transformative legislation, while simultaneously building outside pressure through grassroots movements, public campaigns and community-led activism. This recognizes that meaningful change rarely happens from within the system alone and depends on the active participation of the people.

In practice, building a relational state demands rethinking accountability and measurement. Traditional performance indicators – focused on outputs, efficiency and compliance – are poorly suited to capturing the quality of relationships, the legitimacy of processes or the developmental trajectory of institutions. A relational approach instead calls for developmental or learning-oriented accountability, which asks whether public organizations are becoming more capable, trusted and resilient over time. This requires both new metrics and a new ethos – one that values discretion, empathy and co-creation over control, replication and risk aversion (Kattel et al., 2025b; Kattel and Mazzucato, 2023; Collington and Mazzucato, 2024).

A relational state also requires dynamic capabilities, which enable governments to build coalitions, nurture trust and respond collaboratively to uncertainty. A key capability is the *art of listening* – an essential but often neglected skill in public administration. Listening is foundational to empathy, and empathy is the foundation of effective collective action. Without these capacities, even the most sophisticated policy instruments risk reinforcing distance rather than connection between the state and the people it serves.

4.3 Rethinking business: from shareholder value to collective value creation

The second big change for shaping markets is rethinking how businesses are run, because the type of businesses we have determines the kind of markets we get. If businesses are wed solely to maximizing shareholder value, then we get specific market outcomes: a financialized economy where what matters most are quarterly returns and stock prices. And if the wider concept of *stakeholder value* does not fundamentally address corporate governance, then it just becomes tokenistic without transformation. But if we build corporate models that genuinely align long-term success and value creation with social and environmental value, businesses can become powerful engines of good growth.

These questions are critical because, since the 1980s, corporate profits have become increasingly detached from the social and environmental problems their activities create. In 2021, companies in the S&P Global Broad Market Index were responsible for US$3.71 trillion in unpriced environmental costs – equal to more than 4 per cent of global GDP that year (S&P Global Sustainable1 and Capital Coalition, 2024). What's more, 26 per cent of these companies generated unpriced environmental costs greater than their net incomes (S&P Global Sustainable1 and Capital Coalition, 2024). Through corporate tax cuts, stagnating real wages and privatization, companies have been 'able to focus on maximizing corporate profits without too much concern for the costs of their actions created elsewhere in societies or economies' (Schroders, 2019, p. 6). In the end, governments and communities absorb the costs of these externalities – subsiding low wages through welfare payments, bearing the public health burden of pollution and paying the growing costs of climate change with public funds.

A market-shaping lens suggests these problems are not just about externalities; they are about the structure of the relationship between the state and business. We have become accustomed in Western societies to accepting that maximizing shareholder value is the best a company can do. Ever since Milton Friedman (1970) famously argued that 'the social responsibility of business is to increase its profits', shareholder value maximization has had a tight grip on global market economies. For decades, Friedman (1912–2006) promoted the idea that America's economic performance was declining because the principle of profit maximization was being violated. It was widely held that the only way to ensure that managers would not misallocate resources and that companies would run well was the maximization of shareholder value through a strong market.

Jack Welch, the former CEO of General Electric, was once one of the most prominent advocates of maximizing shareholder value as the primary goal of business. However, in later years, he publicly reconsidered this view, calling the focus on shareholder value 'the dumbest idea in the world' (Welch and Gunther, 2009). Welch came to believe that companies should instead prioritize building long-term value through satisfied customers, engaged employees and strong products. He argued that shareholder returns are the result of these efforts, not their purpose. This shift reflected a broader re-evaluation of short-termism in corporate management.

Nevertheless, the dogma of maximizing shareholder value persists today. The policy of prioritizing short-term returns and stock prices, key drivers of stock options (the main way executives are paid), has resulted in US firms spending over US$7 trillion on buying back their shares (Whitehouse and Wasson, 2022) and has become a central feature of modern capitalism. In 2024, share buybacks by S&P 500 companies reached a staggering US$942.5 billion (S&P Global, 2025). This practice is particularly prevalent in sectors like energy and pharmaceuticals: share buybacks by the fourteen largest publicly traded pharma companies totalled US$747 billion between 2012 and 2021 (Lazonick and Tulum, 2023), meaning that pharma companies prioritized giving returns to shareholders over investing that money back into further research and drug development. The oil and gas sector alone spent over US$136 billion on share buybacks in 2024 and returned even more to shareholders via dividends (more than US$213 billion) over the same period (Deloitte, 2024). Share buybacks are connected to a widening gap between CEO pay and average worker wages (e.g. Anderson, 2023; Tung and Milani, 2018), resulting in an average CEO-to-worker pay ratio for S&P 500 companies of 268 to 1 in 2023 (AFL-CIO, 2024). More generally, pay via stock options has been a key driver of inequality, benefiting the top 1 per cent of income earners (Piketty, 2014). However, the effect and method of boosting shareholder value are not that straightforward, with its impact varying between countries and depending on the institutional rules that shape and govern a particular region (Jensen and Meckling, 1976; Hall and Soskice, 2001).

The idea of shareholder value is based on a mistaken understanding of risk in our economy. It assumes that only shareholders take risks, since they have no guaranteed returns, while workers earn fixed salaries, banks receive fixed interest rates and so on (Jensen, 1986). In reality, this view overlooks the risks borne by other groups. For example, workers are financially vulnerable if wages stagnate, hours are cut or the company fails. Communities also bear risks, particularly social and environmental ones.

And an often ignored fact is that in the history of technological change, the biggest risk taker of all is often the state, investing in the early-stage, high-risk and high capital-intensive phase of innovation (Mazzucato, 2013). In such cases, the probability of failure is high, as any venture capitalist would admit. But when the state fails, the focus is often on government failure, ignoring the many successes from the internet to new forms of energy to the many blockbuster drugs that required early-stage public support. Whereas when the private sector fails, this is seen as part and parcel of risk taking.

This fundamental misunderstanding of risk taking in modern capitalism has consequences which reach far beyond even problems such as huge income inequality. That a critical driver of inequality has been linked with a problematic understanding of which actors are the greatest risk takers implies that combating short-termism (Haldane, 2016) and speculative forms of corporate governance (Kay, 2012) requires reforming finance and corporate governance and rethinking the very models of wealth creation upon which they are based (Lazonick and Mazzucato, 2013; Mazzucato, 2018c).

Stakeholder value

To move beyond shareholder value maximization, the concept of maximizing stakeholder value has taken hold. Oliver Hart, who was awarded the Nobel Prize in economics in 2016, convincingly argued that maximizing market value is not the same thing as maximizing stakeholder value, which itself differs from merely maximizing shareholder value. At a high level, stakeholder value theory provides a basis for firms to see that their responsibilities go beyond maximizing this value to reach a broader range of actors (Jamali, 2008; Mullenbach, 2007). In a related vein, the literature on the varieties of capitalism has highlighted the role of different forms of corporate governance in shaping businesses' response to shareholder pressures and created space for the consideration of stakeholders' interests. Business schools have attempted to define what doing good is by challenging shareholder maximization.

The concept of stakeholder value was first formalized by professor of business administration R. Edward Freeman in his book *Strategic Management: A Stakeholder Approach* (1984), although the concept has earlier roots in the work of other thinkers who reflected on similar ideas without using the term explicitly (Berle and Means, 1932; Dodd, 1932). Some pointed out that the large corporation had become a 'constellation of interests' rather than an instrument in the hands of a single individual or group (Berle and Means, 1932). Others argued that the corporation is a social institution in which the responsibilities of managers must extend beyond the shareholders to include all other groups (e.g. Dodd, 1932). The concept can also be traced back to early discussions of organizational ethics and corporate responsibility (e.g. Clark, 1916). Some scholars include non-human entities (like the natural environment) in this definition (e.g. Starik, 1995) – not unlike the idea of granting legal personhood to rivers.

All this has produced many definitions of the word 'stakeholder'. But for our purposes, a useful formulation is how it encourages companies to do 'good' by thinking beyond their shareholders and instead include 'any group or individual who can affect or is affected by the achievement of an organisation's purpose' (Freeman, 1984, p. 53).*

The formulation is telling because, while the concept of stakeholder capitalism has taken off in recent years, companies usually frame the concept as a means to an end – stakeholder engagement as a productive way of increasing shareholder value in the long run. And although there has been much talk about the social goals and

* Several stakeholder typologies have been proposed. Clarkson (1995) distinguishes between primary stakeholders, with formal or contractual ties (e.g. customers, shareholders), and secondary stakeholders, who lack such ties (e.g. the media, governments, local communities). Phillips, Freeman and Wicks (2003) differentiate between normative stakeholders, to whom firms have moral obligations, and derivative stakeholders, whose interests matter only insofar as they affect the company or its normative stakeholders. Pelle-Culpin (1998) identifies three groups: institutional stakeholders (laws, regulations, professional bodies), economic stakeholders (market actors) and ethical stakeholders (ethical pressure organizations). These typologies are illustrative but not exhaustive.

responsibilities of businesses, the value they create has not been distributed to all actors. For instance, in Larry Fink's 2022 annual address to the CEOs of the companies whose assets his firm manages on behalf of investors, the founding director of BlackRock – the world's largest asset manager – took the opportunity to advocate a more sustainable, socially conscious and forward-looking form of capitalism rooted in stakeholder rather than shareholder value. Yet Fink's vision for stakeholder capitalism, epitomizing the conventional view, focuses far too narrowly on intra-organizational corporate governance and fails to see the wider landscape of extra-organizational relations between different parts of society. It leaves untouched the traditional separation of stakeholder and shareholder identities. Stakeholders are considered and valued only insofar as their inclusion benefits the bottom line – the long-term profits of shareholders, who remain at the top of the pecking order.

The concept of stakeholder value remains weak because it fails to address how value is actually created (Mazzucato, 2022a). This is why I instead adopt the term public value, which better captures the idea that all economic actors co-create value and should be properly recognized and rewarded for their contributions. Too often, stakeholder value is treated as an afterthought – distributing a few crumbs to workers, communities and others – without challenging the underlying theory of value creation that excludes them as equal partners in the process. It has largely relied on moral appeals to business and has not fundamentally changed how firms interact with other actors in the value creation process. At best, it promotes the 'good' of society in an uneven and patchy way. By contrast, public value for the common good considers both who benefits and who shapes its creation (Mazzucato and Ryan-Collins, 2022). It is dynamic, contested and relational, not something imposed from above or fixed. Instead, it must be co-created and renegotiated through democratic processes that engage diverse voices, especially those historically excluded from policymaking spaces.

Even positive initiatives like B Corp (Benefit Corporation) have not fundamentally changed how public and private actors create value together – for instance, ensuring that taxes are paid and that risks and rewards are shared. B Corp is a private certification for for-profit companies that meet high standards of social and environmental performance, accountability and transparency, verified by the nonprofit B Lab. It signals that a business prioritizes purpose alongside profit, balancing the interests of people, planet and shareholders (B Lab, n.d.). Similarly, B Team is a global nonprofit comprised of influential business and civil society leaders (like Virgin Airline's CEO, Richard Branson) who promote responsible business practices that focus on social and environmental wellbeing (B Team, n.d.), but it remains unclear how B Team's framework can address entrenched problems like economic inequality without addressing more systemic change.

Such initiatives are important. But if they are to scale up and change how we 'do capitalism' they must be underpinned by a theory of collective value creation. To share risks and rewards with all stakeholders, instead of just the shareholders, it is critical to start with a different understanding of the collective risks that a society takes – workers, the public sector and community participants. Stakeholder value must embed justice and equity into how value is created from the start, in the design of mutualistic public–private relationships and capital–labour relationships. This can be done, for example, by making sure that prices of publicly funded medicines are capped, by making sure that intellectual property rights are not too wide and strong, by making sure that profits generated by collective effort are reinvested into production instead of share buybacks, and that the public purse gets a share of the upside rather than only covering the downside (Mazzucato, 2018c). We look at this further in Chapter 9.

Indeed, there are 'varieties of capitalism' (Hall and Soskice, 2001) which impact how specific countries govern relationships between business, government, and labour unions. For example, in Scandinavia and in Germany, worker representatives sit on the board of companies and take part in decisions on how companies invest their profits. Indeed, in Germany there have been periods when lower wages were accepted as long as the business promised to make investments in both human and physical capital (e.g.

worker training and innovations) that would increase productivity and hence long-run wages. Of course, as many workers have experienced in practice, there is no guarantee that wages will rise in line with productivity without negotiation and industrial action putting pressure on companies. In many parts of the world the increase in financialization has been matched by wages failing to go up with productivity (Bonizzi, Kaltenbrunner and Powell, 2023).

Environmental, Social and Governance (ESG) metrics are increasingly recognized as critical indicators of a company's long-term sustainability and ethical impact, directly influencing stakeholder value. By integrating ESG considerations into corporate strategy, firms aim to address the interests of a broad range of stakeholders – including investors, employees, customers and communities – thereby enhancing trust, reducing risk and fostering long-term value creation (Freeman, Harrison and Zyglidopoulos, 2018). For example, strong environmental practices can lower regulatory and operational risks, while robust governance ensures transparency and accountability, aligning business practices with stakeholder expectations (Eccles and Klimenko, 2019). However, ESG has also faced criticism as a vehicle for 'value washing', where companies adopt ESG language superficially to appeal to stakeholder concerns without making substantive changes. This critique highlights the risk that ESG metrics may be used more for reputation management than for genuinely delivering stakeholder value, raising questions about the depth and authenticity of corporate commitments (Mazzucato, 2022c).

True stakeholder value must be about how to create value in a way that recognizes the value of workers in production and involves them in decision making, as when trade unions have a seat on a board or in cooperative structures of production where decisions are made collectively. It means examining all the relationships between business and other actors and ensuring that the common good is at the heart of water contracts, property rights, public–private partnerships – including innovation collaborations – financial structures and more. At its heart, stakeholder value should also be about giving a true voice to all actors who create value.

4.4 Rethinking finance: from rent extraction to value creation

A market-shaping view of finance means first making sure that finance serves the economy, instead of the economy serving finance; and second making sure that finance is contributing to the right direction in the real economy – e.g. one that uses fewer fossil fuels. And third, if finance is outcomes oriented, then its structure matters, moving the focus from financial gaps to the quality of finance. Indeed, as we will see, there is plenty of finance, but it is simply often of the wrong type (e.g. too short-term) and misallocated (e.g. going in the wrong direction).

The context is one in which the financial sector has increased its share in the economy relative to other sectors. In Figure 6, we see

Figure 6 The decoupling of the stock market from the real economy

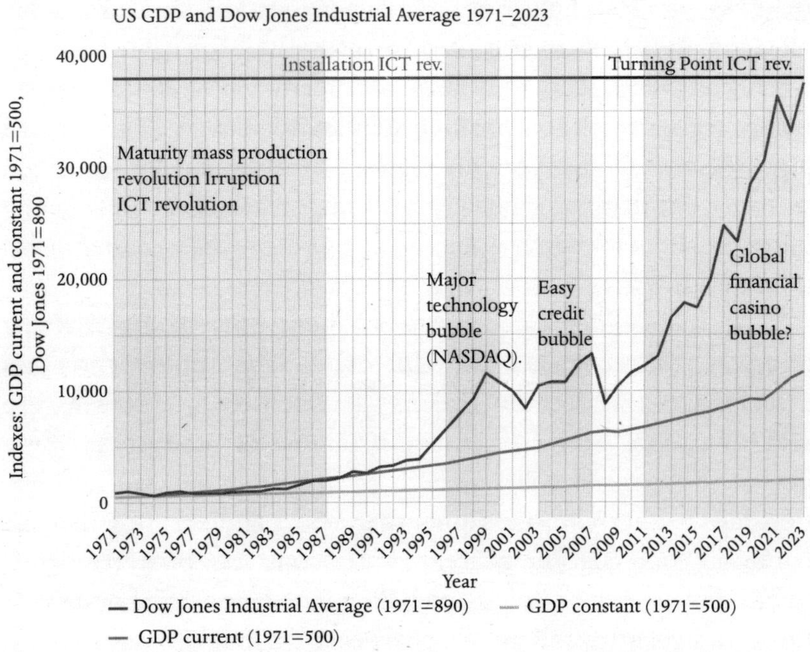

Source: US Bureau of Economic Analysis and S&P Global

the growth of the financial sector has outpaced the growth of the economy as a whole in most of the developed world, driven by the rapid rise of financial services and investment banks.

And over the past forty years or so the stock market has become increasingly decoupled from the real economy – see Figure 7. The growing size of the financial sector and the financialization of our economies point to the need to reduce finance's share of the economy, while making sure that the finance that exists truly serves it.

In theory, finance should be greasing the wheels of industry and commerce and allocating capital efficiently for further investment. Yet in the last fifty years it has been greasing itself. A high percentage of finance goes back to the financial sector, or more broadly finance, insurance and real estate (FIRE), and much of the financial sector simply makes money by shifting existing assets around. In the UK, 80 per cent of finance goes back to FIRE, partly due to the financialization of real estate and speculation that has inflated real estate bubbles in the US – the key factor in the 2008 crash (Ryan-Collins et al., 2012).

Furthermore, finance is often very short-term, making trillions

Figure 7 Global financial assets relative to global GDP

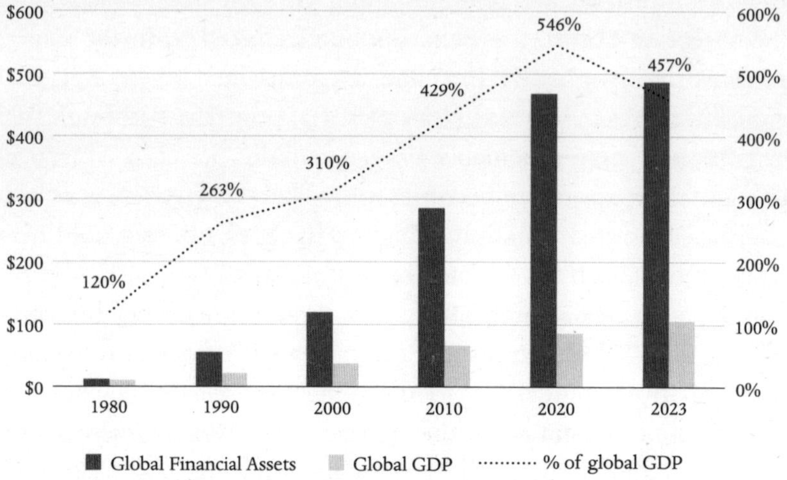

Source: The Transnational Institute (2018), IMF (2025), Financial Stability Board (2024)

from millisecond trades that are just about buying and selling existing assets instead of creating new ones. To make matters worse, private equity firms and similar businesses often exploit patient (long-term) finance, like that in pension funds, to buy up long-term infrastructure such as global utilities and housing, generating fees and rents like a troll under a bridge. This distortion of how capital is allocated was especially evident during recent decades when low interest rates caused financial institutions to search for yields in fee-bearing activities. In *The Value of Everything* (2018c), I looked at the rise of these rents in modern capitalism: from land, to financial instruments, to the structure of patents, to modern algorithmic rents. Brett Christophers (2020) has called this 'rentier capitalism'.

As Perez (2002) argues in her book *Technological Revolutions and Finance Capital*, financial capital plays a crucial role in enabling the transition from one techno-economic paradigm to another, but only when it is redirected from speculative activities towards productive investment that supports innovation and long-term societal goals. Perez's work also shows that periods of systemic crisis constitute critical moments for such redirection. Historically, when speculation, corruption, inequality and populism have intensified, technological revolutions have often prompted state intervention aimed at improving and re-legitimating the socio-economic system. The Victorian boom, the Belle Époque (referred to in the United States as the Progressive Era) and the post-war Golden Age each represent stages in this trajectory of social progress. Although such progress has been undeniably slow, it remains possible. Moreover, substantial improvement becomes more likely when there is a viable roadmap for transformation, which in the present era would need to encompass both the Global South and planetary health.

In this sense, reshaping finance is not about more money, but about aligning financial structures and incentives with the real economy's transformative potential. Key to reforming finance is tackling its short-term nature both indirectly through tax incentives (discussed more below) and directly through more public funds that can help direct patient finance. The latter include institutions designed from the start for the long term. Whereas private investments like venture capital tend to focus on exits within 3–5 years through either a buy-out or an initial public offering, public banks tend to invest with long-term horizons of 10–20 years. Public banks, both national and multilateral, are the best place to do this. There are over 500 public development banks worldwide, about 90 per cent of which are national and 10 per cent multilateral. Collectively, these institutions hold over US$22 trillion in assets (Mazzucato, 2023a; Xu et al., 2021; 2023). The total is even higher if other public financial institutions like pension funds are included, representing a vast pool of capital that could be mobilized to advance the common good.

Governments can use public banks to help steer patient finance towards businesses that are willing to work with governments on their missions, such as net zero objectives. This means that loans need to include conditionalities in the way contracts are structured so that the borrowing companies invest in, for example, greener and more inclusive production methods (Mazzucato and Macfarlane, 2025).

Other types of financial institutions like sovereign wealth funds (SWFs) and community funds also have the potential to be harnessed for the common good if governed correctly. Assets under SWF management have grown from US$1.2 trillion in 2000 to US$13.4 trillion in 2025 (Global SWF, 2025), but their governance varies widely. Despite being publicly owned, many SWFs operate behind closed doors and are driven more by market logic and perceived national interest than by the common good (Cummine, 2013; Maire, Mazarei and Truman, 2021).

On the more local level, community funds offer a potentially transformative approach to finance by creating economic activity while shifting control to local communities. These funds are often designed to meet local needs and empower citizens through direct participation in decision making. By pooling resources at community level, they have the potential to foster economic resilience, social equity and regional development by lending money to those often excluded from traditional financial mechanisms, creating and distributing value through the same mechanism: for example, the

Self-Determination Fund for the First Peoples' Assembly of Victoria, Australia, whose purpose is to help build capacity, wealth and prosperity for current and future generations of first peoples (Self-Determination Fund, n.d.).

Public financial institutions do not automatically serve the common good – they are only as effective as they are designed to be. These institutions are often highly contested spaces, with accusations that they are public only in name, but not really delivering public value. Public value generated will depend on how they are governed – who sets their mission, who holds them accountable and who has a say in decision-making processes (Mazzucato and Macfarlane, 2025). For example, if a public bank or a sovereign fund is replenished with profits made from fossil fuels, its contribution to public value may be called into question. The same applies to lending, which primarily helps large firms or those in particular sectors due to lobbying. Blended finance schemes, which have been created to foster development by deploying public funds to de-risk investments and incentivize private capital to flow towards development objectives, have failed to produce much development finance, generating only about US$15 billion a year (Mazzucato, 2025b). Moreover, the resulting private sector multiplier is very low, at approximately US$0.30 to the dollar. To remedy these shortcomings, more directionality should be embedded into public–private partnerships through tools such as conditionalities placed in public contracts. For example, the loans made to the steel sector in Germany by the German public bank (KfW) were conditional on the sector's reducing the material content of production – which it did through employing reuse, recycle and repurpose throughout the supply chain (Mazzucato and Rodrik, 2024).

From financial gaps to shaping finance

Our focus here is on how to make financing of the real economy more sustainable and inclusive and improve its quality. It is a very different emphasis from assuming that the problem is simply the quantity of finance, rather than the quality. While it is true that the gap between what is needed and what is committed for financing the SDGs is close to US$7 trillion, focusing on this alone means we do not think enough about the structure of the finance, its long-term or short-term nature, the terms of the loans and the 'voice' at the table (Mazzucato, 2025b).

The problem is not the lack of finance but that finance is lost and not directed. By thinking about shaping finance, instead of financial gaps, we can move towards rethinking the global financial system to serve the common good. For example, a financial transaction tax designed to shift finance away from millisecond trades towards long-term investment in the real economy could generate between US$238 and $419 billion a year (Pekanov and Schratzenstaller, 2019). Steering that finance into green incentives could help sustainable transitions instead of worsening climate change. In 2022, governments globally directed an extraordinary US$7 trillion towards fossil fuel subsidies. Fossil fuel price reform could generate US$4.4 trillion in additional revenue by 2030 (though some would likely have to be redirected towards energy cash transfers) (Black et al., 2023). A global wealth tax could generate US$250 billion annually (Zucman, 2024). Closing the tax evasion/avoidance gap could generate an additional US$492 billion a year (Tax Justice Network, 2024). Achieving such shifts, however, depends on political will and governance structures that can overcome entrenched interests and ensure these resources are redirected effectively. That is not easy and will take time.

Using tax policy as a lever to influence the structure and direction of finance is a departure from the role it has long been boxed into: raising revenue and reducing deficits. By adopting more of a market-shaping role, tax can help steer capital towards long-term investments that are aligned with public priorities. Momentum is growing with initiatives like the OECD Global Minimum Tax (GMT), the OECD/G20 Framework on Base Erosion and Profit Shifting (BEPS) and the Bridgetown Initiative (see Chapter 12).*

* The OECD Global Minimum Tax deal proposes a minimum 15 per cent tax on the profits of multinationals with earnings above €750 million. More than 140 countries have committed to implementing the agreement (Torkington, 2024).

Negotiations for a UN Framework Convention on International Tax Cooperation are progressing, in response to the demands and pressure from countries from the Global South. These negotiations explicitly aim to establish a global tax structure that is 'inclusive, fair, transparent, efficient, equitable and effective' and supports sustainable development (UNGA, 2025).

These proposals understand tax as a political instrument to fund a just climate transition and realign financial markets with collective goals. To ensure that these various initiatives have a chance of being effectively implemented, they must be nested within a more holistic, pre-distributive framework of market shaping that ensures the economy is more equitable from the beginning. We discuss co-creation and participation in Chapter 7 and 'pre-distribution' in Chapter 9, and return to these global initiatives in the context of the Common Good Economy in Part III.

4.5 Rethinking labour: from redistribution to pre-distribution

Market shaping is about pre-distribution and making sure symbiotic ecosystems create functional relationships between capital and labour, between public and private actors, and between the state and citizens. In this way, so much energy does not need to be spent on fixing things when they go wrong. In the case of labour, pre-distribution is about ensuring that labour receives its fair share before taxation, rather than relying on redistribution afterwards. It also means having a voice in the direction of change, i.e.

Similarly, the base erosion and profit shifting (BEPS) framework put forth by the OECD and G20 aims to address the activities by which multinationals shift profits to low- or no-tax locations. Under the proposed framework, over 140 countries and jurisdictions are working together to implement fifteen measures to tackle tax avoidance, including the GMT (OECD, 2024a). And the Bridgetown Initiative – led by Barbados and discussed further in Part III – calls for reforms to the international financial architecture to provide Global South countries with debt relief and affordable access to green finance (Bridgetown Initiative, 2024).

the role of labour in the active shaping of markets. Polanyi (1944) described worker struggles as part of a 'double movement', a recurring tension in capitalist societies where market expansion inevitably triggers 'counter-movements' through which society seeks to protect itself from the corrosive effects of commodification. These tensions, rather than being obstacles, can actually help shape markets towards more equitable outcomes by embedding social protections and democratic participation within economic structures. And rather than being only defensive, stakeholder capitalism needs to be about reorganizing boards, with workers having a proactive voice on investment agendas, as they do in many Scandinavian countries, where trade unionists sit on boards.

Such lessons are critical today when it is clear the labour system isn't working. Over the past fifty years, CEO pay in the United States has grown dramatically faster than that of the average worker. In 1965, CEOs earned about twenty-one times more than typical employees, but by 2023 that gap had expanded to roughly 290 times. This widening disparity highlights how executive compensation has surged by over 1,000 per cent since 1978, compared to only 24 per cent growth for workers (Bivens, Gould and Kandra, 2024). Indeed, across the globe most workers struggle to secure a liveable wage and are often unable to cover basic needs, like decent housing and adequate healthcare. In some cases, the gap is even wider. For instance, Starbucks CEO Brian Niccol reportedly received US$95.8 million in compensation after taking the role in September 2024, more than 6,000 times the company's median employee salary of US$14,674, many of these employees occupying insecure hourly and part-time positions (Batish, 2025).

Precarious working conditions are even more prevalent in the Global South. In many low- and middle-income countries, a large proportion of people work in the informal economy – more than 75 per cent in sub-Saharan Africa and between 50 and 74 per cent in Central America (ILO, 2024). These workers often lack basic protections like minimum wages, social safety nets or the right to organize, making them highly vulnerable to exploitation and economic shocks (ILO, 2024). Guy Standing (2011) describes this growing class of workers as the *precariat* – people trapped in unstable employment without security or voice in shaping their livelihoods. As global supply chains increasingly rely on this kind of precarious work, the divide between those who create value and those who benefit from it continues to grow.

What this shows is a labour system that values people according to their hierarchical position and market power, not on the effort they put in or whether their work supports the kinds of jobs essential to building a flourishing society. If we are serious about creating an economy rooted in the common good, we must therefore fundamentally rethink how labour is structured. This means redesigning institutions and protections to give workers voice, dignity and agency – and reward the types of work our society needs. Without that, we will stay stuck in a system where growth is not shared, and social divisions keep deepening.

Of course, workers have been fighting for better conditions for a long time. Labour unions have played a crucial role in this struggle, fighting for so many things we take for granted today: weekends, holiday pay, sick pay, the right to organize, and banishing all the 'bads' like child labour. That fight continues today. For instance, after hearing about their new CEO's huge compensation package, Starbucks workers across the US launched a wave of strikes, following years of demands for higher wages, more-predictable schedules and safer workplaces. Since late 2021, Starbucks workers have led a significant unionization movement, with over 500 US outlets – representing more than 12,000 baristas – voting to unionize as Starbucks Workers United. Despite extensive pushback by the company, workers have persisted in striking and fighting for better working conditions (Sainato, 2025). Their efforts have sparked a deeper conversation about how workers can reclaim power and shape the labour market to deliver more equitable and sustainable outcomes.

However, unions are often not enough on their own. In fact, in some cases, unions have been influenced or captured by political interests, which has limited their effectiveness. In addition to organized labour, civil society movements have also been critical for change. Feminist movements transformed workplace norms by challenging pay discrimination, demanding parental leave and validating the social value of care work. Anti-racist movements have expanded fair hiring practices and pressed firms to take diversity seriously. Environmental movements have built broad public coalitions that place renewable energy at the heart of industrial and policy strategy, proving that citizen activism can steer markets. These examples show that shaping the economy is not just up to governments or companies – it can happen through the collective efforts of workers and the broader society. What is critical is to make sure that such conditions are embedded in all contracts from the beginning. For example, the CHIPS and Science Act, introduced by President Biden in 2022, included requiring companies benefiting from government contracts to pay fair wages and improve working conditions (Mazzucato and Rodrik, 2023).

New ways of owning and running workplaces are also giving workers more power and voice to shape a fairer labour system. This is about co-creation. In Germany, as mentioned previously, co-determination laws require large companies to allocate a significant portion of their supervisory board seats to employee representatives. This system, known as *Mitbestimmung,* ensures that workers have a voice in key corporate decisions – from strategic planning to social policies – which helps balance the interests of employees with those of shareholders. Companies with co-determination tend to invest more in job security, worker training and long-term sustainability, rather than focusing solely on short-term profits (Fulton, 2020). And contrary to the fears expressed by many economists, there is no evidence that co-determination reduces investment, productivity, longevity or other measures of company performance (Jäger, Noy and Schoefer, 2022).

Similarly, the Mondragón cooperative in Spain offers a useful example of worker ownership and democratic governance in action. Founded in the 1950s, Mondragón is a federation of cooperatives where employees are also owners who participate directly in decision making through elected councils. Profits are shared among members, and the cooperative prioritizes employment stability, social welfare and community development over traditional short-term shareholder value (Whyte and Whyte, 1991). This model demonstrates how solidarity-based ownership can align business success with the wellbeing of workers and their communities.

Improving working conditions is not just about justice – it is also good for the economy. As Keynes (1936) argued, higher employment and incomes boost demand, which supports investment and growth. When workers have secure jobs and fair pay, they spend more, creating a positive cycle that benefits the whole economy. So, investing in labour is investing in stability and growth.

These ideas fit with the broader vision of the common good economy. Markets cannot be shaped for collective benefit if work remains precarious and unequal. History shows that when workers and civil society organize, they can do more than merely protect themselves from market failures: they can help shape markets towards fairer and more sustainable outcomes. From demands for safer workplaces and fair pay to campaigns for anti-discrimination and climate action, collective efforts have demonstrated the capacity to reshape economic priorities around shared values. An economy that serves the common good will depend on strengthening these efforts – empowering workers and civil society to build a more dignified and sustainable future of work.

Conclusion

The economics of the common good requires moving away from fixing market failures and government failures towards actively shaping how markets are governed. This is about how to steer markets, govern institutions and, especially, how to conceptualize the underlying values and relationships in the economy. That is why the theory here respects but differs both from the work of the commons in economics, and from the work of communitarians in philosophy. The commons concept still sees the government as a regulator and focuses on why governments fail (including being captured). Its solution is more bottom-up community involvement to govern resources outside the realm of public–private partnership. However, this sort of governance design is harder to scale beyond the local level once we enter the territory of grand challenges which require changes to the design of policies, corporate governance, public–private partnerships and global cooperation.

At the same time, communitarians, such as Michael Sandel, differentiate the idea of the common good from market mechanisms, claiming that the good life can only be achieved by building on the attributes of moral reflection, civic responsibility and community engagement. This requires treating caring activities, for example, as non-market activities. While of course some activities should not enter formal markets (e.g. one can debate whether water, care and education should be market driven or publicly financed), the common good economy can help redesign those very market systems that many who believe in the common good are sceptical about. Limiting the common good to 'non-market' activities means the problematic market system itself remains intact. Rather, the radical agenda is to enshrine the idea of the common good in how advanced capitalist economies are structured. The questions in this chapter include what the common good means for how we structure public sector institutions, for how corporate entities are governed (shareholder or stakeholder capitalism?), for how financial markets function (for themselves or for the real economy?) and for what they mean for people (workers and civil society more generally).

To address these questions, we must look at the actual actors in those systems, how they are governed and how they inter-relate. Pursuing the common good thus means all actors must seek the 'good' in their interactions and relationships. But how can we know whether this is being achieved? How can we make sure the concept of the common good is not captured by a minority?

To do so, we move to Part II with reflections on how a common good 'compass' can help us work together in different ways, with common good principles (elements of the compass) helping to *shape markets* with explicit directionality, creating value collectively, and putting the common good at the heart of all relationships so that the characteristics of ecosystems are as important as the rate and direction of economic growth.

PART II

The Elements of the Common Good

If we look at the whole picture, we're bound to feel hopeless and helpless . . . but once we realise that even small actions cumulatively can make a big difference, we can start taking action to make the world a better place.

– Jane Goodall (1934–2025)

5.

An introduction to the common good compass

Markets are always shaped. The question is how to shape markets towards the common good, with clear principles that guide the way in which all economic actors interact. If steering the economy towards the common good is like setting out in a sailing boat, then various forces may shift our course in different directions. Indeed, as we have seen, there are multiple ways to talk about 'good' in economics, from the commons, to the public good, to the public interest and, of course, to the rhetoric around stakeholder value, collective action and shared purpose. A compass is thus indispensable. Without one, we may end up drifting wherever the strongest gust – or loudest actor – pushes us. With it, we can continually reorient ourselves even in rough seas towards a direction that prioritizes collective flourishing.

Part II of the book therefore begins with a 'compass' that can be used to ask different questions from those that are usually posed. It is not about which market failure is to be fixed, but the direction we want our economy to sail in. It is not about setting that direction in a technocratic way but rather about asking how the destination can be deliberated together. Instead of using patents to incentivize innovation, the question is how to govern knowledge. And instead of one actor 'de-risking' another, the question is how both risks and rewards can be socialized in equitable ways.

Navigating the economy towards the common good is not only a matter of vision – it also requires practical tools for action. Markets, institutions and social norms do not automatically align with the common good. They are shaped by the institutions and tools we design, the rules we set, the incentives we create and the interactions we enable. This means that achieving shared goals depends as much on how we organize economic relationships as on what those goals are. In other words, the challenge is not only to decide the direction we want to head in, but also to embed common good principles into the very structures and practices of the economy that allow that direction to be realized.

To translate this vision into practice, I introduce here five elements of a compass which together comprise a unifying foundation on which an economy for the common good can be built. Like Ostrom's design principles, the five elements identify key features that are required for systems to align collective action with the common good. Each element addresses a core dimension of economic life, providing principles for shaping markets, institutions and relationships in ways that align with the common good.

The first element, **purpose and directionality**, promotes outcomes-oriented policies that promote the common good. The second element, **co-creation and participation**, allows different stakeholders in the economy to participate in debate, discussion and consensus building on the desired direction. The third element, **collective learning and knowledge sharing**, helps design true purpose-oriented partnerships that drive collective intelligence and the sharing of knowledge. The fourth element, **access for all and reward sharing**, ensures that the benefits and risks inherent to economic activity are equitably distributed among stakeholders, whether through equity schemes, royalties, pricing or collective funds. The fifth element, **transparency and accountability**, ensures public legitimacy and engagement by upholding commitments among all actors and by aligning on clear evaluation mechanisms.

The aim is to use the compass to help steer the economy towards collective flourishing. Table 4 considers how the five elements of the common good compass relate to the more traditional way in which neoclassical theory looks at collective action.

The compass can complement other holistic metrics, dashboards

Figure 8 A common good compass

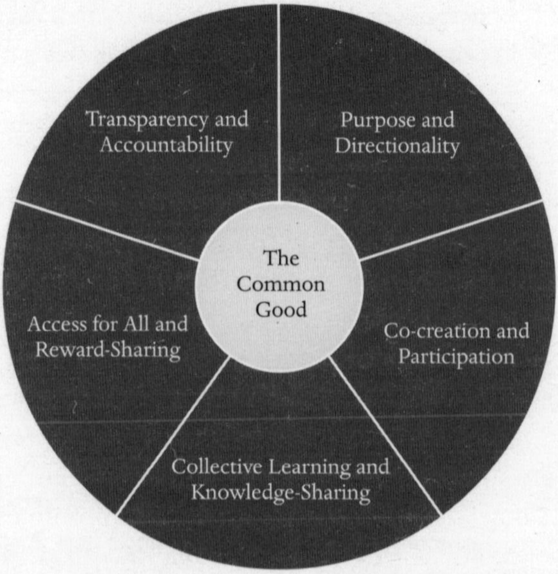

Source: Mazzucato (2023b)

Table 4 A comparison of the common good compass with neoclassical collective action theory

Principles	Economics of the common good	Neoclassical collective action theory
Purpose and directionality	Directional and outcomes oriented with collective goals and an emphasis on long-term public value creation.	Individual utility maximization assuming all actors are rational and should prioritize efficiency and profit. Directionality is revealed.
Co-creation and participation	Co-creation and participation are embedded in economic processes and decision making is inclusive and democratic.	Market driven and decentralized with collective action emerging as a by-product of individual decisions rather than deliberate processes.

Collective learning and knowledge sharing	Collective learning and transparency through open access and purpose-oriented partnerships, with IP structured to maximize collective intelligence.	Information asymmetry and individual strategies, with actors pursuing IP rights to protect private interests.
Access for all and reward sharing	Access for all and reward sharing based on collective value creation, with the benefits from investment and innovation distributed equitably.	Acceptance of inequality and power imbalances, justified through a market-determined approach to 'value' and 'productivity'.
Transparency and accountability	Transparency and accountability, with mechanisms to ensure public legitimacy, enforce commitments and align evaluation with shared goals.	Focus on correcting market failures after they occur, with limited accountability focused on addressing inefficiencies rather than fostering ongoing legitimacy.

Source: Author's creation

and tools. It moves beyond the principles in Ostrom by bringing principles of collective action to the centre of how capitalist actors interact, not only in cases where there are government and market failures but also in large cases like a global vaccination programme, the design of digital public infrastructure or the construction of international financial institutions. While the theory of the commons has offered an alternative to the market–state dichotomy, it stopped short of challenging the underlying assumptions that sustain this divide, particularly the view of the state as primarily interventionist and corrective. How market shaping informs all goal-oriented relationships is the purpose of our compass.

Critically, the compass must help us achieve the goals that countries have set themselves, such as the SDGs, established in 2015 by the United Nations and adopted by all 193 member states. These goals provide a global framework for assessing national wellbeing by encompassing seventeen interconnected goals that address economic, social and environmental dimensions. Several countries, including Finland, Iceland, New Zealand, Scotland and Colombia, have developed 'wellbeing dashboards' rooted in the SDGs to inform policymaking and track progress beyond GDP. Notably, Goal 17 on Partnerships for the Goals emphasizes international cooperation, multi-stakeholder collaboration and knowledge sharing as essential to achieving sustainable development. This global, goal-oriented perspective is closely aligned with the first principle of the common good compass. Together, the SDGs can promote inclusive, systemic and collaborative policymaking aimed at long-term societal transformation. How those goals resonate locally – taking into consideration context and genuine participation – is critical to ensuring that the ultimate outcome fosters more inclusive societies.

Where the common good compass pushes us further is in giving much more attention to the details of the interactions between human beings and organizations on the way towards mission accomplished. The common good is not only about the goal but the way it is achieved, and the five elements together allow us to hold the concept of the common good accountable.

With a compass, every element is understood in relation to the other – you cannot go south if you do not know which way is north. And as with the SDGs, there is no point in tackling one goal in isolation: to address SDG 13 on climate change, we might electrify transport, but if we end up using too much water to extract lithium for the needed electric batteries, we will impede progress on SDG 6 (ensuring water for all). Solving one challenge while hindering progress on another will not take us in the right direction.

Similarly, with the common good compass, the focus cannot just be on one element. For example, a public bank driven by the common good must have a clear direction (element 1); its governance should be co-created so that diverse voices – including those from the Global South in the case of multilateral development banks – can influence how funding is allocated (element 2); and loan contracts should ensure both knowledge sharing and equitable distribution of rewards (elements 3 and 4); while the processes for disbursing funds should be fully accountable and transparent (element 5). Similarly, the design of digital platforms – when guided towards social or environmental good – needs to adhere to these elements. The compass can focus the questions asked: What is the platform's true goal? How is it governed? And how are the benefits shared? If we focus on only one or a few elements, the system risks reproducing the very inequalities and inefficiencies it was meant to address.

The remainder of Part II approaches each element in turn, taking inspiration from parts of the world where seeds of the common good are revealed. Learning from these experiences is key. Jane Goodall's quote at the start of Part II reminds us that we need to learn from examples, and be inspired by meaningful actions, no matter how small. But ultimately, unless we can scale such actions, and render them key to how the system works, the current economic system remains intact. The compass helps us both recognize those actions, but also teach us how to reach that cumulative and systemic learning and impact Goodall calls for.

Conclusion

The common good compass derives from a market-shaping view of the state that understands how to create public value through collective action, with symbiotic interactions. The five elements should be used to challenge and redistribute power more equitably across society, which can create more fertile ground for nurturing the common good.

By emphasizing purpose and directionality, co-creation and participation, collective learning and knowledge sharing, access for all and reward sharing and transparency and accountability, the common good compass pushes us to design dynamic and outcomes-oriented systems and assess how existing ones may fall short.

The common good is not utopian. In fact, many of its elements are already evident in our society – consider the multiple ways in which goal orientation, collaboration and benefit sharing happen in our everyday lives. Yet these seeds cannot bear fruit because there is no guiding compass to systematize these experiences and scale them across an economy. In the next chapters of Part II we gather insights on each element from real-world examples – from how some public banks operate, to how energy communities work, and how some digital platforms are structured. None of these are perfect, but each offers valuable lessons about the properties and nuances of the common good, informing us how we might expand such practices across the broader economy.

6.
Purpose and directionality

Hope can feel hard to come by when we look at the scale of today's global challenges. But it doesn't have to be this way. Seeds of solutions already exist in the many actions, projects and movements taking place all around us. Across communities, organizations and institutions, people are working together to solve problems and to design a fairer and more sustainable economy.

To see this clearly, we need to change our perspective. Rather than focusing only on what is broken, we can start noticing where meaningful change is already happening. The seeds of transformation are everywhere: in libraries and youth centres, community-owned energy projects, social enterprises, and new governance models that value participation and care. Each may seem small on its own, but together they point to the possibility that our economy can be built around the common good.

Recognizing these existing efforts is crucial. Change rarely comes from a single breakthrough or policy. It grows through the accumulation of actions that begin to align around shared principles and goals. The challenge is to connect these efforts into a more coherent framework capable of scaling and sustaining transformation.

This is where the common good compass comes in. It provides on the one hand a structure to align and scale what is already happening, establishing a clear direction and holding the system accountable to make sure that those who use the common good term do not use it in vain. Purpose and directionality – the first element of the compass – are where this process begins.

In the economy this is critical. The obsession with the rate of economic growth has led us to overlook something more important: the direction of that growth. Every economy has a direction, whether government gets involved or not. A deregulated economy has a direction. A financialized economy has a direction. An economy based on unsustainable business practices has a direction. But these are not *good* directions if they result in inequality, climate change or biodiversity loss. Recognizing that all economies already move in some direction invites us to ask: who sets the direction, how is it determined, and does it serve the long-term interests of society or just a select few?

Purpose and directionality, our first element of the common good compass, mean moving beyond the narrow, growth-only mindset towards actively deciding where we want the economy to go to serve the common good and aligning policies and business behaviour to get there. If an economy is working towards a specific societal goal, every instrument – from tax incentives to direct funding through grants or procurement contracts – should be aligned to make progress in that direction. And the way businesses create value, and profits, needs to be aligned from the beginning, rather than correcting for mistakes at the end, or doing good in tokenistic ways (e.g. corporate social responsibility). In practice, rather than simply 'levelling the playing field', this means *tilting* the playing field so that moving towards the goal becomes easier. It is not about rewarding some actors over others, but about creating incentives that mobilize all actors towards a desired outcome.

This is the essence of shaping markets we discussed in Part I: moving beyond repairing what is broken and towards actively designing the future we want, using policy tools as incentives to reorient public and private investment and collaboration towards shared goals. This chapter explores how the concept of 'mission orientation', on which I have written much (Mazzucato, 2018a/b; 2021), can provide the economy with that clear sense of purpose and directionality – and how making it explicit means it can also be contested.

6.1 Mission orientation

Discussing the direction of economic growth, rather than simply its rate, begins by identifying the key problems economies seek to address – many of which are already articulated in frameworks such as the SDGs and in national climate or health strategies. The real challenge lies in translating these broad ambitions into concrete missions that can guide and coordinate action across sectors. Missions are ambitious, clear and time-bound objectives that mobilize cross-sectoral solutions to resolve challenges (Mazzucato, 2021). By starting from the question 'What is the problem we want to solve?', missions give economic activity a clear direction, aligning diverse actors towards shared goals, such as tackling climate change, expanding digital inclusion and improving health equity. In the next chapter we will look at how missions are set, and how that process can be as participatory as possible through a common good lens. Here we ask more about what it means to direct economic growth via a mission-oriented approach.

To be effective, missions must meet five specific criteria (Mazzucato, 2018a). They should (1) be bold and inspirational with wide societal relevance; (2) set a clear, targeted, measurable and time-bound direction so progress is clear; (3) be ambitious yet realistic; (4) encourage cross-disciplinary, cross-sectoral and cross-actor innovation; and (5) involve multiple, bottom-up solutions. When governed with confidence, missions can forge new partnerships between government, business and labour, breaking down a country's biggest challenges into more manageable policy priorities and reorganizing production, distribution and consumption to achieve them. If done right, they are meant to enable bottom-up experimentation towards mission accomplished.

Mission-oriented approaches have been widely used by the military–industrial complex but are far less common when it comes to addressing social problems. It is not a coincidence: when a goal is seen as urgent, governments tend to adopt outcomes-oriented tools (such as advance purchasing agreements) and even create money out of thin air to meet those goals. This is different from budgets for climate, health and other societal challenges which are viewed as limited, often pitting them against each other – more spending on health means less for climate. In recent years Germany has faced intense scrutiny over the costs of its climate transition, with every euro for renewable energy and green infrastructure dissected in the name of fiscal prudence. Yet, when defence spending surged past €100 billion after 2022, questions of affordability and efficiency seemed to fade into the background. Economic discipline is demanded for protecting the planet, but rarely for preparing for war. It is also interesting that the military has more confidence than other sectors to deliberatively seek the right kinds of partnerships with business to ensure prices and intellectual property support their security objectives. While the military may invest in health-related technologies to protect soldiers and ensure it is available to all of them, civilian health systems are often less coherent: despite significant public funding for medicine development, many people cannot access the medicines their own taxes helped create (Angell, 2004; Mazzucato, 2018a).

Mission-oriented contracts are more ambitious than those oriented to simply support a sector. Space missions require many sectors to innovate to solve problems, not to simply be subsidized or 'de-risked'. The Apollo programme required NASA to work with private sector actors willing to innovate in an outcomes-oriented way, in industries as different as nutrition, materials and electronics. For this reason, NASA's head of procurement, Ernest Brackett, changed procurement policy from a cost-plus model to a challenge-oriented (or outcomes-oriented) model, with incentives for innovation and quality improvement. The change sparked a wave of solutions to problems that needed to be solved to get men to the moon (and back): What would astronauts wear? How would they send data from the lunar module back to mission control? What would they eat? How would they go to the toilet? The answers produced innovations still widely used today, from new materials and software to baby formula, nappies, home insulation and camera phones. This culture of experimentation stimulated technological and organizational change, enabling NASA to fulfil its mission and promote economic growth. Dynamic growth relies on precisely this kind of experimentation, trial and error and learning by doing (Mazzucato, 2013; 2018a; 2021).

But missions should not be left to the military. Societal challenges deserve the same outcomes-oriented approach with the same ambition and system-wide coordination. A common good approach demands that responsibility for societal wellbeing be embedded at the centre of government and economic policy, rather than treated as peripheral or siloed. A critical issue like care, for example, cannot be confined solely to the Ministry of Health, while the Treasury or Finance Ministry continues to view investment in care as merely increasing government deficits. As long as economic models remain stuck in this market-fixing mindset, creating a truly caring economy will be nearly impossible. The divide between academics and practitioners who focus on the welfare state – concerned with care and redistribution – and those interested in the 'innovation state' – concerned with value creation – is a false dichotomy. In reality, care and value creation are deeply intertwined: investing in care work strengthens the economy and society as a whole. And, as many feminist economists have argued, transforming our economies into caring economies would mean fundamentally redesigning how government functions across all ministries and reshaping the relationships between business, government and civil society.

Organizations like the EU have already begun adopting a mission-oriented approach. For example, the EU's Horizon programme has embedded mission-oriented thinking into its innovation policy, selecting five mission areas (Mazzucato, 2018b; 2019a):

1. **Adaptation to climate change:** Aiming to guide at least 150 communities through understanding climate risks, developing pathways for preparation and implementing innovative solutions by 2030.
2. **Cancer:** Improving the lives of more than 3 million people by 2030 through prevention, cure and, for people affected by cancer including their families, to live longer and better.
3. **Climate-neutral and smart cities:** Delivering 100 climate-neutral and smart cities by 2030 and ensuring that these cities act as experimentation and innovation hubs to help all European cities to follow suit by 2050.

4. **A soil deal for Europe:** Establishing 100 living labs and lighthouses to lead the transition towards healthy soils by 2030.
5. **Restore our oceans and waters:** Protecting and restoring our oceans and waters through innovation and action by 2030.

Translating missions like those set by the EU's Horizon Programme into practice cannot be done without an all-of-government approach, with mission-oriented policymaking enabling cross-sectoral alignment. To be effective, mission governance should sit above all individual government entities, coordinating efforts across these bodies and the wider ecosystem. Indeed, in the EC, missions had limited impact because they did not go to the centre of the EC cabinet; they remained in the Directorate-General for Research and Innovation. A green deal would require the DGs responsible for innovation, energy, transport, telecommunications, agriculture and more to coordinate together.

Missions should not be mistaken for top-down mandates in which governments simply impose objectives through regulation and wait for results. Instead, a mission-oriented approach should act as a dynamic interface between the public sector, private sector, labour and society at large, creating space to collectively design, implement and govern the missions (Mazzucato and Kattel, 2020). This model creates opportunities for effective citizen participation, sparking civic engagement and a shared sense of purpose. As we will explore in the next chapter, engaging citizens in defining, implementing and evaluating missions is essential for strengthening commitment and ensuring they genuinely serve the public interest.

The mission-oriented approach differs from narrow, sector-based industrial or economic policies by concentrating on concrete problems that demand system-wide transformation (Mazzucato, 2018a; 2021). The common criticism of industrial strategy as 'picking winners' (in the sense of favouring particular sectors or actors, which critics argue governments cannot do well) does not apply here. In a mission-oriented approach, what is being 'picked' is not a sector or company, but rather the shared challenges that all sectors must work on together to solve. Here, the state incentivizes action among all actors towards meeting a mission – rather than supporting individual actors.

For instance, in collaboration with the Economic Commission for Latin America and the Caribbean (ECLAC) and GIZ, Germany's international development agency, I examined how a mission-oriented approach could be used to tackle the climate crisis in the region (Mazzucato, 2023c). A central part of the mission is to establish 100 carbon-neutral cities across LAC by 2030, aligned with broader climate and sustainable development goals.

As shown in Figure 9, this mission requires coordinated investment and innovation across multiple sectors. Developing a sustainable energy matrix including solar, wind, hydro and other renewables will provide the backbone for low-carbon urban systems. Clean electric mobility solutions, deployed in both urban and rural areas, can reduce emissions, improve air quality and enhance connectivity to economic opportunities. In agriculture and livestock, carbon-neutral practices such as regenerative farming, sustainable cattle raising and urban–rural supply chain integration can capture carbon, conserve biodiversity and strengthen food systems (Mazzucato, 2023c).

Focusing on these cross-sectoral areas can mobilize economy-wide collaboration and innovation across sectors including infrastructure, transport, recycling, digital services, energy, materials, education and agriculture. This mission is about more than just reducing emissions; it has the potential to transform urban and rural landscapes, stimulate investment in sustainable industries and create more resilient regional economies (Mazzucato, 2023c).

For a mission-oriented approach to be effective, governments need to deploy the full range of policy levers at their disposal. This goes beyond just focusing on developing a public investment strategy to include the wider institutional levers of markets – from regulatory frameworks (such as environmental standards) to skill development and public procurement. On the supply side, governments can act as investors of first resort (rather than lenders of last resort), funders and regulators, providing clear direction to innovation. On

Figure 9 A mission-oriented approach to carbon-neutral cities

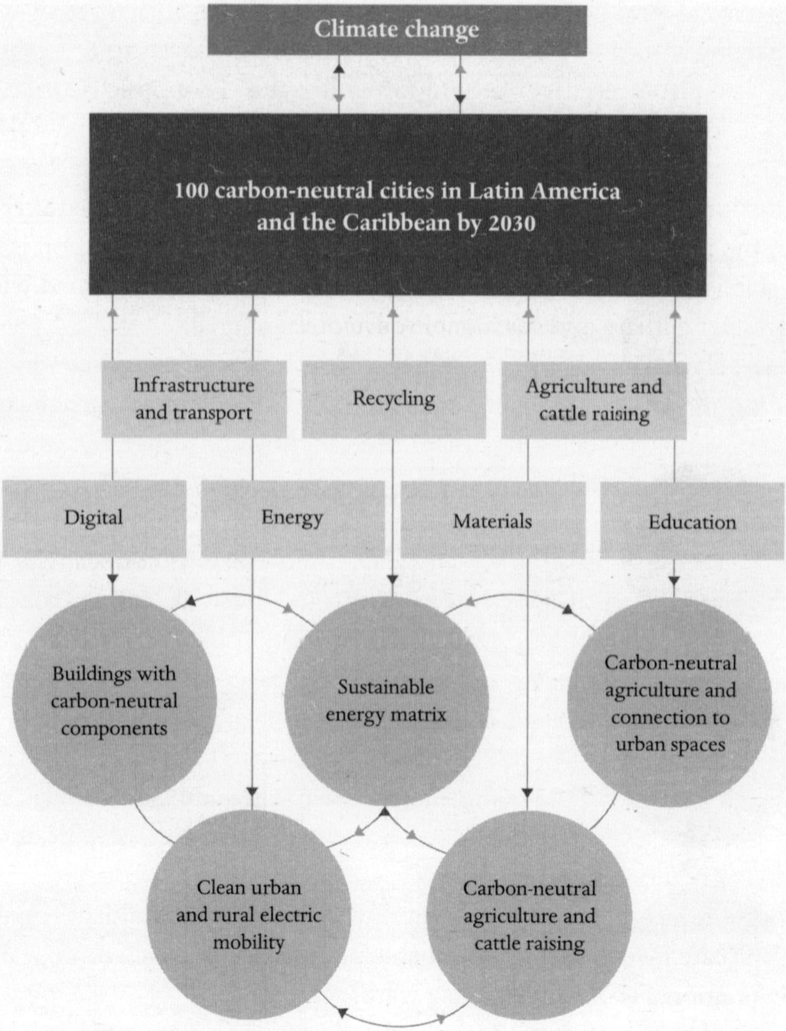

Source: Mazzucato (2023c)

the demand side, governments can use procurement policies to stimulate innovative solutions in areas ranging from public transport to housing. The idea is not to subsidize specific sectors, but to catalyse transformation across all sectors in pursuit of social goals.

Figure 10 A new culture of public procurement

A NEW CULTURE OF PROCUREMENT

	OLD MINDSET	NEW MINDSET
Neutral to intentional	Procurement processes should aspire to be neutral and objective because that makes them fair	All processes embed values; procurement processes should reflect the values and intent of the commissioning authority
Risk to uncertainty	Public service requirements are knowable and specifiable; to the extent that there are unknowns, they are quantifiable risks	The social systems that commissioners work within are complex and outcomes are fundamentally uncertain
Transactional to relational	The contracting relationship is predicated on purchasing agreed deliverables (whether inputs, outputs, or outcomes)	Commissioners are selecting who they want to work with as much as what they want to be delivered, and therefore trust and shared values are critically important
Risk management to risk leadership	Risks, especially around legal challenge and value for money, should be minimised as much as possible	Risk is an inherent part of change and innovation, and senior leaders should be challenged on not taking enough risk as well as taking too much risk

Source: Mazzucato and Wainwright (2024)

For example, climate action requires coordinated innovation from sectors as diverse as digital, nutrition, transport and construction.

To achieve these goals, governments must transform how they use the tools at their disposal. For instance, as shown in Figure 10, they must adopt a new mindset around procurement. They need to move beyond the outdated idea that neutrality and objectivity automatically make processes fair and recognize that every decision carries values. Procurement decisions should therefore intentionally reflect the government's principles and ambitions. This also requires accepting that public service requirements are not always fully knowable or precisely specifiable. Public systems are complex, unpredictable and highly interdependent, meaning outcomes cannot be entirely controlled in advance. Governments must also reframe procurement from a purely transactional process to a relational one, focusing as much on who they choose to work with as on what is delivered. Finally, they must rethink their approach to risk. Rather than striving to eliminate it, risk should be treated as an essential component of learning, innovation and progress. Figure 10 summarizes how procurement would need to change to be more mission oriented, from a focus on costs to a focus on outcomes. It comes from a study we did on outcomes-oriented procurement, with procurement commissioners in Camden Council, London (Mazzucato and Wainwright, 2024).

6.2 Directed growth: combating false trade-offs

There is often a false trade-off between solving problems and focusing on growth. Clear and ambitious missions can mobilize public and private sector investment to tackle urgent societal challenges while generating growth in the process. However, for this to work, policies must be designed not as giveaways but as tools to leverage greater public and private investment, since growth ultimately depends on the aggregate level of investment. Indeed, it is not a coincidence that many low-growth economies are low-investment economies.

The point here is not to seek investment for its own sake, but to channel it towards achieving well-defined and ambitious missions, whether in health, AI or climate adaptation. When framed as opportunities that demand coordinated public and private action, missions can stimulate innovations whose dynamic spillovers drive 'directed' growth. A climate change mission, for instance, will require breakthroughs in a wide range of areas, such as energy, nutrition, materials, transport and digital services, spurring growth and producing benefits well beyond the immediate challenge. Investments that are too narrowly focused or confined to a single sector, by contrast, are unlikely to generate these wider spillovers.

A key question, then, is what kind of investments are necessary to solve societal challenges and how those investments should be valued afterwards. The answer lies in moving beyond traditional cost benefit analyses towards dynamic metrics that capture the spillovers across an economy, a topic we turn to in Chapter 10. It is crucial to create the fiscal space necessary for governments to invest by understanding the future value of these investments in expanding productive capacity and generating higher tax revenues. The conventional orthodoxy of 'fiscal rules' which dictate that yearly expenses match yearly tax revenue is misguided and even harmful. Moving policy away from this constraint is critical to taking a long-term approach, since much of the benefits of public investment are not immediate.

Mission-oriented school meals

Outcome-oriented policies, as ambitious as those that got us to the moon, can be normalized to everyday goals, such as providing a healthy, tasty and sustainable meal to all schoolchildren in a country (Mazzucato and Doyle, 2025). If done right, such a policy can improve health and educational outcomes in the short term but also generate long-term economic returns by fostering a healthier population while catalysing investment in local manufacturing and sustainable agriculture. Such a policy can create spillovers that benefit health, the environment and the economy at the same time, showing how a social programme is not only about reducing inequality but can become a driver of wider economic transformation, influencing everything from sustainable land use to cleaner transport practices. The question is then how to scale the lessons of such a policy, so that outcomes-oriented procurement becomes central to all social goals, from sustainable mobility to healthy populations, which by stimulating innovation bridge the gap between welfare policy and industrial strategy.

Sweden is a leading example of how school meals missions can encourage innovation and change (Mazzucato and Doyle, 2025). The country is aiming to be the first fossil-free welfare nation in the world (Fossil Free Sweden, 2021), looking to enhance wellbeing (alongside reaching net zero emissions) by 2045 (Fossil Free Sweden, 2024). Sweden has identified the food system as critical to fulfilling this mission. A key tool is public procurement to support sustainable food systems (Mazzucato and Wainwright, 2024). The Swedish innovation agency, Vinnova, has partnered with the National Food Agency to run several pilot projects exploring how procurement can shape markets for healthy and sustainable school meals (Vinnova, 2021). As part of this effort, the municipality of Vellentuna ran a 'reverse procurement' pilot where local suppliers offered school lunches based on the availability and seasonality of ingredients. This shifted sales from being demand driven to being aligned with local seasonal production, resulting in healthier and more sustainable meals for students (Livsmedelsverket, 2023a). The programme also included co-designing solutions with schoolchildren and staff, ensuring that meals matched their preferences and wellbeing needs (Livsmedelsverket, 2023b). By involving students and staff in these decisions, the programme increased meal uptake, reduced food waste, and led to greater awareness of healthy diets and sustainable food systems.

Sweden is not alone. Brazil also demonstrates how procurement can link access to healthy and sustainable school meals with an industrial strategy that creates local market opportunities for agricultural producers (Mazzucato and Doyle, 2025). The government is using public procurement – worth an estimated 12–15 per cent of GDP (MGI, 2023) – to build domestic markets for innovative products and services that address the country's most pressing challenges, while simultaneously creating opportunities for businesses and strengthening domestic productive capacity (Mazzucato, 2024a). The National

School Feeding Program is central to this strategy, providing all schoolchildren with healthy and sustainable meals and legally requiring that at least 30 per cent of funding for school meals goes to family farms, supporting sustainable local agriculture. This strategic use of public purchasing is possible thanks to the 2021 New Bidding and Contracting Law, which shifted procurement away from prioritizing the lowest cost and towards selecting purchases based on sustainability, benefits to local economies and the inclusion of marginalized groups (MGI, 2023), thereby aligning Brazil's procurement with broader societal missions (Mazzucato, 2024a).

In the UK, there is also growing recognition that school meals are an effective poverty reduction strategy that can also improve health and education outcomes, while presenting a market opportunity for agrifood industries. Some UK regions are already taking the lead. For example, the Mayor of London, Sadiq Khan, has extended funding for free primary school meals through 2024–5 in response to the cost-of-living crisis (Mayor of London, 2023).

To make sure that school meals are healthy, tasty and sustainable, governments must interact with private actors in food, drinks and agriculture differently by setting clear goals that require companies to innovate. In doing so, they must invest, and since investment is a key driver of growth, outcomes-oriented procurement in school meals can help increase both wellbeing and economic growth. Examples of this kind show that it is wrong to think that there is a crude trade-off between societal wellbeing and economic growth and that human suffering may be the price to pay for economic growth. If growth is directed, it can stimulate innovation towards shared goals, boosting productivity and prosperity along the way.

Conclusion

Growth is not necessarily good – it depends on its direction and how it is produced. Embedding purpose and directionality into economic policy is a vital first step for achieving good growth through the common good economy. Defining clear, ambitious missions can mobilize public and private actors towards shared societal goals, driving innovation and inclusive, sustainable growth, and in so doing combating the false trade-off between achieving growth and solving societal problems. They can both be done together. Examples from the EU's Horizon programme to national initiatives in Sweden and Brazil demonstrate how mission-oriented policies can create dynamic spillovers that benefit health, the environment and the economy simultaneously.

However, setting missions is not enough. Politics often obstructs governments from adopting the common good as the central goal of the economy. Governments risk capture by private interests through lobbying, campaign financing, misinformation and other pressures that distort policy choices. Without addressing these structural and political forces, mission-setting risks becoming a technocratic exercise disconnected from real power that shapes policies and limits transformative change. We can see powerful resistance to policy that favours the common good in contemporary economies – not all purely capitalist – across the world.

One of the best ways to prevent capture – in addition to having rigorous metrics for guiding government investments and holding officials accountable – is to ensure that government-led missions are co-created with citizens, embedding their experiences and making them active participants in mission design, implementation and evaluation. This participatory approach strengthens legitimacy and helps missions genuinely to serve the public interest. This is the topic we turn to next.

7.
Co-creation and participation

So, who decides what direction an economy takes, and what missions we pursue? If the answer is a dictator or a handful of people, we are far from advancing the common good. In fact, we are moving in precisely the opposite direction. The second element of the common good compass is therefore about ensuring that our vision of the common good – what goals are worth striving for and how we implement them – emerges from genuine co-creation and participation among all stakeholders. This means giving people ownership of the agenda rather than being just a voice in someone else's plan, reflecting also the emphasis of the late Pope Francis on the 'principle of subsidiarity'.

As we saw in Chapter 3, Aristotle understood this well. For him, the ultimate purpose (*telos*) of human life was to flourish (*eudaimonia*), which could only be achieved through the cultivation of virtues that arise from active participation in public life within the *polis*. In his view, the *polis* was far more than a city state; it was the arena where humans, as 'political animals', could collaborate, deliberate and govern as equals.

Building on Aristotle's insights, modern thinkers, including communitarian philosophers and proponents of the collaborative economy discussed in Part I, emphasize that co-creation and participation are not only about cultivating the virtues that lead to human flourishing, but also about collectively defining the common good itself. Clarifying the values we want our society and the economy to embody and determining together how to bring that vision to life is key.

Brazilian scholar Paulo Freire (1970) linked co-creation and participation directly to societal transformation. For him, these practices are central to learning and a powerful means of empowerment. By reflecting and acting together – what he called praxis – people can transform both themselves and the world around them. His 'theatre of the oppressed' made this idea tangible, demonstrating how collective creation could liberate marginalized groups and help them reclaim their voice in society. Participation and co-creation, therefore, are essential for setting shared goals and creating the conditions that make freedom and transformation possible.

At the same time, co-creation and participation have a very practical dimension. When diverse groups are genuinely engaged, they produce better results. They avoid groupthink, challenge blind spots and introduce ideas that might otherwise remain hidden (Page, 2007; Phillips, 2014). Constructive disagreement, often voiced by minorities, sharpens reasoning and fosters more creative outcomes (Mannix and Neale, 2005). Equally important, these processes build a sense of ownership. When people help define a problem and develop and implement solutions, they see them as theirs rather than something imposed on them. Co-creation and participation are a path to societal transformation, as Freire emphasized, and a means for more effective and inclusive decision making.

Since the writings of Friedrich Hayek (born 1899), economists have long thought about how discovery happens through growth dynamics (Hausman and Rodrik, 2003). But discovery does not only happen via price signals (see Nelson and Winter, 1982, for an excellent critique) but by working together – often the search for one thing leads to the discovery of something totally different, as serendipitous processes in science teach us. A common good compass must help to nurture processes which are about *learning to learn*. This is important so that the processes of directionality and co-creation are not technical but truly participatory, and the delicate balance between direction setting and bottom-up processes is one that fosters learning. Indeed, any open system that is susceptible to feedback effects is one that must be flexible and agile. It could be that the participatory processes lead to a change in the direction set. But too much change also makes it hard to 'learn by doing' as the doing keeps changing.

In this chapter, we explore how co-creation and participation can shape the design and implementation of policies like missions, putting the common good at the centre of economic and political activity.

7.1 Citizen participation

It is often assumed that democratic systems already secure participation through elections, since elected representatives are expected to reflect citizens' priorities and values. Yet, as political scientist Honorata Mazepus (2018) argues, legitimacy in political decision making is not guaranteed by elections alone. Elections represent only a small, though vital, part of the wider practices of co-creation and participation needed to shape political and economic policy. She identifies three interconnected dimensions of political legitimacy:

1. **Input legitimacy**, or 'government *by the people*', refers to the mechanisms by which citizens can participate in governance and influence decisions, most commonly through elections. It ensures that authorities' actions align with citizens' authentic preferences, values and needs.
2. **Throughput legitimacy**, or 'government *with the people*', focuses on the quality and inclusiveness of the decision-making process itself. It emphasizes transparency, fairness and participatory procedures that allow stakeholders to shape policy decisions throughout the entire policy cycle. This is where the bulk of co-creation and participation takes place.
3. **Output legitimacy**, or 'government *for the people*', concerns the results of governance – the effectiveness of policies and institutions in achieving common goals and delivering tangible benefits to society.

This broader understanding of co-creation and participation in governance is essential to avoid 'participation washing'. These practices are not about sending people forms to fill out but, as Freire insisted, about co-creating spaces from the beginning: setting priorities together, framing questions collectively and leaving room for experimentation rather than imposing top-down answers. For participation to be genuine, three criteria are essential: transparency in how decisions are made, inclusivity to ensure marginalized voices are represented, and empowerment so that engagement has real influence and is not just tokenism. These principles echo Ostrom's work on governance and collective action. Co-creation and participation are most meaningful when they strengthen communities, broaden equity and sustain long-term practices.

Yet co-creation and participation don't happen automatically. Their success depends on the readiness of both institutions and citizens (Voorberg, Bekkers and Tummers, 2014). On the institutional side, governments must provide the infrastructure that makes them possible. This includes clear communication channels, training for officials and citizens and – perhaps most importantly – leaders willing to treat citizens as genuine partners. Too often, participation breaks down here. Risk-averse bureaucracies tend to see citizen involvement as messy or uncontrollable, and defensively keep decision making behind closed doors.

Citizen involvement is sometimes structured through citizens' assemblies, a representative group of ordinary people, selected by sortition, who deliberate on public issues and make recommendations to guide policy decisions. Such assemblies try to embody a more democratic and participatory approach to policymaking, ensuring that diverse voices shape collective priorities. They have roots in ancient Athenian democracy, where random selection was used to ensure political equality and prevent domination by elites. The modern form re-emerged in the late twentieth and early twenty-first centuries, notably in countries like Ireland, Canada and France, where assemblies have addressed issues such as constitutional reform and climate policy. Their growing use reflects a broader movement towards deliberative democracy, aiming to rebuild trust between citizens and institutions (Smith, 2009).

However, the effective participation of citizens requires both willingness and capacity. Education levels, family circumstances and personal characteristics all shape whether people step forward. Citizens must also be aware of their ability and opportunity to influence public policy. Just as importantly, co-creation and participation depend on social capital, broadly defined by sociologists as the social relationships and networks that shape how people relate to one another. Social capital is critical for building sustainable relationships between public organizations and citizens. Where such conditions are weak, responsibility falls back on public institutions to strengthen them – whether through outreach, supportive policies, finance or the appointment of 'policy entrepreneurs' who can build bridges across communities (Voorberg, Bekkers and Tummers, 2014).

Theories of social capital show that collaboration relies on shared norms, mutual recognition and the negotiation of differences across social boundaries (Bourdieu, 1986; Putnam, 2000). This may help explain why collaboration is often easier among people who already have things in common, yet this can also lead to people being stuck in siloes. If collective intelligence is strongest when people from different backgrounds, networks and perspectives come together, deliberate effort must be made to create new networks rather than relying only on existing ones. Without such efforts, participation and co-creation processes risk reproducing inequality, as power disparities and dominant interests can become institutionalized. Who is invited, whose knowledge is valued and who bears the burden of coordination are crucial to success.

Beyond building social capital and developing more inclusive processes, co-creation and participation in designing and implementing missions can happen through structured, iterative engagement. This includes collaborative workshops, focus groups and participatory design sessions where stakeholders actively contribute to defining problems, generating solutions and testing ideas. Digital platforms can also complement in-person activities by widening participation, encouraging dialogue and scaling initiatives to reach larger and more diverse audiences. Importantly, these methods should not treat citizens as passive respondents but as partners with valuable input, ensuring that their knowledge, perspectives and priorities directly shape the mission and its implementation. By embedding these practices at every stage of the policy cycle, organizations can transform participation into a dynamic, co-creative process that enhances outcomes while strengthening community ownership.

When these conditions are met, co-creation can transform mission design and implementation into a process that builds community, promotes equitable participation and produces sustainable outcomes. By actively involving citizens and stakeholders from the beginning, public organizations can design missions that are socially legitimate and more innovative, resilient and widely supported. A strong example of co-creation that has scaled beyond the local level is the European Union's Horizon Europe 'Mission on Climate-Neutral and Smart Cities' (the EU Cities Mission). This mission aims to help 100 European cities become climate neutral by 2030, not just through top-down funding but via deep citizen engagement and co-creation processes (Conway, 2024). Cities like Amsterdam, Copenhagen and Mannheim have integrated residents, local businesses and community groups in designing transition roadmaps – using citizen assemblies, participatory budgeting, and open data platforms to co-develop mobility, energy and housing solutions. What makes it notable are its mission-oriented design (clear societal goal + cross-sector coordination) and its scalability: the approaches developed in the 100 'mission cities' are meant to be replicated in thousands of other European municipalities, embedding co-created climate governance across the continent.

Co-creating Missions in Camden

Camden, a London borough, is known for its cultural diversity and vibrant communities, but it also faces high levels of economic inequality. Some areas are home to affluent residents and thriving businesses, while others struggle with poverty, under-resourced housing estates and reliance on food banks. This mix made Camden an ideal setting for experimenting with co-creating missions aimed at addressing the borough's most pressing challenges.

In 2020, the Camden Renewal Commission was established to enable residents to shape the borough's priorities (Camden Council, 2022). The Commission, which I co-chaired with Camden's Leader at the time, Georgia Gould, brought together a diverse cross-section of the borough as commissioners, including residents, voluntary organizations, businesses and academic institutions, reflecting Camden's cultural and social diversity.

To achieve genuine citizen participation, the Commission launched 'We Make Camden', a participatory process that convened citizen assemblies, resident associations and even 'citizen scientists' to discuss which missions mattered most to them. Conversations ranged from broad questions, such as what sustainability should mean for the borough, to more specific concerns, such as how sustainability initiatives could benefit residents of housing estates and their communities.

Listening carefully to residents, the Renewal Commission developed a set of four missions for the local council to implement to support the borough's development:

Mission 1: Borough-wide diversity in positions of power. By 2030, those holding positions of power in Camden should be as diverse as the community.

Mission 2: Opportunities for young people. By 2025, every young person must have access to economic opportunity that enables them to be safe and secure.

Mission 3: Access to food for all. By 2030, everyone in the borough must have access to nutritious, affordable and sustainable food.

Mission 4: Sustainable neighbourhoods. By 2030, Camden's estates and their neighbourhoods should be healthy, sustainable and unlock creativity.

A defining feature of the Camden process was redistributing power so that residents co-designed and implemented initiatives rather than passively receiving services. For example, work on the food access missions transformed the borough's food banks into green food cooperatives, where people benefiting from food distribution also took responsibility for ordering and organizing the food distribution through a cooperative structure. This experience showed that increased self-worth, dignity and mutual respect were the result of putting people in the driving seat of these initiatives.

The Commission also made sure that areas such as outcomes-oriented procurement were led by users and workers (Mazzucato and Wainwright, 2024). In particular, procurement for adult social care in some housing estates was redesigned to include both those receiving care and those providing it in decisions about what procurement should look like. As part of this process, the Commission developed the 'Mission Incubator', which updated service specifications to focus on missions through four workshops that brought together officers from Adult Social Care, the Estates Mission and the Procurement Service alongside residents and workers. One of the main recommendations that emerged was that care workers should be seen as place shapers – not just service deliverers – leveraging their knowledge and experience to improve the environments of those they support.

The youth mission followed the same approach. While youth centres are vital community spaces, simply funding them was not enough. Young people had to be actively involved in design and governance of these centres to ensure they met the needs and interests of different age groups – for instance, teenagers, whose needs differ from those of younger children. It is not enough merely to fund a place for a community; the community itself must have a genuine role in shaping how that space is created and run. We look at the role of community spaces further in Part III.

Participation of Indigenous people and local communities in the Amazon

A complementary example to that in Camden can be found among Indigenous people and local communities in the Amazon. Co-creation here is not about outsiders 'saving the rainforest' but about placing Indigenous people and local communities at the centre of decisions that shape their future. The Amazon Fund, established in 2008 and managed by the Brazilian Development Bank (BNDES), illustrates this approach, though it is far from perfect. Widely regarded as a pioneering model for climate finance, its purpose is to channel voluntary international and domestic donations into non-reimbursable projects (meaning funded projects do not require repayment of the money provided) focused on forest conservation, environmental monitoring and sustainable development. The Fund has approved more than 124 projects valued at US$920 million (BNDES, 2025).

The Fund is governed by two main bodies: a multi-stakeholder Guidance Committee (COFA) and a Technical Committee (CTFA). COFA brings together representatives from federal agencies, Amazonian state governments, civil society and Indigenous groups to provide strategic direction and oversee resource allocation. CTFA, composed of independent scientific experts, verifies emission reductions reported by supported projects. Importantly, all projects must meet strict eligibility criteria, including the documentation of free, prior and informed consent from any Indigenous communities affected by project activities (BNDES, 2025), formally embedding Indigenous participation in its governance.

Despite this inclusive framework, meaningful participation remains a challenge. A mid-term review conducted in 2019 found that mechanisms intended to facilitate participation – such as technical workshops and COFA meetings – were frequently inaccessible to Indigenous organizations because of their language, format and technical complexity. As a result, community-based actors often struggled to influence project design or engage substantively in governance processes (Gómez Garcia et al., 2019). Civil society representatives on COFA have also expressed frustration over their limited influence in BNDES decision making, and members of CTFA have noted that their role is largely confined to validating emissions data at the end of each year, with little opportunity to contribute to strategic planning (Zadek, Forstater, and Polacow, 2010). Strengthening mechanisms for Indigenous and community-led engagement – not only in project execution but also in shaping and evaluating strategic investment priorities – is crucial for reinforcing the Fund's legitimacy, accountability and long-term impact.

The Amazon Fund example shows both the potential and the limits of co-creation in mission-oriented initiatives. While Indigenous people and local communities possess critical knowledge of the Amazon's ecosystems and can contribute to innovative conservation practices, structural barriers often prevent them from fully exercising decision-making power. Meaningful empowerment requires not only consultation but also the redesign of governance mechanisms to reduce these barriers, strengthen community-led engagement and ensure that local actors can influence project priorities, design and evaluation. And it is not enough to invite stakeholders to the table; they must be truly valued. For example, the initiative of the Bolsa Verde by the Ministries of the Environment and Finance in Brazil is an attempt to recognize the role that traditional communities have played for centuries in preserving biodiversity in the Amazon. Paying them to both recognize and continue doing this work is not redistributive but pre-distributive. Experiences like this underscore that co-creation is not automatic; to achieve greater legitimacy and impact, it must be actively nurtured, adapted to local realities, and supported by both institutional commitment and inclusive process design.

7.2 Community-led governance of land, water and energy

Governing shared resources is often framed as a problem of scarcity and conflict, yet Ostrom (1990) showed that communities can and do manage the commons effectively when they design their own rules and actively participate in their implementation. The following examples – from water to land to energy – demonstrate how collective governance turns co-creation and participation from abstract concepts into practical approaches that foster the common good.

Water

Community participation in water management shows how local actors can reclaim essential resources as commons. In the late 1990s, Bolivia's adoption of neoliberal economic policies led to the privatization of water, triggering widespread outrage in Cochabamba, a city in the country's centre. The government handed control of all water sources to a foreign consortium – causing prices to skyrocket – and even criminalized activities like rainwater collection and use of community wells. In response, farmers, factory workers, academics and small business owners came together to form the Coordinadora por la Defensa del Agua y la Vida (Coalition for the Defence of Water and Life). This cross-sector coalition organized mass protests that forced the government to reverse the privatization in April 2000. The coalition's success was a turning point in the defence of water as a common good, challenging the belief that the market should govern essential resources (Hines, 2021; Tomba, 2023).

Following the victory, residents of the San Pedro Magisterio neighbourhood in Cochabamba took water management into their own hands. In partnership with international NGOs, they formed a water cooperative to build and operate a local wastewater treatment plant in 2015, tackling severe pollution in the River Rocha. The project reflected the community's deep commitment to environmental stewardship, solidarity and self-management. The cooperative's success was built on its participatory governance. Through regular assemblies, residents made decisions on tariffs, coordinated maintenance and collectively managed the plant (Orellana López, 2018). Despite initial scepticism from the municipal utility authority about the community's technical capacity, the project proved highly effective and became a model for other communities along the river (Minelli, 2018). It demonstrated the power of collective ownership and local knowledge in fostering a more equitable and sustainable approach to managing shared resources.

A similar dynamic occurred in Terrassa, a city in Catalonia, Spain. In 2015, the citizen platform Taula de l'Aigua de Terrassa in Catalonia launched a Social Pact for Public Water campaign to re-municipalize the city's water service after seven decades of private management. In December 2016, the Terrassa City Council voted to regain control over the water supply, creating a new public water utility company, Taigua, alongside the Observatori de l'Aigua de Terrassa (Terrassa Water Observatory). The Observatory is a participatory, autonomous body responsible for conducting studies and advising the City Council on all matters related to municipal water management. Composed of representatives from political groups, technical staff, business representatives, community organizations and unions, the Observatory is a permanent participatory space. Citizens, municipal representatives and staff from the public utility company can co-design strategies for transparent, socially just and sustainable water management, reclaiming water as a common good (Planas and Martínez, 2020).

Land

Community struggles over land reveal how the value of shared spaces can be recognized, defended and legally secured through collective action. Wandsworth Common in south London illustrates how communities can assert the significance of public land for local life and well-being, and how this understanding has underpinned its management over time. Ownership of Wandsworth Common changed hands many times over the centuries, with the aristocratic Spencer family taking control in 1763. Although privately owned, local residents were allowed to use the Common, but the family eventually considered closing it off or selling it. In the late 1860s, fierce opposition, led by resident John Charles Buckmaster, arose as the community mobilized to protect access. Residents organized committees, distributed flyers and launched letter-writing campaigns. One pamphlet called on working men and others in London to resist the loss of common land, concluding with an appeal to collective action: 'We must all pull together – and may you long enjoy, in your spare time and holidays, the pleasure of breathing the pure air of UNENCLOSED WANDSWORTH COMMON!' (Wandsworth Heritage Service, 1870a).

By April 1870, the committee had successfully raised £5,000 to challenge Earl Spencer in court. By October, they reached a resolution securing 'the Common for the public enjoyment, in perpetuity, under a popular and efficient management' (Wandsworth Heritage Service, 1870b). This resolution was formalized by the 1871 Wimbledon and Wandsworth Common Act, which transferred the land to public ownership and enshrined the community's stewardship in law. Later, the Commons Act 2006 reinforced these protections, ensuring that Wandsworth Common continues to benefit the public in perpetuity.

Today, this legacy endures, though it is geographically specific. The formal protections and community management apply primarily to Wandsworth Common, rather than all open spaces in the borough, while other parts of Wandsworth are experiencing gentrification and private redevelopment. To maintain the Common, Wandsworth Borough Council has established formal partnerships with the community. While Enable Leisure and Culture (Enable LC), a not-for-profit organization, handles day-to-day maintenance of the Common, elected volunteers from the Management Advisory Committee and the Friends of Wandsworth Common collectively oversee and care for the land so residents can enjoy it. The structure of the Committee and the Friends group also strengthens accountability measures between the Council, Enable LC and the local community. Together, these structures ensure that Wandsworth Common remains an attractive, well-stewarded public space, reflecting the enduring legacy of community action.

Energy

Energy communities provide another compelling example of co-creation and citizen participation. These communities bring together diverse stakeholders – including energy service providers, energy producers, citizens, public officials, engineers and social movements – at federal, regional and local levels to co-produce and share in the rewards of renewable energy. Energy is a key resource for our modern economies, and while renewable energy represents the future, its potential cannot be realized without governance structures that avoid replicating the extractive models of traditional energy systems. Energy communities offer a powerful model for encouraging renewable energy production while ensuring that its benefits are shared locally.

The town of Wolfhagen in Germany demonstrates the potential of this approach. Following the municipalization of the local energy company Stadtwerke in 2006, the town engaged a wide range of stakeholders to build consensus on transitioning to 100 per cent local renewable energy (Baasch, 2015). To address opposition to wind power installations, the town worked directly with local climate activists and residents to integrate community concerns into planning and implementation processes (Matschoss et al., 2022). The result was greater local acceptance of the wind farms and increased citizen involvement in energy production.

In 2013, to ensure residents could benefit from the transition to renewables, the town and its residents launched the cooperative BürgerEnergieGenossenschaft (BEG) Wolfhagen. A quarter of the Stadtwerke's shares were sold to the cooperative, and the city used the money to build needed infrastructure (Baasch, 2015). By 2019, BEG Wolfhagen had grown to 800 members and was valued at nearly €4 million (Russell, 2019). Today, it holds a 39.68 per cent stake in the local energy company and has nearly 1,000 members (BEG Wolfhagen, n.d.).

As a cooperative, BEG Wolfhagen requires local energy customers interested in membership to purchase 500 euros' worth of shares, payable over two years to ensure inclusivity. Once shares are purchased, members can participate in cooperative governance and receive annual dividend payments (up to 6 per cent). The remaining surplus supports the Energy-Saving Fund, which finances energy-related projects and initiatives within the community, including providing free electricity to vulnerable residents. BEG Wolfhagen's governance model goes beyond traditional civic engagement, allowing residents to actively shape decisions around energy production and also share in its benefits. We delve further into this idea of reward sharing in Chapter 9.

Conclusion

The second element of the common good compass highlights that real progress towards shared societal goals depends on active participation and empowerment of diverse voices, especially those historically marginalized. From the streets of Camden to the heart of the Amazon, the experience is that the success of purpose-driven policies, like missions, depends on processes that are transparent, inclusive and grounded in mutual respect. Co-creation and participation are equally important when managing common resources, like water, land and energy, ensuring that their use benefits the public while fostering a sense of ownership and dignity among all involved.

Examples from Cochabamba, Catalonia, Wandsworth and Wolfhagen show that when communities have real power to shape their futures, the policies and innovations that emerge are not only fairer and more sustainable, but also more resilient and responsive to local realities. The cases presented in this chapter are not perfect and may be criticized for not going far enough, but they are powerful seeds for change, showing how systems can leverage participation and co-creation to advance the common good. For these seeds to take root and bear fruit in the form of lasting transformation, collective learning and knowledge sharing are essential – a subject we explore next.

8.
Collective learning and knowledge sharing

Platforms like Wikipedia, GitHub and Foldit illustrate how collective intelligence can create knowledge and solve problems at a scale impossible for any single individual. Governments and NGOs have similarly harnessed collective intelligence to tackle complex societal challenges. For instance, the UN's World Food Programme has used crowdsourced mapping and data platforms to improve disaster response and humanitarian aid delivery, while city governments have deployed digital platforms to engage citizens in urban planning and policymaking. These initiatives demonstrate that large-scale collaboration, when structured effectively, can produce practical knowledge and solutions that no single organization could achieve alone.

Yet collective intelligence is profoundly shaped by political, economic and power dynamics that determine who controls knowledge and who can access it. Political institutions and governance structures influence which actors are included in decision making and whose knowledge is recognized as legitimate. Economic factors, such as funding, intellectual property rights and market incentives affect who can generate knowledge, how widely it can be shared and whether certain groups can afford to participate. Power dynamics, both formal hierarchies and informal social or cultural influence, shape whose perspectives dominate and whose contributions are marginalized.

Because of these constraints, the success of collective intelligence depends not only on bringing people together but also on creating the right conditions for collaboration. This means setting appropriate incentives, building effective networks, sharing knowledge in the right form and amount, and cultivating trust among participants, all while accounting for cultural and interpersonal dynamics.

This chapter examines key domains essential to fostering collective intelligence, the third element of the common good compass. I highlight how a knowledge governance approach to intellectual property rights, data and non-extractive use of Indigenous knowledge can ensure that collective learning and knowledge sharing are done according to a common good approach.

8.1 Knowledge sharing

The economist Joseph Schumpeter (1883–1950) argued that innovation is the main engine of growth in capitalist economies. Companies succeed not just by competing on price, but by creating and applying new knowledge, which makes the way knowledge is shared and managed critical for economic growth. Traditionally, intellectual property rights, such as patents, have been seen as incentives for innovation by protecting inventors from copycats and allowing them to profit from their inventions. Yet innovation depends on more than these incentives – how knowledge is shared and governed is equally, if not more, important. Intellectual property rights are central to knowledge governance, but if they are too broad, too strong or applied too early, they can slow innovation by limiting the sharing of knowledge essential for generating new ideas (Mazzoleni and Nelson, 1998).

Historical evidence shows that innovation can thrive even without intellectual property rights. For example, a survey of chief R&D executives at 100 US firms asked what proportion of inventions developed between 1981 and 1983 would not have been created without patent protection. The results showed that 60 per cent of pharmaceutical inventions and 38 per cent of chemical inventions depended on patents, but for most other sectors the figure was below 20 per cent. Some industries, such as motor vehicles and textiles, reported that none of their inventions would have been affected by the absence of patents (Scherer and Ross, 1990). Even with the high reliance on patents reported in pharmaceuticals, there is evidence that innovation in that sector flourished before today's stringent intellectual property regime (Dosi et al., 2023a; 2023b). This suggests that while patents may matter in certain sectors, a world without patents would still be a world rich in innovation.

In a contrary direction, key scholars have found that overly rigid patent systems may actually stifle innovation or lead to unintended negative consequences (Boldrin and Levine, 2013). Typically, mature industries turn towards patents only after their initial stage of rampant growth as their growth potential stagnates and market power becomes more concentrated. The software industry is a sector where intellectual property protections were historically minimal (Scherer and Ross, 1990). A prime example of this is the Linux operation system launched by Linus Torvalds in 1991, which has evolved into a cornerstone of global IT infrastructure, powering everything from servers to smartphones to supercomputers. The cause of its success has not been patent protections or commercial monopolies but a dynamic open source ecosystem, shaped by user needs, voluntary contributions and distributed governance. Thousands of developers around the world contribute to Linux under non-restrictive licences, permitting rapid iteration and wide adoption (Mustonen, 2003). This model demonstrates how innovation can flourish – and even dominate a sector – when knowledge is shared widely.

Yet today, overly restrictive intellectual property rights are widespread. Contemporary intellectual property regimes also remain rooted in, and often reinforce, colonial structures. Modelled on Western laws and favouring Western interests, they can act as mechanisms of economic control when applied in countries of the Global South.* While many scholars have highlighted the drawbacks of intellectual property rights, reforms have been limited (Machlup, 1958). This is in part due to how patents have continued to be justified in terms of fixing markets (e.g. underlying information asymmetries) and not shaping them through a knowledge governance lens linked to specific outcomes (e.g. using knowledge to foster an economy that is more

* For a detailed discussion of intellectual property and colonialism, see Merson (2000), Rahmatian (2009) and Birnhack (2021).

inclusive and competitive). Indeed, even the Schumpeterian and evolutionary schools, despite their focus on the innovation systems, have struggled to debunk the dominant economic view of markets, in which public institutions (e.g. innovation agencies or public labs) are primarily seen as correcting system failures related to knowledge production and diffusion (Rikap and Lundvall, 2021; Nelson, 2022). To support wider knowledge sharing, intellectual property rights must be understood according to the way they are governed and not just as mere incentives for innovation (WHO, 2023). Veblen's (1908) notion of knowledge as 'common stock' is particularly instructive, framing knowledge as cumulative and collective rather than as an individual possession. From this perspective, patents can act as 'a detriment to the community at large', limiting how innovations are applied and developed. Reforming the intellectual property system to encourage knowledge sharing could foster greater collaboration, drive innovation and help tackle some of today's complex challenges. Achieving this requires a new legal framework for patents and other intellectual property that better balances private incentives with collective interests. To foster collective intelligence, patents should be weak (easy to license), narrow (not too wide for strategic reasons) and not far too early in the innovation chain (so they are still open to research).

The following two examples illustrate how knowledge sharing can function effectively in practice, highlighting approaches that leverage collaboration while navigating the constraints and opportunities of intellectual property.

COVID-19 vaccine development

The global vaccine market is segmented. Vaccines in the Global North are largely supplied by global pharmaceutical corporations, which have the power to generate substantial profit margins by charging high prices for new vaccines. In contrast, vaccines in the Global South are primarily supplied by manufacturers that operate on a low-price, high-volume and low-margin model, making substantial investment in the R&D prohibitively difficult. In both cases, the state will often play a significant role in vaccine supply and delivery, though countries in the Global North often have greater fiscal capacity, whereas countries in the Global South rely heavily on donor support. These structural disparities became abundantly clear during the COVID-19 pandemic, which exposed significant inequities in vaccine access for the Global South. While global distribution of vaccines was far from perfect, innovative collaborations emerged to reshape R&D and production models, aiming to improve access and equity.

Of all the vaccines produced during the pandemic, only one embodied an outcomes-oriented approach in the design of the public–private partnership: the collaboration between Oxford University and AstraZeneca (sometimes referred to as 'Vaxzevria'). In this model, early-stage developments by Oxford were transferred to AstraZeneca for final development, manufacturing and distribution. Within this arrangement, the UK government embedded conditionalities in the Vaxzevria Supply Agreement, requiring vaccines to be delivered at cost (Mainc, 2020). As stated in the Agreement: 'AstraZeneca shall use Best Reasonable Efforts to mitigate and reduce the Cost of Goods during the Term of this Supply Agreement' (GHIAA, 2021). These terms significantly enhanced the UK government's ability to guarantee vaccine access for all UK citizens (Mazzucato, Stratton and Williams-Eliyesil, 2025).

After the pandemic, different attempts were made to learn the lessons on how to make sure Global South countries are able to produce their own vaccines: for example, the creation of the mRNA Vaccine Technology Transfer Programme (Dutt, Mazzucato and Torreele, 2024). Its main purpose is knowledge sharing to increase the capacity of Global South countries to produce their own vaccines. By distributing technology across multiple production sites in the Global South, the programme seeks to decentralize and diversify mRNA vaccine manufacturing, counter extractive intellectual property practices and ensure that early-stage, high-risk public funding is conditional on knowledge sharing and equitable access.

The pandemic thus created key lessons on how rapid policy

responses can be used to create not only outputs but also outcomes that shape the innovation landscape. Urgent global health needs can realign incentives and foster unprecedented cross-sector collaboration (Mazzucato and Li, 2021). Different modes of partnerships, including knowledge sharing and materials transfer, can coexist and complement one another in accelerating innovation. However, we should not need an emergency such as COVID-19 for incentives to knowledge sharing and development to advance the common good.

Knowledge sharing and the Seed Treaty

Another example of knowledge sharing is the International Treaty on Plant Genetic Resources for Food and Agriculture (ITPGRFA) – often referred to as the Seed Treaty (FAO, 2001). Established by the UN Food and Agriculture Organization and adopted in 2001, this global agreement creates a multilateral system for the sharing of plant genetic materials crucial to food security and sustainable agriculture. The Seed Treaty enables countries to freely access a pool of over sixty important food crops and forage plants, including staples like rice, wheat and maize, which have been cultivated, bred and improved upon over centuries by farmers across the globe.

This model directly challenges the dominant intellectual property rights paradigm, where private actors seek exclusive rights over seeds, often derived from the very genetic materials they now restrict access to. Instead, the Seed Treaty recognizes plant genetic resources as a global common good, co-created and maintained by farmers, researchers and public institutions. The agreement facilitates access to these resources and requires the fair and equitable sharing of benefits – such as the results of research and any commercial gains.

From a common good perspective, the Treaty represents a shift in governance from a system based on ownership and enclosure to one based on stewardship and reciprocity. It reflects the co-creation and participation we discussed in the previous chapter, ensuring that smallholder farmers and Indigenous communities – who are often the original custodians of these genetic resources – are included in decision-making and benefit-sharing processes. Moreover, it promotes transparency and accountability, the final element of the common good compass, in how plant knowledge is managed, circulated, and used to support food sovereignty and climate resilience.

This model illustrates that global knowledge-sharing agreements, when designed around public purpose, can reshape economic incentives and legal norms towards more inclusive, sustainable outcomes. It also reinforces the point that innovation ecosystems should not only produce technological progress but must also institutionalize fairness in access and distribution – something that the Seed Treaty operationalizes through international law.

8.2 Data access and digital equity

While the digital economy presents many opportunities, for example greater communication and access to data, it has also increased the opportunities for rent extraction. When rents are captured through the way that algorithms are designed, my co-authors and I have called this 'algorithmic rents' (O'Reilly, Strauss and Mazzucato, 2024). Dominant digital platforms act as gatekeepers of user attention, giving them enormous power over their ecosystems of suppliers who rely on that attention for visibility. Unsurprisingly, these platforms often exploit this position to prioritize profits, frequently disregarding user preferences, promoting paid information over more relevant content or subtly manipulating user attention through design choices. Together, these dynamics mean we are in an era of 'digital feudalism' (Mazzucato, 2018c; 2019b; 2025c), a system in which the digital economy enables a small number of actors to extract profits from the innovations generated by many.

This is why I don't like the term 'tech bro' to describe the male owners of the richest tech companies. In most cases, the technology at the heart of their success was not invented by them. They simply learned how to position their companies to extract as much value as possible from platforms and innovations that were primarily built on publicly funded research and technologies (Mazzucato, 2013). Once those rents accrued, they were able to recruit many researchers from public institutions into their private companies. That dynamic is very different from one in which one individual personally funds and develops new technologies on their own. Technology development is never a one-person show. It is a truly collective process.

This is a vital issue because in the twenty-first century, knowledge and innovation are more important than ever due to how much knowledge is available through digital platforms. Data governance is therefore not simply a technical or legal issue: it is a fundamental question of how we organize and distribute knowledge and value in an increasingly data-driven economy. In a world where data is the engine of innovation and economic growth, governance must move beyond serving the narrow interests of the private sector to addressing broader concerns of equity and access. A new framework for data governance should prioritize two dimensions: knowledge sharing and reward sharing. Knowledge sharing ensures that valuable insights derived from data are accessible to all, enabling collaboration and collective problem solving.

Conceptually, data and technology are not neutral or created in isolation. They emerge from socio-political contexts. The principles underlying the development of technology – whether it prioritizes private value, public value or the common good – can significantly shape the design and impact of these technologies. Practically speaking, today's societies run on software, whether it be digital systems that coordinate vaccine distribution, provide social welfare, manage identity records, make payments, pay wages or share medical data. These types of systems are 'digital resources' which make up a new type of infrastructure and which different societal actors can leverage for many possible uses (Mazzucato, Eaves and Vasconcellos, 2024).

Digital Public Infrastructure (DPI) – a layer of infrastructure that sits above hardware and internet protocols and underpins the functioning of modern markets and societies – is emerging as one of the defining features of this century. Like roads, electricity and water systems, DPI forms the backbone of our collective life. For much of the past two decades, the digital agenda had focused narrowly on service delivery, administrative efficiency and enabling private sector innovation. But today, DPI is increasingly recognized as the 'railways of a digital economy' – a shared infrastructure that connects people, supports the delivery of essential services and rights, and promotes inclusion (Mazzucato, Eaves and Vasconcellos, 2024).

In practice, invocations of 'public interest' and 'public oversight' in the case of DPI have often failed to distinguish it from private digital platforms that also claim to benefit society or are subject to regulation. What is needed is a clearer understanding of what constitutes public value in the context of DPI and how that value is intentionally created and sustained. Without this framing, it is impossible to ensure the transparency and accountability of the most important technological changes of the twenty-first century.

Two lenses are commonly used to assess DPI's public value creation: attributes and functions. Attributes refer to the technical features that make infrastructure scalable, flexible and open – such as interoperability, modular design and open source code. These features support dynamic efficiency* and reduce fragmentation across digital ecosystems. Functions, on the other hand, refer to the roles DPI plays in society: fostering community and social relationships, enabling economic activity, guaranteeing essential capabilities and enhancing overall quality of life.

While both are important, they are not sufficient. A system can be technically open and functionally useful yet still fall short of advancing public goals or being governed in ways that promote the common good. Instead, a third lens is needed: the common good elements discussed in this book, which focus not only on outcomes

* Dynamic efficiency as an economic concept refers to an economy's or firms' ability to innovate and improve over time, leading to better-quality products, lower costs and enhanced consumer welfare in the long run.

but also on the processes and institutional arrangements through which value is shaped, distributed and sustained.

Collective learning and knowledge sharing imply that DPI should be conceived of as a site of continual experimentation and feedback. Open source platforms such as the Modular Open Source Identity Platform (MOSIP) enable global collaboration and localized adaptation. By supporting shared infrastructure that evolves through distributed contributions, such models institutionalize collective intelligence and align innovation with long-term public value.

All five common good elements are needed to provide a governance framework that turns DPI from a promising technological concept into an institution of the common good. But the key point here is that people who contribute data have a stake in the value generated from its use. It is essential that data governance be reimagined as part of a broader social contract – one which guarantees that the gains of the digital economy are distributed in ways that promote the common good. Proper data governance can facilitate 'data sovereignty' or 'digital sovereignty', where citizens have full control over their data and greater independence from private sector actors. We now turn to two examples of how this can happen.

Barcelona's digital transformation

Barcelona has become a global leader in digital sovereignty, offering a model that puts citizens at the centre and promotes open, transparent and collaborative government. Initially, at the forefront of the smart city movement between 2011 and 2015, Barcelona partnered with tech giants to manage urban infrastructure through a citywide operating system that primarily benefited private interests. However, the election of Ada Colau as mayor in 2015 marked a radical shift which rejected a corporate-led digital transformation in favour of distributed technological sovereignty and participatory democracy. Under her leadership, Barcelona recast the smart city concept, positioning technology to serve citizens rather than extract value from them.

Barcelona's Digital Plan, launched in 2016 with an annual investment of €75 million, aimed to place democratic control at the heart of data governance. A central feature of this plan was the creation of a 'data commons' that saw data as a shared resource for collective benefit. The city adopted open source software, established ethical standards, and created new governance structures which emphasized transparency, accountability and public control. Key developments included the creation of CityOS, a 'data lake' where all municipal data is consolidated; the establishment of a Municipal Data Office to oversee infrastructure and engage stakeholders; and a significant upgrade to the city's open data portal to improve accessibility and value. Through these initiatives, Barcelona established an inclusive framework that enabled citizens to engage directly with data, ensuring that its benefits were more equitably distributed.

Transitioning to a data commons also demanded new forms of citizen control over data. Rather than serving solely commercial interests, the DECODE project sought to put societal benefits at the top of the list by enabling citizens to control the terms of access, use and purpose through distributed ledger technology.* This model of data sovereignty demonstrated how democratic principles can guide digital tools to serve the common good, promoting a fairer and more inclusive digital future (Monge et al., 2022).

One illustrative DECODE pilot involved Internet of Things technology that allowed citizens to measure environmental factors like noise and pollution levels in their homes. But participants were concerned about potential misuse of their data – such as private companies profiling homes based on pollution exposure and potentially affecting property values or insurance costs – and wanted greater control over how their data was shared. To address this concern, the project introduced cryptographic technology and flexible data-sharing rules to enable citizens to share data at varying levels

* Distributed ledger technology includes infrastructure and protocols that allow data to be replicated, shared and synchronized across multiple sites, geographies or institutions.

of detail with different stakeholders so that valuable environmental data could inform city policies while citizens retained full control over its use.

Barcelona's experience highlights the key role cities can play in shaping democratic data governance and how well positioned they are to institutionalize data sharing for the public good (Bria et al., 2023). Many cities already collect significant data – from mobility flows to air quality – but this data is often locked within private platforms. An alternative is for anonymized data to be openly available to researchers, civil society and citizens to support common good uses as with the DECODE pilot. Projects like the SynchroniCity project, funded under Europe's Horizon 2020 programme, have leveraged European cooperation to help smart cities to exchange data using shared standards, powering innovation in mobility, waste management and energy efficiency in other cities like Milan and Helsinki (Bria, Timmers and Gernone, 2025).

Europe's digital sovereignty: EuroStack

Europe's current digital stack is built on seven interconnected layers that together form the continent's digital ecosystem. At the base are resources, including minerals, energy and skilled labour, which provide the foundation for all digital infrastructure. Chips include processors and memory technologies, essential for powering digital systems and ensuring secure supply chains. Networks connect Europe internally and to the wider world through cell towers, fibre-optic cables and undersea links. Connected devices and Internet of Things (IoT) – from smartphones and laptops to industrial sensors – collect and share data in real time. Cloud infrastructure provides secure storage and computing power. Software platforms, applications and algorithms drive digital interactions and cybersecurity, while data and artificial intelligence process information and generate insights (Bria, Timmers and Gernone, 2025).

Large parts of this stack are currently owned or managed by external actors. Over 80 per cent of Europe's digital infrastructure and technologies are imported, and 70 per cent of foundational AI models are developed in the US, leaving Europe vulnerable to both security and commercial risks. To address this, the 2025 EuroStack initiative proposes an ambitious plan to reduce dependence on external technologies and strengthen Europe's digital sovereignty by building its own digital stack. Realizing this vision will require significant investment, with EuroStack expected to need around €300 billion over the next decade (Bria, Timmers and Gernone, 2025).

EuroStack is grounded in seven core principles designed to ensure Europe's digital stack operates ethically, is resilient and adaptive, and delivers lasting value to all stakeholders. *Sovereignty and security* aim to keep critical infrastructure under European control and protect it with robust privacy and security measures. *De-proprietarization and interoperability* promote open source technologies that work seamlessly together, reducing dependence on foreign systems and encouraging collaboration across Europe. *Sustainability* ensures digital systems are energy efficient and environmentally responsible, in line with Europe's climate goals. *Data as a common good* treats information as a shared resource, supporting innovation while safeguarding people's rights and societal interests. *Decentralized sovereign infrastructure* combines distributed computing with central systems to make networks more efficient, resilient and under European control. *Inclusive governance* establishes fair rules and accountability, balancing immediate needs with long-term independence. Finally, *strong democracy* ensures digital technologies not only avoid harm but actively support democratic values and empower citizens (Bria, Timmers and Gernone, 2025).

Building on these principles, EuroStack proposes a set of interconnected initiatives to create a resilient and independent digital stack: EuroChips, EuroConnect, SovereignCloud, DataCommons, EuroOs and SovereignAI. EuroChips proposes developing European-made semiconductors to strengthen supply chains and technological independence. EuroConnect proposes developing fast, secure and energy-efficient pan-European networks, preparing the continent for 5G, 6G and future connectivity. SovereignCloud proposes establishing a European-controlled cloud and edge infrastructure for AI, data storage and high-performance computing, supporting both public and private sectors. SmartEurope IoT proposes creating interoperable devices and systems, powering smart cities, industrial automation, renewable energy and advanced manufacturing. DataCommons proposes offering secure platforms for data sharing, treating information as a common good while promoting innovation. EuroOS, including a Digital ID Wallet and Digital Euro, proposes giving citizens and businesses secure, privacy-first access to services and payments. Finally, SovereignAI proposes developing ethical AI solutions tailored to Europe's linguistic, cultural and sector-specific needs, supporting healthcare, education, climate monitoring and other strategic areas (Bria, Timmers and Gernone, 2025). Together, these components aim to build a secure, sovereign and innovative European digital ecosystem that balances technological independence with collaboration, sustainability and the protection of citizens' rights.

While acknowledging how bold this initiative is, some caution that full ownership of the digital stack may not always be practical or even desirable. Bracken, Eaves and Wronski (2025) argue that defining sovereignty as owning every layer of a stack can overlook how digital ecosystems typically develop as platforms and emerge from services, not the other way around. In this view, rather than pursuing a single monolithic stack, Europe might gain more by prioritizing interoperability, open standards and user-driven services that can generate both resilience and long-term value. This approach, they argue, can be reinforced through conditionalities for digital companies. For example, European countries could require that tech companies operating within their jurisdiction ensure their services are interoperable.

A balanced approach based on the common good elements – particularly collective learning and knowledge sharing, and access for all and reward sharing (discussed in the next chapter) – may be the most effective: Europe should prioritize interoperability and use conditionalities to secure stronger agreements with tech companies, while also increasing ownership of critical parts of the stack to safeguard the region's sovereignty and security.

8.3 Valuing Indigenous knowledge

The way that knowledge functions as a resource to be owned and exchanged often reinforces hierarchies of power and value between those who generate knowledge and those who profit from it. Across fields such as biotechnology, data science, environmental management and cultural research, the extraction of knowledge mirrors broader patterns of exploitation and inequality. Information is often taken from communities or ecosystems, transformed into technical data or intellectual property, and circulated within global markets far removed from its original context. The language of innovation and development frequently conceals these dynamics, presenting appropriation as progress and masking the unequal relations that shape who controls and benefits from knowledge.

The experience of Indigenous peoples provides a clear illustration of these dynamics. Their knowledge of ecosystems, climate and biodiversity has long been extracted by researchers, governments and corporations, often without consent, recognition or fair compensation. Indigenous communities insist that their ancient knowledge is central to their survival and identity and must be protected as a fundamental right. They also argue that when their knowledge benefits external groups, they should have control over its use and benefit from any resulting gains. While international law increasingly acknowledges these claims, most protections remain weak, and scientific and commercial interests often override them.

For decades, Indigenous peoples have petitioned for the recognition of their cultural and sovereignty rights. Appeals to the League of Nations and the UN have been consistently rejected as threats to national sovereignty. While the UN Charter (1948) supported self-determination for colonies, it did not extend these rights to

Indigenous peoples within nation states. The ILO Convention 107 (1957) recognized certain Indigenous rights but framed them as individual rather than collective, promoting them primarily to integrate Indigenous peoples into modern labour pools. A shift came with the UN's study on Indigenous discrimination (1994), which recommended legal protections for traditional laws, land ownership and self-governance. This led to the formation of the Working Group on Indigenous Populations, which reviewed the evolution of standards concerning the rights of Indigenous peoples. A draft declaration on the rights of Indigenous peoples, begun in 1988, has also been influential in shaping international Indigenous rights.

The Convention on Biological Diversity (CBD), in effect since 1993, recognizes the deep connection between Indigenous communities and biological resources and advocates fair benefit sharing. Article 8(j) of the CBD calls for respecting, preserving and maintaining Indigenous knowledge relevant to biodiversity conservation and sustainable use; promoting its broader application with the approval and involvement of Indigenous communities; and ensuring equitable benefit sharing from its use (Mauro and Hardison, 2000).

Debates continue over the scope of these obligations. Indigenous representatives argue that preserving Indigenous knowledge requires recognizing rights to land, language, religion and culture. Yet many parties have sought to limit these rights. Additionally, existing intellectual property laws are often seen as inadequate for protecting Indigenous knowledge, prompting calls for new laws that better recognize community rights and diverse traditions. Some progress has been made. Non-binding agreements have been used to promote Indigenous rights, and the Rio Declaration (1992) highlights the importance of Indigenous participation in sustainable development. Moreover, research protocols, such as those under the Arctic Environmental Protection Strategy (1991), mandate community consent. Indigenous groups have also developed their own policies, including the Kari-Oca Declaration (1992), the Mataatua Declaration (1993) and the Inuit Tapirisat's *Principles for Negotiating Research Relationships in the North*, to regulate research in their territories. However, Indigenous communities say that these are often ignored.

Good practices are emerging at the local level. The Robustas Amazônicos Initiative, in the Matas de Rondônia in Brazil, exemplifies the power of partnerships to promote both economic and environmental sustainability by integrating Indigenous knowledge with modern agroforestry techniques for sustainable coffee production. The region includes more than 60 per cent of the state's coffee-growing areas and generates 83 per cent of Rondônia's coffee production. Thanks to technological adoption and the integration of Indigenous knowledge (Rosa Neto, 2024), productivity has increased by almost 500 per cent over the last two decades. The initiative has also benefited Indigenous communities by fostering sustainable development and economic opportunities while preserving their cultural heritage and traditional knowledge. Indigenous knowledge is essential for ensuring that development is sustainable and inclusive, respecting cultural practices and land rights while promoting conservation.

At the international level, building on the CBD, the Nagoya Protocol (2010) is a major step forward in regulating access to genetic resources and ensuring the fair and equitable sharing of benefits arising from their use. While the CBD introduced the core principles of access and benefit sharing (ABS), it left many of its provisions open to interpretation and uneven implementation. The Nagoya Protocol addresses these gaps by implementing legally binding commitments, establishing a more coherent and enforceable international framework. Among its important features are the requirements for free, prior and informed consent and mutually agreed terms, which are intended to be safeguards to ensure that access to genetic resources – and the traditional knowledge associated with them – is granted transparently, ethically and with appropriate compensation.

In doing so, the Protocol seeks to rebalance global inequalities. It empowers biodiversity-rich but resource-constrained countries and recognizes the rights of Indigenous peoples and local communities as essential stewards of genetic material and cultural knowledge. By placing these obligations within a broader vision of biodiversity as a shared global good, the Nagoya Protocol repositions access as a structured, reciprocal process – one that links scientific and commercial use with conservation, equity and justice (Morgera, Tsioumani and Buck, 2024).

Despite its promise, it is important to note that the Nagoya Protocol was established primarily by the decisions of state representatives rather than by Indigenous peoples and local communities themselves. This gap highlights the need for an intermediary institutional framework that reflects and is guided by the standards, practices and knowledge systems these communities have developed. A common good economy framework can help ensure that governance mechanisms are not only legally binding but also culturally legitimate and socially just. The G9 alliance, a coalition of Indigenous and local organizations from the nine countries of the Amazon basin established during the 2024 UN Biodiversity Conference in Cali (Silva, 2024), could benefit from a stronger framing in order to perform this role by providing both structure and representation that align with the rights and worldviews of Indigenous peoples throughout the entire value chain of knowledge and value creation.

Conclusion

This chapter has shown that collective learning and knowledge sharing – the third element of the common good compass – depends on how knowledge is created, governed and shared across multiple domains. Intellectual property rights, the digital ecosystem and knowledge extraction all present both challenges and opportunities for fostering collective intelligence. Examples such as Barcelona's data commons and initiatives like the Nagoya Protocol demonstrate that when knowledge is managed inclusively, it can generate social, economic and environmental benefits while empowering communities. By moving beyond narrow ownership models towards collaborative knowledge governance, we can harness this collective intelligence to tackle complex societal problems and ensure that its benefits are shared by all – a critical topic we turn to next.

9.

Access for all and reward sharing

How economies are structured reflects ideas about who creates value and how benefits should be distributed. While it is often assumed that only business creates value, all the different people who labour (whether in factories, hospitals or schools) are of course key to value creation. This does not mean dismissing the role of business, but it does mean widening our understanding of value creation across all economic actors and making sure that rewards are shared accordingly.

In fact, it is precisely by not recognizing the collective aspect of value creation, that rewards and resources are often captured by a few hands. If it is recognized that investments in technological change trace their origin to publicly funded research, this should be reflected in how property rights and prices are structured. Similarly, natural resources in the Global South – part of a population's collective wealth – should benefit all, not just a small group. And if during an economic crisis banks are bailed out with public funding (as they often are, including during the 2007–8 financial crash), once they are up and running again, the gains should flow back to taxpayers with a risk-adjusted interest rate. When value is understood as collectively created, businesses can play a much more constructive and inclusive role in the economy by rewarding their employees, paying their taxes and contributing fairly to the societies that enable their success.

Recognizing this is also crucial because the creation of value extends well beyond firms and the state to the everyday contributions of people and communities. Citizens generate vast amounts of value, including data that they create every day when using apps, yet it is mainly the technology companies that monetize that data. Cultural innovations, from blues and jazz to modern hip hop, have generated trillions globally, but the communities that created them see little of the returns. Indigenous knowledge has informed pharmaceutical breakthroughs and sustainable practices, yet those communities almost never benefit. From the legacies of colonialism to modern-day capitalism, the risks and efforts are widely shared, but the rewards are captured by narrow groups.

Addressing this imbalance requires action on two fronts: redistribution and pre-distribution. Redistribution is the more familiar approach, relying on measures such as progressive taxation, social spending and public investment to correct inequalities that already exist. Pre-distribution, by contrast, seeks to prevent such inequalities from emerging in the first place. While both are vital, pre-distributive strategies are especially important because they embed fairness and a commitment to the common good into the foundations of the economy, rather than relying on corrective measures after the fact. And this is not just a matter of fairness or ethics: excessive inequality also undermines economic productivity, dampens social mobility and weakens the foundations of a well-functioning economy.

This chapter explores both approaches, which complement each other in building an economic system where collective effort yields collective rewards. I also highlight the role of public finance institutions (e.g. public banks or wealth funds), showing how they can ensure broad access to resources and shared benefits once resources are mobilized through both redistributive policies and pre-distributive measures.

9.1 Redistribution and taxation

When *Forbes* magazine began tracking global billionaires in 1987, it identified 140. By 2025, that number had shot up to 3,028 (Forbes, 2025). Together, these individuals now hold US$16.1 trillion in wealth – more than the GDP of every country in the world except the United States and China (Burleigh, 2025). At the top of the list sits Elon Musk, whose fortune stood at US$342 billion in April 2025 and has since more than doubled to US$775 billion in February 2026 (Forbes, 2026). This is equivalent to the combined annual income of an astonishing 707.8 million people living in extreme poverty today.

Much of this wealth accumulation is not the result of effort or merit, despite what some might like to believe. Instead, it reflects systemic structures that perpetuate unequal reward sharing and limited access – a legacy rooted in colonialism and extractivism. As economist Thomas Piketty illustrates in *Capital in the Twenty-First Century* (2014), the wealth of owners of capital tends to grow faster than the economy itself because returns on capital consistently outpace returns on labour. In other words, the rich get richer simply by owning assets ('passive income') rather than through work. As I have argued, these dynamics have been further amplified in recent decades by the financialization of the economy and the structure of the modern knowledge economy, where the public often assumes the risks through investments in research and subsidies for emerging industries, while private actors capture the rewards through expansive intellectual property regimes (Mazzucato, 2013; 2018c).

Gabriel Palma (2019) highlights the tangible costs of inequality for government finances and overall economic efficiency. He shows, for example, that allowing inequality to persist forces states to spend precious resources picking up the mess. Palma distinguishes between 'market inequality' – the level of inequality before taxes and transfers, or what the market delivers on its own – and 'income inequality', which reflects a nation's level of inequality after redistributive fiscal policies are applied (measured via household disposable income). Income inequality, he argues, better captures citizens' lived experience, while market inequality reflects the competitive and dynamic forces shaping the economy. Palma also demonstrates a strong link between growth, market inequality and returns on capital: in countries where mainstream macroeconomic policies dominate – such as light-touch financial regulation, low corporate taxes and high levels of rent extraction – the top 10 per cent have little incentive to invest productively because they can earn higher returns through speculative financial investments. By contrast, when governments pursue competition-inducing Keynesian policies – as seen in much of East Asia today, and in OECD countries in the post-war era – productive investment is stimulated, because people cannot chase astronomical financial returns. He further notes that the growing rate of market inequality alongside stagnating growth and productivity in advanced economies contributes to what he calls 'reverse catching up', where highly unequal middle-income countries in Latin America and Africa can outperform some high-income nations in terms of productive investment and social outcomes.

To counter these structural inequalities, most progressive economists and policymakers advocate redistributive measures that transfer wealth and resources from the most affluent segments of society to those with less, through tools such as progressive taxation, social spending and public investment. For instance, Piketty, Saez and Zucman (2023) argue that an optimal tax system should combine progressive income, wealth and inheritance taxes – a framework they describe as the 'ideal triptych'. While elements of this model exist in many modern democracies, they stress the need for systematic reinforcement and global coordination to make it fully effective. Piketty (2022) has also proposed using revenues from wealth and inheritance taxes to fund a minimum universal inheritance scheme, so that the poorest 50 per cent of children receive an inheritance that would secure a fairer start in life.

Beyond redistribution, taxation can also serve other important purposes. It can build the financial muscle required for states to implement actions for the common good and can help give purpose and directionality to the economy. Tax regulations can steer finance towards more productive activities that advance the common good and incentivize productive entrepreneurship through measures such as lower taxes for hiring labour and higher taxes on financial transactions. Nevertheless, while taxation and other redistributive policies are essential, they are not enough on their own, because by the time they are applied rewards have already been distributed unfairly, without adequately recognizing the collective effort that underpins economic activity. This is why pre-distribution is discussed in the next section, as a way of setting relationships right from the start. But before that, we take a closer look at different types of taxation, which are some of the most direct and potentially transformative tools for addressing extreme inequality today.

Income tax

A progressive income tax is one where the rate of taxation increases as income rises: those who earn more pay a higher percentage of their earnings. Progressive income taxes are among the most established tools for redistribution, though rates vary widely by country. In countries such as Belgium, with strong progressive systems, top tax rates can exceed 50 per cent, whereas in lower-income-tax economies such as Chile or Colombia, earners may pay less than 20 per cent (OECD, 2025). When effectively enforced, progressive income tax not only generates government revenue but also funds social programmes, poverty reduction strategies and infrastructure that support broader development.

However, in the Global South, where informality rates are high, taxation faces persistent challenges. For instance, in Latin America, high levels of inequality are compounded by the scale of the informal economy, which accounts for almost half of regional employment (47.6 per cent). The numbers are even higher in countries like Peru (72 per cent) and Ecuador (68 per cent) (ILO, 2025). With so many workers operating outside the formal tax system, revenue collection remains limited.

Moreover, the ultra-wealthy rarely rely on wages or salaries as their primary source of income. Their wealth is largely derived from assets, investments and corporate profits. As a result, even highly progressive income taxes capture only a fraction of their total resources. In addition, high-income individuals often exploit loopholes, offshore accounts and other avoidance strategies, further reducing the effectiveness of income taxation in addressing extreme inequality.

These realities show that while income tax is essential, it is insufficient on its own to counter the concentration of wealth at the very top. To meaningfully reduce inequality, it must be complemented by capital gains and land taxes, wealth taxes and corporate taxation, which target the unearned income and accumulated assets that make up the bulk of wealth among the richest individuals.

Furthermore, some argue that high income taxes hurt innovation – they need only look at one of the most innovative periods in US history to discover the opposite. Under the presidency of General Dwight Eisenhower (1953–61), who was not only a Republican but also previously a military general, the top marginal taxation rate was famously over 90 per cent. And yet this was the same period in which some of the most innovative programmes, which businesses greatly benefited from, were funded, such as DARPA and NASA. The point is not that tax hurts or benefits innovation; the point is that ideologies that argue against taxing high incomes in the name of innovation have no empirical evidence.

Corporate taxes

Unlike income taxes, which target salaries and wages, corporate taxes target profits. This makes them crucial for capturing the economic value generated by companies that benefit from public infrastructure, legal frameworks and educated workforces. By strengthening corporate tax rules alongside wealth taxes, governments can help ensure that both profits and accumulated assets contribute fairly to public revenue and play a role in reducing inequality.

Statutory corporate tax rates vary widely across the globe. In 2024, the OECD average was 21.1 per cent, a substantial decline from 28 per cent in 2000, reflecting decades of international competition for investment. Some jurisdictions have no corporate tax regime or apply a statutory rate of zero, including Anguilla, the

Bahamas, Belize, Bermuda, the British Virgin Islands, the Cayman Islands, Turks and Caicos, Bahrain, Guernsey and Jersey. Others maintain low rates, such as Barbados, Hungary and the United Arab Emirates, where the corporate rate is 9 per cent. In contrast, higher-tax economies such as Colombia and Malta impose some of the highest corporate tax rates in the world at 35 per cent (OECD, 2024b). However, statutory rates often overstate the actual tax paid. Effective corporate tax rates – which take deductions, exemptions and credits into account – can be much lower, particularly for multinational corporations, highlighting significant gaps in the system.

A central challenge is international tax avoidance. Multinational enterprises frequently shift profits to low- or no-tax jurisdictions through transfer pricing, intellectual property arrangements, headquarter arrangements and other financial mechanisms. Estimates suggest that over US$348 billion is lost annually worldwide due to such strategies, disproportionately affecting developing countries with smaller tax bases (Tax Justice Network, 2024).

In response, global reforms have emerged. The OECD / G20 Inclusive Framework introduced a global minimum corporate tax of 15 per cent for multinational enterprises, which is expected to generate up to US$200 billion in additional revenue annually (OECD, 2023). Around sixty-five countries have enacted legislation to implement this measure, but some major economies, including the United States, have pushed back. For example, President Trump has threatened to retaliate against countries that impose the global minimum tax on US companies, putting progress in this area at risk (Bunn and Bray, 2025). Strengthening tax rules, closing loopholes and coordinating internationally remain essential to ensure that economic gains from corporate activity are shared more fairly, rather than accruing disproportionately to owners and shareholders.

Capital gains and land taxes

Given that most executives in companies earn income not based on fixed salaries but on stock options whose value changes on the basis of stock price changes, it is capital gains taxes (CGT), not income, that often matter the most. CGT are levied on the increase in value of assets when they are sold. Individuals pay capital gains taxes when they sell an asset such as stocks, real estate or crypto. Attention to CGT can help to prevent wealth from accumulating disproportionately through financial investments rather than labour. In practice, however, many countries tax long-term capital gains at lower rates than income and offer exemptions or deductions, primarily benefiting high-net-worth individuals. For example, in the UK, the top marginal income tax rate is 45 per cent, while the top rate for capital gains is 32 per cent (Gov.uk, 2025). As a result, wealthier individuals are incentivized to prioritize capital gains over earned income, reinforcing inequality.

These lower CGT rates are often justified on the grounds that they encourage saving, investment and entrepreneurship by increasing the after-tax return, though the evidence for these claims is mixed. Studies suggest that in some countries, capital gains tax relief leads to investment flowing abroad rather than domestically, and there is little evidence that tax breaks for the sale of closely held businesses meaningfully stimulate entrepreneurship (Hourani and Perret, 2025).

Land and property taxes provide a mechanism that can help reduce inequality by taxing wealth concentrated in land ownership rather than income. Properly designed, land taxes discourage speculative accumulation and reduce intergenerational inequality by ensuring that inherited or acquired wealth contributes to society.

Wealth taxes

Wealth taxes have gained popularity in recent years as they target an individual's total net worth, including income, financial assets, land and other property, making them a more comprehensive tool than income, capital gains or land taxes alone. Taxing wealth is often portrayed as a radical innovation, yet it has a long history. Denmark pioneered a progressive wealth tax as early as 1903, soon followed by countries such as Norway, Luxembourg, Colombia and Nicaragua

(Ola, 2024). Over the course of the twentieth century, a handful of other countries – from Argentina to Japan – experimented with various forms of wealth taxation, aiming to raise public revenues and address inequalities (Saez and Zucman, 2019a). Many of these early attempts were ineffective and eventually repealed. Generous exemptions, widespread avoidance and evasion, and high administrative costs led to very narrow tax bases, limiting their ability to raise revenue and reduce inequality (Ola, 2024). This failure was not inevitable – it resulted from political choices that consistently favoured the wealthiest by leaving loopholes, weak enforcement and acceptance of tax competition from other countries (Saez and Zucman, 2022).

Today, only a few countries – including Norway, Spain and Switzerland – maintain net wealth taxes (Ola, 2024), though the idea is regaining global attention thanks to economists like Piketty, who has helped shift the debate by highlighting the structural forces driving wealth concentration (Piketty, 2014; 2022). To avoid the shortcomings of earlier attempts and remain effective in the twenty-first century, Saez and Zucman (2022) propose key components for a more effective wealth taxation plan. First, the tax should target the ultra-wealthy by setting high exemption thresholds, which reduces administrative burdens and helps to mitigate political opposition. Second, robust third-party reporting and prefilled tax returns are essential, as compliance rates are significantly higher when financial institutions – rather than individuals – report asset information. Third, for difficult-to-value assets such as private businesses, taxpayers could pay in kind by transferring shares to the government, which would then auction them. This mechanism would establish a market-based valuation and, in some respects, make wealth taxes easier to administer than taxes on land, which tends to be less divisible.

Implementing a robust wealth tax has faced strong opposition from wealthy individuals and will require substantial political will and coordinated international action. Current wealth tax rates in countries that have them typically range from 0.2 to 2.5 per cent, falling short of what is needed to address today's extreme wealth concentration. Estimates suggest that rates of at least 6–8 per cent would be needed merely to prevent concentration of wealth growing even further (Piketty, Saez and Zucman, 2023; Piketty, 2022). Reaching such levels will require collective efforts to confront entrenched interests. In France, for instance, a proposal popularly known as the 'Zucman tax', after its author, economist Gabriel Zucman, which advocates a 2 per cent annual tax on net wealth exceeding €100 million, has faced significant hurdles. Although it was approved by the National Assembly in February 2025, the Senate rejected it in June 2025, citing concerns over capital flight, economic competitiveness and potential legal challenges. At first glance, this may seem like an insurmountable obstacle. Yet history shows that when there is a will, there is a way. Indeed, we see how easily global funds can be traced when sanctions are placed on an individual or country. Coordinated action is possible – it just requires political will.

Financial transaction taxes

Financial transaction taxes (FTTs) target trades in financial markets, such as the buying and selling of stocks, bonds, derivatives and other financial instruments. Unlike income or corporate taxes, FTTs focus on the rapid, high-volume movements of capital that often generate profits for a small segment of wealthy investors while contributing little to the real economy.

Because financial markets are dominated by institutional investors and high-net-worth individuals, FTTs support redistribution by ensuring that revenues from these transactions come disproportionately from the wealthiest. Estimates suggest that a global FTT of just 0.1 per cent could generate up to $420 billion annually – enough to fund public goods, infrastructure, climate action and social programmes (Pekanov and Schratzenstaller, 2019). Moreover, beyond revenue generation, FTTs can steer financial activity towards more productive uses. By penalizing short-term speculation and high-frequency trading, they encourage investors to prioritize long-term investment, sustainable business practices and productive entrepreneurship in the real economy. In this way, FTTs act not only as a fiscal tool but also as a mechanism for shaping financial markets to better serve the common good.

Around forty countries – including major economies such as Japan, Germany, Italy, France, China, Brazil, India, South Africa, Chile and the UK – either currently implement FTTs or have done so in the recent past. In the United States, a small transaction tax is already in place, with the revenue used to fund the Securities and Exchange Commission. Implementing an FTT at the national level would require only modest administrative adjustments, as financial institutions already have extensive reporting obligations. However, even at the national level, strong political consensus is needed to overcome resistance from powerful financial interests. Expanding such a measure internationally would demand an even higher degree of coordination and cooperation among countries.

A comprehensive tax framework

Income, capital gains, land, wealth, corporate and financial transaction taxes together form a multi-layered, complementary system for redistribution. By addressing both earned and unearned income, as well as asset appreciation, these measures provide the fiscal foundation for more equitable societies. Their effectiveness, however, depends on coordinated international action and strong political will, as entrenched interests have historically impeded reform. This reality underscores the importance of pre-distribution as a complementary strategy. By shaping fairer economic relationships from the start, pre-distribution supports more balanced power dynamics and, in many contexts, may be more politically feasible than relying solely on redistributive measures. Combined with a robust tax framework, it offers a stronger and more sustainable approach to reducing inequality and promoting social justice.

9.2 Pre-distribution and conditionalities

As important as redistributive policies are, they remain reactive, addressing inequality only after it emerges. By contrast, pre-distribution seeks to shape markets so that economic outcomes are fairer by design, ensuring that the dynamics of wealth creation and distribution are right even before the tax system is required to intervene. When pre-distributive systems work well, inequality is less likely to arise, reducing the reliance on constant redistribution to repair the damage. Pre-distribution requires us to rethink how we understand value to be produced in the economy. Since value is never created by a single actor alone, rewards should be shared more fairly among all contributors from the start. This principle applies broadly across production, services, care work, cultural sectors and technological development alike.

Critical to pre-distribution is the use of conditionalities in contracts, to ensure ecosystems are defined by reciprocity of the kind we discussed in Chapter 4. This can be achieved through strategic conditions attached to public finance that incentivize progress towards specific goals. Conditionalities can take many forms, from minimum wage and price requirements to environmental targets such as energy efficiency, or profit sharing with the public sector. While often implicit in industrial policy, conditionalities are most effective when made explicit and embedded into a coherent strategy for creating public value (Laplane and Mazzucato, 2020; Mazzucato, 2022b; Mazzucato and Rodrik, 2023). For example, companies benefiting from publicly funded health research should be forced to keep prices low and not create patents that are too wide and strong, leaving them hard to license.

This does not mean the state should set prices or take exclusive ownership or control in ways that could block progress, which is rarely the case. Instead, the state's role is to enable and stimulate value creation across the economy. By retaining a portion of the value it helps generate, the state can secure resources to reinvest in future initiatives and projects.

For example, leading tech companies (sometimes referred to as FAANG, i.e. Facebook, Amazon, Apple, Netflix and Google, or MAGA, i.e. Meta, Amazon, Google and Apple) have captured a disproportionate share of income produced through collective effort (Lekkas, 2025). Indeed, as I argued in *The Entrepreneurial State*, most of the technology that fuelled Silicon Valley was publicly financed (Mazzucato, 2013). And today, with the emergence of artificial intelligence and the data economy, these corporations rely on billions of users who contribute data, content and feedback to their platforms and products. Yet the resulting financial rewards are largely privatized, accruing to a small group of owners and investors rather than being shared more broadly with the communities and public institutions that helped generate that value.

The problem extends beyond user contributions. Government grants and subsidies have also helped these companies, yet taxpayers rarely benefit from the profits. For example, US National Science Foundation (NSF) grants helped fund Google's algorithm and Facebook has received US$785 million in disclosed state subsidies, mostly for data centres, including a US$355 million deal with the state of Georgia, US$150 million packages from Utah and Texas, and US$41 million from Oregon (Subsidy Tracker, n.d.). In the future, such grants and subsidies could include clauses ensuring that when public funding generates large profits, a portion flows into a public wealth fund to support future innovations.

A similar principle applies to government loans. In 2009, the US Department of Energy (DoE) issued nearly identical loan guarantees to Tesla (US$465 million) and Solyndra (US$500 million), a solar panel manufacturer. While Tesla succeeded, Solyndra declared bankruptcy just two years later, attracting intense public scrutiny. The US government suffered the public backlash and cost from Solyndra's failure but received nothing from Tesla's success. Under the original agreement, the government would only receive three million shares if Tesla failed – a counterintuitive arrangement, since public stakes in struggling companies rarely benefit taxpayers.

A more effective approach would have granted the government shares only if Tesla succeeded, allowing taxpayers to benefit from the company's growth. Tesla's share price, which was around $9 in 2009, then ranged between $258 and $479 in 2013, meaning that a public stake could have generated substantial funds to cover Solyndra's losses and support future investments. The cases of Tesla and Solyndra highlight how, by not recognizing its role as a public venture capitalist, the state often ends up socializing risks while privatizing rewards.

Beyond taking equity stakes, the government can incorporate conditionalities into its contracts as a pre-distribution tool to ensure that societal benefits are built in from the start. A clear example is the US 2022 CHIPS and Science Act, which aimed to bolster domestic semiconductor manufacturing by providing approximately US$53 billion in incentives for research, development, manufacturing and workforce development (CHIPS stands for 'Creating Helpful Incentives to Produce Semiconductors'). The Act was designed to expand production and shape how the benefits of public investment are distributed – diversifying manufacturing locations, strengthening supply chain security, creating jobs, driving innovation, and promoting resilience and inclusivity (Mazzucato and Rodrik, 2023).

Access to CHIPS funding came with conditions that influenced value distribution upfront. For example, the Act prohibited government funds from being used for stock buybacks or dividends and favoured applicants committed to avoiding buybacks more generally. Recipients with projects exceeding US$150 million were required to share profits with the government above a certain threshold and provide plans for childcare for facility and construction workers. Proposals also had to align with programme priorities such as workforce development, R&D investment and energy- and water-efficient supply chains.

It is interesting to note that some, especially those who adhere to the 'abundance' agenda (Klein and Thompson, 2025), claim that such conditions can impede investment and innovation. The abundance critique is that there are abundant opportunities to grow being held back by excessive regulation, planning and conditions of the sort mentioned above which can create inertia in the system. But this view can also exaggerate the problem. All contracts are designed. The challenge is to include in their design conditions of reciprocity. If there are too many conditions, of course, that can push the system overboard and stifle entrepreneurship. But the opposite extreme just leads to deregulation and markets that only increase profits, and extractive behaviours. And indeed, there are plenty of examples where regulation and conditions are precisely the factors that stimulate innovation, because they require businesses to invest and innovate in order to receive subsidies or incentives. Ultimately, there is a disagreement here whether scarcity comes from friction in the system or from underinvestment and extractive behaviours.

Indeed, one could argue that conditionalities could go further than they did with CHIPS. While the rules aimed to boost production and create better-quality jobs, they applied only to certain sectors, limiting their pre-distributive impact. For example, minimum wage standards applied only to labourers and mechanics, not all categories of workers. Similarly, although proposals required commitments to community engagement, recipient firms were not required to give community stakeholders a formal role in decision making. CHIPS could have strengthened its pre-distributive effect by mandating worker representation on company boards and implementing agreements protecting the right to organize (Mazzucato, 2025d).

Such considerations are critical today when advances in artificial intelligence (AI) are making a few companies very rich, notwithstanding that significant public investment powered early developments in AI, particularly in speech recognition, along with neural networks. Government agencies like DARPA were not just passive funders of basic research: they actively shaped the direction and pace of innovation (Mazzucato, 2013; Laplane and Mazzucato,

2020; Mazzucato and Rodrik, 2023). In the 1970s, DARPA's Speech Understanding Research (SUR) programme funded pioneering work at Carnegie Mellon University, MIT and Stanford Research Institute, leading to systems like CMU's 'Harpy' that achieved near-human levels of recognition for a 1,000-word vocabulary. Throughout the 1980s and 1990s, DARPA continued to invest in language and learning technologies through programmes such as the Strategic Computing Initiative and Spoken Language Systems, laying critical groundwork for the voice assistants commonly found today in phones, cars and smart speakers. These investments were not immediately commercial, but they built the high-risk, long-term infrastructure that private firms later capitalized on. Far from being peripheral, the state catalysed the AI revolution by taking early bets on technologies that would only become commercially viable decades later.

Since taxpayers bore the early risks that made today's AI breakthroughs possible, it is both reasonable and necessary to ensure that AI systems serve broad societal goals rather than narrow corporate interests. This could involve establishing public missions to guide AI development – such as advancing healthcare, climate action or democratic participation – while embedding public value conditions into funding, procurement and regulation. Publicly funded institutions could also retain a stake in the value created, whether through equity, licensing or public data ownership. In this way, AI's trajectory can be shaped not just by profit incentives but by deliberate, democratic choices about the kind of future we want these technologies to build.

These examples illustrate how pre-distributive measures can take many forms, operating either directly – through profit-sharing mechanisms such as equity or royalties – or indirectly, through conditionalities, including requirements on profit reinvestment, pricing or knowledge governance. A more comprehensive overview of the types of measures that can be used to establish fairer relationships from the start could include:

Direct pre-distributive measures:

- **Revenues beyond taxation.** The government can claim a share of the financial gains resulting from public investments, which it can use to cover the inevitable losses and make future investments. Compared with the indirect measures discussed below, direct profit sharing can better generate directionality of innovation and enhance the flexibility of managing recouped revenues. The choice of a profit-sharing mechanism and its intended form of public return should be aligned with the financing instruments selected to support innovation (Laplane and Mazzucato, 2020).
- **Revenues from natural resources.** Communities in resource-rich countries should receive a more equitable share of the benefits from extractive industries, both because these industries often exploit collective resources and because of the social and environmental risks they incur. In Chile, for example, national sustainability targets have made continued lithium extraction conditional on adopting less water-intensive processes and ensuring the financial benefits from mining activities are shared with local communities (Gobierno de Chile, 2023).
- **Equity stakes.** Governments can take equity stakes in companies that it helps to finance. This has been done in countries with public venture capital funds (e.g. Yozma in Israel, or the CIA's In-Q-Tel fund) or by public banks (e.g. European Investment Bank, KFW bank in Germany, BNDES in Brazil). The idea is that a public fund is rewarded for its high-risk investments through shares or other forms of stakes with a gain if the investment succeeds. Such rewards can then be used to replenish the fund so that it can cover losses and invest in future rounds. Such policies gained some traction during the COVID-19 recovery, with many arguing that governments should be

taking equity stakes in the companies they supported with bailouts (Hockett, 2020). But rather than seeing this only as an issue during a crisis-related bailout, the bigger question is how the government, as a public investor of first resort, necessary for innovation-led growth, can secure a fair return from the risks it takes. Equity stakes offer one possible solution.

Indirect pre-distributive measures:

- **Pricing-capping schemes.** When public investments lead to innovations, governments should protect taxpayers by adopting pricing-capping regulations. In the US, Section 203 of the 1980 Bayh–Dole Act provides for powers of this sort. The Act established the US government's 'march-in' right over pharmaceuticals if, among other reasons, patent holders that benefited from public funding fail to satisfy the 'health and safety needs' of consumers (Sampat and Lichtenberg, 2011). Although this provision has been widely discussed (Davis and Arno, 2001; Korn and Heinig, 2004), it has not yet been implemented. Another way to ensure competitive prices is through competition and antitrust policies, which may be far less tolerant of monopoly prices than has been the case in the US over the past forty years (Stiglitz, 2017). While President Biden began to introduce a framework in 2023 that would allow march-in rights (King & Spalding, 2023), the law did not pass and the second Trump administration has explicitly rejected their use.
- **Conditions on reinvestments.** Governments can also negotiate conditions on requiring that profits be reinvested into the real economy, either through regulation or attached to financing contracts. For example, the creation of Bell Labs resulted from antitrust conditions imposed on AT&T by the US Department

of Justice (Brumfiel, 2008). In 1925, as a condition for retaining its monopoly over the phone system, AT&T was required to reinvest a share of its profits in research. Similar approaches are used in defence-related procurement through 'offset agreements', which mandate the creation of specific commercial, industrial or technological benefits. In Sweden, for instance, such agreements have been explicitly used to promote the military aircraft industry (Eliasson, 2017).

- **Knowledge governance.** Several measures can advance the creation and diffusion of knowledge essential to tackling challenges such as climate change and poverty, as discussed in detail in the previous chapter. One is to reform the IP system so that it aligns with broader institutional requirements, allowing multiple actors to access and use knowledge (Henry and Stiglitz, 2010). This involves ensuring that patents are used for productive rather than financialization purposes and are narrow in scope and duration (Mazzoleni and Nelson, 1998; Frischmann and Lemley, 2007). IP can also be managed strategically through flexibilities under the World Trade Organization agreement on Trade-Related Aspects of Intellectual Property Rights (TRIPS). For example, governments may choose to issue compulsory licences to obtain access to knowledge and/or price reductions on proprietary goods. In the 2000s, this was used to promote access to medicines in Brazil, India, Indonesia and South Africa, to facilitate genetic diagnostic tests in France and to procure antibiotics for defence purposes in the US (McNeil, 2001; Reichman, 2009). Where IP blocks the creation and diffusion of knowledge that is key for competitors – through refusals to license or defensive patenting behaviour – competition and antitrust policies may help, as applied by European authorities (Motta, 2004). These measures can be further supported by alternative incentives such as prize schemes, which reward investment in socially beneficial areas without resorting to excessive pricing or overly stringent IP protections.

Together, these direct and indirect pre-distributive measures demonstrate that a wide range of tools is available to establish fairer partnerships from the outset and to shape economic outcomes before inequalities arise. By combining profit sharing, equity stakes, reinvestment conditions, pricing regulations and knowledge governance, governments can ensure that both risks and rewards are more fairly distributed while promoting innovation and public value.

We now turn to a mechanism that illustrates how resources gathered through pre-distributive and redistributive measures can be used to benefit entire communities: public wealth funds.

9.3 Public funds

Public wealth funds are particularly interesting because they both create wealth and redistribute it. Moving beyond traditional grants, loans and loan guarantees, public wealth funds are publicly owned, independent and actively governed entities that maintain ownership of firms and assets. They operate with long-term horizons and aim to maximize value for the public sector. Notable examples exist throughout the world: the Norwegian Government Pension Fund Global (GPFG), Temasek in Singapore and ÖBAG in Austria, and at a local level the Camden Public Wealth Fund in England, HafenCity Hamburg Gmbh in Germany and the Cassa Depositi e Prestiti in Italy (Detter, Fölster and Ryan-Collins, 2020). Scholars generally classify public wealth funds into five types: national wealth funds, public venture capital funds, public climate funds, regional development funds and urban wealth funds (Detter, Fölster and Ryan-Collins, 2020).

Norwegian Government Pension Fund Global

A particularly strong example of a national wealth fund is the Norwegian Government Pension Fund Global (GPFG) – often called the Norwegian Sovereign Wealth Fund. Established in the 1990s to manage surplus revenues from Norway's petroleum sector, the GPFG was designed to ensure that profits from oil extraction would benefit both present and future generations, rather than becoming short-term windfalls for private corporations or the state. Now one of the largest wealth funds in the world – with assets of more than US$1.5 trillion – its earnings finance public services and social welfare while preserving capital for the long term (Cummine, 2013).

The GPFG operationalizes the principle that if the public assumes the risks of innovation – through early-stage R&D, infrastructure, regulation or resource management – it should also share in the rewards (Mazzucato, 2013). In doing so, it stands in stark contrast to extractive models, where risks are socialized and rewards privatized, undermining economic justice and innovation ecosystems. Beyond this, its governance demonstrates a strong commitment to transparency, ethical guidelines and intergenerational equity, directly linking to the common good element of transparency and accountability, which I discuss in the next chapter.

The GPFG also challenges conventional neoclassical theories of public goods and risk management, which typically view the state as a corrective force rather than an active market shaper. In Norway, the state is a mission-oriented investor, deliberately steering the economy in the interest of collective, long-term welfare. While the fund is financed through oil revenues – raising concerns about fossil fuel dependence and environmental impacts – it demonstrates how sovereign wealth funds can be used to invest in alternative income streams, such as returns from green innovation, renewable energy or public digital infrastructure, to support a just transition to decarbonization.

Public wealth funds can also operate at the local, urban or regional level. Urban wealth funds, for example, aggregate real estate assets into a fund for urban renewal and housing projects, maximizing the value and crowding in investment (Detter, Fölster and Ryan-Collins, 2020). Community funds offer a transformative approach to finance by shifting control to local residents. By pooling resources and involving citizens in decision making, these funds foster economic resilience, social equity and community-led development.

Camden Community Wealth Fund

The £30 million Camden Community Wealth Fund in north London exemplifies this approach. The Fund, created as part of the Camden Renewal Commission discussed in Chapter 7, offers repayable loans, equity finance and business support to local individuals, organizations and enterprises to support economic development. Its overarching aim is to recognize collective value creation by predistributing wealth and reducing inequality across the borough (Mazzucato et al., 2022a). The Fund is capitalized with a £30 million long-term capital allocation from the Council, primarily resourced through business rate retention and capital receipts generated by the borough's Community Investment Programme. While the long-term goal is an evergreen fund of £30 million, it launched in 2025 with an initial £4 million pilot dedicated to youth-led enterprises and increasing diversity in positions of economic power (Camden Community Wealth Fund, 2025). A central feature of the Fund is its commitment to co-designing investment strategies with the community. While traditional financial models concentrate decision making among so-called 'investment experts', Camden's model places residents – particularly those historically excluded from access to capital – at the centre of the process. Community representatives help design, develop and implement the fund, ensuring lived experience shapes each stage of decision making. A Community Engagement Forum connects the Fund to the broader community, providing a platform for open dialogue that keeps local needs and aspirations at the heart of its operations. Moreover, a Community

Guidance Group strengthens this participatory framework by offering applicants feedback and advice, helping them refine proposals before seeking investment (Mazzucato et al., 2022a; Camden Community Wealth Fund, 2025). By embedding community participation at every stage, the Camden Community Wealth Fund redistributes resources and empowers residents to shape and participate in their local economy.

Copenhagen's By & Havn Development Corporation

Another illustrative city level example is Copenhagen, which leveraged a public wealth fund to transform itself from a depopulating manufacturing hub into one of the most liveable cities in the world (Katz and Nowak, 2018). In the 1970s and 1980s, Copenhagen faced severe budgetary shortfalls, high unemployment, an ageing population, rising welfare and housing costs, and a poverty rate of nearly 20 per cent due to deindustrialization and suburbanization (Andersen and Winther, 2010; Katz and Noring, 2017). In response, national and local governments collaborated to create the Ørestad Development Corporation in 1992, leveraging unused public land for commercially and socially beneficial development. The national government provided the land, while the local government implemented intelligent zoning policies to meet local commercial, housing, transportation and social needs.

The Corporation's first major project was a metropolitan transit line, which set the stage for further commercial and residential developments. This collaboration effectively created a public wealth fund to aggregate land for urban renewal and housing projects, maximizing its value while generating public benefits. In 2007, the Danish government and the city of Copenhagen merged the Ørested Development Corporation with another publicly owned development corporation, forming the By & Havn Development Corporation. Despite its being privately operated, local and national governments set its objectives, placing it in a unique position to create public value.

At the heart of the Corporation's success is its relationship with the Danish government and the city of Copenhagen. The government transfers land to By & Havn, which is then re-zoned for commercial and residential use. As land value increases, the Corporation borrows public funds on favourable terms to finance transit and other infrastructure development on publicly owned land. The cycle allows it to service its debt while maximizing public value. The Corporation also uses contract conditionalities with private developers. For example, it levies additional property taxes on developments within fifty metres of new metro stations to capture increases in property value due to public investment. Beyond this, By & Havn invests 25 per cent of its revenue into public spaces, infrastructure and quality of life initiatives for Copenhagen residents (Bruns-Berentelg, Noring and Grydehøj, 2020).

These efforts have contributed to Copenhagen's economic revitalization and helped the city earn recognition as the Sustainable City of the Future at the 2009 COP 15 climate summit (Katz and Nowak, 2018). By & Havn Development Corporation shows how the concept of the common good can be used to steer and shape the economy towards the collective goals of equitable land development. However, despite its successes, some of its projects, such as the North Harbour development, have met resistance. While the law requires the project to support Copenhagen's efforts to be carbon neutral by 2025 and that 25 per cent of housing must be set aside for social housing for low-income residents (Katz and Nowak, 2018), climate activists, scientists and city residents raised environmental concerns related to construction activities (Peters, 2021), leading the Danish Climate Movement to file an injunction against the development (Nugent, 2023). As Copenhagen is on the front line of climate change, By & Havn Development Corporation will need to continuously navigate tensions between environmental sustainability and urban development.

The strength of public wealth funds, such as those in Copenhagen and Camden, lies in their potential to democratize economic power. By helping to shape markets and benefit local communities, these funds promote more equitable sharing of rewards and access for all, better positioning them to advance the common good. However, public wealth and community funds do not automatically achieve these outcomes – they must be deliberately designed to do so. Governance models for public wealth funds vary widely, and many still mirror private sector logic that prioritizes market performance over democratic participation. To genuinely serve the common good, public wealth funds must embed transparency, accountability and community involvement at their core.

Conclusion

Ensuring that economic systems deliver both broad access and fair reward sharing requires a dual approach: redistribution and pre-distribution. Redistributive measures, such as wealth taxation, remain vital tools for correcting inequalities that have already emerged. However, relying solely on redistribution is insufficient, as it does not prevent inequities from arising in the first place. Pre-distributive strategies, such as equity stakes and conditionalities, shape economic relationships and structures from the outset, ensuring that risks and rewards are equitably shared.

Public wealth funds illustrate the potential of combining redistribution, pre-distribution and participatory governance. They show how collective resources – from land to public investment capital – can be strategically managed to generate both social and economic returns for the wider community. By embedding democratic decision making, long-term planning and ethical investment criteria, these funds demonstrate how value creation can benefit everyone and result in improved environmental outcomes.

Implementing these measures is of course far from easy. Policies that challenge concentrated wealth and power inevitably encounter resistance from those whose interests are most directly affected. Overcoming these barriers requires meaningful community participation and co-creation. Involving citizens and local stakeholders in the design, governance and oversight of redistributive and pre-distributive measures, while building broad public support, helps ensure that they are successful. Transparency and accountability are equally critical: they help maintain trust, prevent capture and reinforce the legitimacy of policies aimed at advancing the common good. This is the topic we turn to next.

10.
Transparency and accountability

The fifth and final element of the common good compass is transparency and accountability, because without them, the common good cannot be fully realized. At its core, transparency means making visible what is often hidden: who does what, who owns what, who benefits and what trade-offs are involved. Accountability ensures that those in power can be held responsible for their actions and that promises made are kept. Together, these principles create the conditions for trust – between citizens and governments, across sectors and among the many actors involved in the economy. These ideas go back to Aristotle's vision of the *polis*, in which civic life depends on knowing and debating how decisions are made and by whom. In modern governance, the same principles apply. Legitimacy depends not only on outcomes, but also on transparent processes and accountable actors.

Transparency and accountability are the glue that holds the other four compass elements together, ensuring that resources, profits and decision making are visible, fairly managed and able to be contested. Whether it is water being extracted and distributed, data being used by tech companies or energy generated from community-owned resources, it is essential to know who benefits, how profits are shared and what governance structures are in place. For instance, tracking the use of publicly contributed data – such as Wikipedia content used by OpenAI – ensures equitable reward distribution, while in water infrastructure, transparency requires clarity on construction costs, reinvestment in system resilience, shareholder dividends and consumer charges. Corporate governance more broadly must reveal ownership, profit allocation and the use of collective investments.

Although Environmental, Social and Governance metrics (ESG) have gained traction,* progress has been uneven: environmental criteria have advanced, but social and governance dimensions lag behind. Transparency is also crucial in limiting the influence of lobbying, as even sectors like renewable energy have sometimes concealed pressures on governments, leading to lost tax revenue and tougher trade-offs in public goods allocation. In all these cases, AI could either strengthen transparency and fairness or exacerbate inequalities, highlighting what is at stake in accountable governance.

To understand how transparency and accountability work in practice, this chapter breaks them down into four key parts. First, we examine rules, which establish the legal and institutional basis for holding people accountable and promoting fairness. Yet rules alone cannot guarantee accountability, which is why we next consider the importance of strong institutions with dynamic capabilities to enforce those rules, adapt to new challenges and prevent the misuse of power. Building on that, we explore how transparency makes the exercise of power visible, enabling citizens to engage meaningfully and hold actors responsible. Finally, we look at how to measure progress because, even with good rules, strong institutions and open systems, we may still be tracking the wrong things. Accountability requires metrics that assess not just how much growth occurs, but also its quality and who benefits from it.

10.1 *Setting the rules of the game*

Transparency and accountability depend on clear, enforceable rules that set expectations for the behaviour of all actors – governments, private entities and individuals alike. These rules create predictable

* Environmental, Social and Governance metrics are quantifiable measurements used to evaluate a company's impact on sustainability and various ethical issues. They are used to track progress, report to stakeholders, and inform investment decisions by assessing a company's performance on a range of non-financial factors.

and stable conditions that strengthen democratic governance and embed society's core values – whether protecting private property or pursuing the common good – into the structures that shape public life, including markets. As Polanyi (1944) and Pistor (2019) argue, legal and economic systems are inseparable: markets are not self-contained entities but shaped and sustained by governance and legal frameworks.

Two key legal traditions that have been instrumental in codifying commitments to the common good are human rights law and constitutional law. Together, they provide the institutional architecture with which actors can be held accountable and are critical for ensuring that the common good remains a central guiding principle of political and economic activity. Beyond this, the common good can also be advanced through sector-specific policies, contracts and agreements that hold individual actors accountable.

Human rights as a foundation for the common good

Human rights establish universal, legally binding obligations aimed at protecting the dignity and freedoms of all individuals. The Universal Declaration of Human Rights, adopted in Paris in 1948 and signed by representatives of forty-eight countries, affirms that all people are born free and equal in dignity and rights. It guarantees fundamental freedoms, including equality, freedom from discrimination, and the right to life, liberty and security. It also recognizes social and economic rights – such as the right to housing, education, work and participation in society without injustice.

Despite their foundational importance in guiding state actions and protecting fundamental rights, human rights principles are often seen as separate or an afterthought of economic governance, where private interests continue to dominate. As a result, significant gaps remain in the realization of these rights globally. About 4.5 billion people lack access to essential health services, over 2.2 billion people lack safe drinking water and more than 270 million children remain out of school worldwide (WHO, 2025; UNDESA, 2025). To uphold the common good and ensure everyone has access to essential services, human rights must be repositioned not as abstract ideals, but as concrete, enforceable standards that guide the behaviour of all economic actors and shape the policies governing them.

Take the right to housing. Today's global housing crisis stems from deep structural issues, including market deregulation, the financialization of housing and chronic underinvestment in public infrastructure. The core of this crisis is the treatment of housing as a commodity, available only to those who can afford it, rather than as a basic human right to which all are entitled.

Recognizing housing as a human right creates a binding responsibility to guarantee that everyone has adequate access (Mazzucato and Farha, 2023). In our work, my co-author Leilani Farha and I have unpacked the right to housing into a set of actionable components that define what governments, and other actors, must do to safeguard it – and how they can be held accountable for doing so (see Figure 11 below). Guided by the Declaration, we identify the necessary relationships among financial institutions, developers and municipal authorities to create housing systems that are affordable, sustainable and conducive to community wellbeing – for instance, by ensuring proximity to work, schools and safe public spaces.

Crucially, this human rights framework guides the development of policies and practices by setting clear standards for transparency and accountability. For instance, accountability here entails a duty for governments to take continuous and effective measures to implement the right to housing. This accountability also extends to private sector actors and the complex interactions between public and private institutions, ensuring all contribute towards the shared goal of housing for all (Mazzucato and Farha, 2023).

Transparency is indispensable to making accountability effective. It is important that governments systematically collect and publish quantitative and qualitative data – including information on housing inequalities, discriminatory barriers and the impact of specific policies. Progress should be assessed against clear, time-bound targets, focused on outcomes such as the delivery

Figure 11 Human rights characteristics of the right to housing

Affordability
Housing is affordable if it is proportional to household income, not measured against what the market can command, and if the costs of housing do not threaten the attainment of other basic needs.

Habitability
Housing must be kept in good repair providing inhabitants with adequate space and protecting them from the elements, structural hazards, and threats to health.

Cultural Adequacy
Housing, through its construction methods and materials, should enable residents to express their cultural identity.

Location
Housing must be located within reach of vital amenities and sources of livelihoods, including employment opportunities, healthcare facilities and educational establishments. Housing should also only be built in areas that are safe to live, in particular away from sources of pollution.

Right to Housing

Sustainability*
Low or zero emissions housing, that is built with regenerative & sustainable materials, and that adequately protects against climate-related disasters and weather.

Accessibility
Adequate housing must be sustainable and fully accessible for those who need it, in particular people who are vulnerable and marginalized.

Security of Tenure
For tenure to be secure states must adopt legal protections against, for example, forced eviction harassment, or other threats; increases in rent causing unaffordability; construction or renovations causing displacement; or a change of ownership resulting in eviction or displacement.

Availability of services, materials facilities, & infrastructure
Housing must contain the facilities that are needed to ensure comfort and wellbeing. This includes access to safe water, sanitation, heating, cooking and washing.

Each of these components is key to a home being adequate, and without even one of them quality of life significantly declines. For more information on the characteristics of adequate housing, please refer to the UN Committee of Economic, Social & Cultural Rights General Comments No. 4 and No. 7, or Fact Sheet 21.

* Sustainability has recently been recognised by the UN Special Rapporteur on the right to housing, but is not included in the definition under international human rights law.

Source: Mazzucato and Farha (2023)

of secure, dignified, affordable and decarbonized housing. Oversight will be incomplete if it fails to include the entire housing ecosystem, encompassing private developers, investors and financial actors, all of whom should be held accountable for meeting human rights obligations. Furthermore, transparency is essential for community engagement, enabling individuals to express unmet needs and propose practical solutions, thereby building trust and increasing the legitimacy of housing strategies (Mazzucato and Farha, 2023).

Figure 11 shows how a human-rights-based approach – within a broader common good framework – provides the legal and institutional foundation that embeds transparency and accountability into economic systems (Mazzucato and Farha, 2023). The success of such an approach depends on whether governments hold themselves and other actors accountable to their human rights obligations and responsibilities and monitor their progress towards achieving the common good. The use of human rights to enforce global accountability – within both national governments and international institutions – is also reflected in global public good discourse (e.g. Kim, 2013). This highlights the critical need to further explore the intersection of human rights governance and the common good.

Embedding the common good into constitutional frameworks

While international human rights law provides a universal foundation for accountability, constitutions aim to secure these rights in national legal systems and broaden their reach. Constitutions are blueprints for political structures and expressions of a society's values and normative aspirations. When oriented towards the common good, they can oblige the state to actively shape the economy in ways that promote collective wellbeing. This perspective moves beyond interpretations of constitutional law that focus primarily on procedure, the protection of private property and the rule of law. Instead, it understands constitutions as normative instruments intended to ensure that political and economic activity advances democratic, social and ecological objectives.

Some legal systems already enshrine a constitutional commitment to the common good. For instance, Article 151 of the Bavarian Constitution states that 'all economic activity serves the common good', while the Colombian Constitution defines the state as a 'social state based on the rule of law'. These examples show that the common good can be much more than a moral aspiration and become a binding legal duty, guiding the design, implementation and evaluation of public policy.

This normative orientation has deep philosophical roots, going back to thinkers discussed in Part I such as Aristotle, Aquinas and even Adam Smith (Dierksmeier, 2016), each of whom maintained that the legitimacy of economic activity derives from its contribution towards a greater purpose or *telos*. Modern constitutional models that place the common good at their core continue this long intellectual tradition, while addressing today's pressing challenges like inequality, the climate crisis and democratic erosion.

A recent and highly instructive example is Chile's attempted constitutional reform, which came out of mass social protests over inequality, extractivism and weak democratic accountability. The 2022 draft constitution sought to reorient the Chilean state around social rights, plurinational democracy and ecological stewardship. While it was ultimately rejected in a national plebiscite, partly because public trust in the Constitutional Convention had eroded amid political polarization and misinformation, one of its most transformative proposals was to recognize water as a non-commodified common good and a fundamental human right, reversing decades of privatized water regimes established under Pinochet. By shifting water governance from market-based allocation to democratic and ecological oversight, the draft embodied a common good orientation in both principle and legal design. And although it failed, the process ignited a national and global debate on how constitutions can prioritize public values over market primacy.

More broadly, these examples demonstrate that constitutional recognition of the common good can create powerful mechanisms of legal accountability and transparency. Constitutions that embed the common good make the co-creative role of the state legally binding. They authorize and require governments to pursue mission-oriented policies, institutionalize citizen participation and govern markets in ways that deliver long-term societal benefit. Constitutional mandates, for example, can compel states to justify budgetary decisions against measurable social and environmental outcomes.

Several countries explicitly recognize water as a public or common good in their constitutions, framing it as a right or a resource to be protected for all. This does not mean that the problem is solved, but at least the constitution can be leaned on during disputes. In Bolivia, the constitution declares water a public and communal good, guaranteeing access as a human right and prohibiting its privatization. Ecuador's 2008 Constitution similarly recognizes water as a fundamental human right and mandates its management in the public interest. South Africa guarantees everyone the right to sufficient water, placing responsibility on the state to ensure access. In Colombia, water is considered a public utility, with constitutional provisions requiring the protection of water sources as part of environmental stewardship. European constitutions do not explicitly declare water a common good, though EU law and national frameworks typically treat it as a regulated public service.

Other legal agreements that support the common good

Finally, while embedding the common good in a constitution is ideal, it is not the only way to promote it. Even without a constitutional mandate, the common good can be advanced through sector-specific policies, contracts and agreements, which can also hold individual actors accountable. For example, in housing programmes, councils could require developers on publicly owned land to meet defined housing standards, cap rents and reinvest into community amenities such as art centres.

10.2 Cultivating the capacity to govern

Even the strongest rules cannot lead us to the common good without the institutional capacity to implement and enforce them. A central challenge for this fifth element is identifying the rules needed to guide behaviour and determining who is responsible for upholding them – and whether those tasked with implementation and oversight, particularly in the public sector, have the capacity to do so effectively. Rules are necessary, but without the tools, knowledge and resources to act, they are insufficient.

As Rosie Collington and I argue in *The Big Con* (Mazzucato and Collington, 2023), the public sector's growing reliance on outsourcing over the past several decades has steadily eroded its internal capacity. As core functions have been handed over to external consultants and contractors, governments have often lost the ability to effectively manage, direct or even understand the systems for which they remain formally responsible.

By transferring key strategic and analytical functions to private actors, they have lost control not only over implementation but also over their ability to learn. Consultancy firms often come in with pre-packaged solutions, producing reports that disappear into filing cabinets rather than contributing to institutional capacity or collective problem solving. This is knowledge extraction and leaves the public sector dependent and disempowered.

With outsourcing expanding in both scale and scope, transparency and accountability mechanisms have also been affected (Mazzucato and Collington, 2023; Kattel and Mazzucato, 2018). Opaque contracts and diffuse responsibilities make it difficult to know who is making decisions and whether those decisions serve the common good. In many cases, this has created extractive relationships that erode public trust and delegate decision making to external actors who have not been democratically elected.

Strengthening public capacity means not only reducing dependency on external consultants but also creating systemic conditions that enable public entities to regain their ability to govern. Collington and I propose the following solutions:

1. Capping the use of strategic consultancy. Governments must set clear boundaries around the use of consultants, particularly for core strategic, policymaking and operational functions. Consultancy should never replace the public sector's ability to think and act for itself.
2. Reinvesting in internal capabilities. There is a need for long-term investment in public sector skills, especially in areas like digital infrastructure, procurement, data analysis and systems thinking. This must include training, recruitment and retention strategies to build a resilient, confident workforce.
3. Establishing public learning institutions. Just as we invest in science and research institutions, we need public institutions devoted to learning – places where civil servants can share knowledge, evaluate policies and collaborate across departments and sectors.
4. Building better frameworks for collaboration. When governments do engage with external partners, these relationships must be transparent, accountable and designed to support knowledge transfer into the public domain. Contracts must incentivize capability building, not dependency.
5. Strengthening public sector confidence. Underpinning all of this is a cultural shift. Governments must believe in their own power to shape markets, direct innovation and lead social transformation. That confidence must be rebuilt from within – through knowledge and practice, not outsourcing.

Reinvesting in internal capacities is especially critical, as governments need to develop dynamic capabilities to address some of the biggest challenges we face today. *Dynamic capabilities* refer to the skills and competencies that enable governments to adapt the focus of their resources, processes and teams to address existing challenges and create solutions for emerging vulnerabilities, while operating within and leveraging their own structural conditions and constraints (Kattel et al., 2025b).

One key initiative in this area is the Public Sector Capabilities Index (PSCI), developed by myself and others at the UCL Institute for Innovation and Public Purpose with support from Bloomberg Philanthropies, which aims to provide a global measure of city government capabilities, helping them assess and strengthen their dynamic capabilities. The index was developed through engagement with city governments across the world – including Bangladesh, Brazil, Finland, India and South Africa – through hundreds of expert interviews. Urban experts, including academics, philanthropic foundations and development banks involved in or funding city initiatives, were also consulted. These discussions helped refine the understanding of dynamic capabilities, identify existing data sources, explore approaches for assessing capabilities in city governments and clarify the value the PSCI could provide as a tool for improvement (Kattel et al., 2025b).

From this research, five key dynamic capabilities have been identified:

1. Cultivating strategic awareness: identifying and understanding problems and potential opportunities through horizon scanning, foresight, research, co-creation, external feedback and central government directives.
2. Adapting focus areas: balancing priorities with flexibility to address unforeseen needs through manifesto planning, foresight, decision making, risk identification and participatory processes.
3. Building coalitions: fostering partnerships to maximize resources and impact through networking, commissioning and procurement with academia, NGOs, private sector actors, and city and national governments.
4. Transforming teams: reshaping skills, resources and ways of working for effective delivery through recruiting new

talent, restructuring teams, tracking progress, robust evaluation and redesigning processes.

5. Embedding experimentation: creating a culture of continuous learning and innovation by actively considering evidence of impact, testing what works and using prototyping, trials, innovative procurement and participatory methods.

PSCI research has shown that these dynamic capabilities are critical in helping cities address complex challenges under significant constraints. For instance, in Freetown, Sierra Leone, a city of over a million people, the City Council has faced growing demands over the past decade, including addressing service deficits such as waste management and urban mobility while also tackling long-term issues such as climate change and sustainable development. In response, Mayor Yvonne Aki-Sawyerr launched Transform Freetown in 2019, a bold development plan designed to foster climate resilience, sustainable urban development and economic growth. The plan was created with input from over 15,000 Freetonians and identified eleven priority sectors for the city. The council's core administration of roughly 550 people works alongside a Mayor's Delivery Unit of 30–50 handpicked staff responsible for implementing Transform Freetown, supported by newly created roles such as a Chief Heat Officer to help tackle the climate crisis (Freetown City Council, 2023; Kattel et al., 2025a).

Given that Freetown faces significant constraints, including fiscal dependence on external donors, low civil servant salaries, limited skill development, inadequate data systems and political frictions with central government, the council has leveraged international partnerships and invested in developing dynamic capabilities to make Transform Freetown a reality. The city is cultivating strategic awareness through stakeholder engagement to identify urgent service needs and long-term vulnerabilities. It is adapting focus areas by balancing immediate priorities, such as waste management, with longer-term climate and development goals. It is also building coalitions with international donors and development partners to mobilize critical resources for key initiatives. The city is transforming teams by bridging the gap between the Mayor's Delivery Unit and the core administration through peer learning and targeted recruitment. Finally, the city is embedding experimentation through participatory budgeting, policy trials and digitalization of the tax system, strengthening fiscal resilience and accountability (Freetown City Council, 2023; Kattel et al., 2025a).

Similarly, in Seattle, USA, a city of over 700,000 residents, the city government faces complex challenges, including housing affordability, equity, community and neighbourhood development, climate sustainability and the opioid crisis. Seattle enjoys considerable autonomy under a strong mayoral executive system but still requires close coordination with state and federal authorities. To address these challenges, the city has invested in cultivating strategic awareness through data collection, analysis and stakeholder engagement to understand emerging urban pressures and inform policy decisions. It is adapting focus areas by prioritizing immediate needs, such as homelessness and public health crises, alongside long-term initiatives like climate resilience and infrastructure planning. The city is building coalitions with universities, technology companies and philanthropic organizations to mobilize expertise and resources while carefully managing partnerships to avoid over-reliance on external consultants. It is also transforming teams through staff training, role development and cross-department collaboration to strengthen internal capacity. Finally, Seattle is embedding experimentation by piloting data-driven policies, testing new service delivery models and evaluating outcomes to continuously improve decision making and urban management (Kattel et al., 2025a).

These examples demonstrate that by cultivating strategic awareness, adapting focus areas, building coalitions, transforming teams and embedding experimentation, cities are better equipped not only to tackle immediate and long-term challenges but also to reinforce institutional transparency and accountability. Cities that invest in strengthening their organizational capacity and learning processes are more capable of implementing policies and are better positioned to disclose decisions, monitor performance, justify choices and respond to public input. In turn, transparent governance fosters public trust and strengthens political legitimacy, creating feedback loops that hold both public and private actors accountable.

10.3 Creating transparency mechanisms

Accountability depends on the rules of the game, the institutional capacities to uphold them and the ability for others – especially the public – to see and understand what is happening. Transparency is essential here. It enables institutions to be monitored, decisions to be traced and outcomes to be assessed in relation to public commitments.

What is more, transparency is a catalyst for participation. As explored in Chapter 7, co-creation requires that citizens not only have a role in the process but also the information and context necessary to engage meaningfully. In this way, transparency and participation are mutually reinforcing: timely, relevant and accessible information empowers citizens to hold those in power accountable, while participatory processes help define what kinds of information matter most and how they should be communicated. Together, transparency and participation help create the conditions for democratic legitimacy and responsive institutions that support the common good.

Fiscal transparency in Porto Alegre and beyond

Fiscal transparency is a powerful example of democratic accountability. One of the earliest and most inspiring illustrations of this comes from Porto Alegre, Brazil. Since 1989, its pioneering participatory budgeting process has invited citizens to decide how public funds are spent. Through neighbourhood assemblies, residents review budgets, prioritize projects and hold officials accountable. The process has increased transparency in municipal finances and empowered marginalized communities, enhanced social inclusion and improved public services (Santos, 1998). Building on Porto Alegre's example, in

2012 more than 100 civil society organizations from fifty-six countries endorsed the Dar es Salaam Declaration on Budget Transparency, Accountability and Participation, asserting that citizens have a right to clear, accessible information about public spending – and to be fully involved in shaping budget decisions. This declaration helped mainstream budget transparency as a global standard. Following it, countries such as Kazakhstan and South Africa have experienced significant policy shifts: in Kazakhstan, disability-related spending rose thirteenfold due to civil society advocacy, and in South Africa budget transparency was central to securing court-mandated funding for HIV / AIDS treatments, extending life-saving drugs to over a million people. In both cases, fiscal transparency enabled marginalized groups to mobilize for policy change, demonstrating that when information reaches the right hands it can help redistribute resources and advance the common good (World Bank, 2013; Harrison and Sayogo, 2014).

Digital transparency in Taiwan

Digital tools have also reshaped the landscape of transparency – sometimes with transformative results. Under the leadership of Audrey Tang, Taiwan's digital ministry pioneered what she called 'radical transparency' by publishing transcripts of nearly all meetings online – including those with lobbyists – as well as using open source software and open repositories for government documents. These efforts enabled citizens to contribute directly to improving public systems and holding decision-makers accountable (Tang, 2024; Melendez, 2024).

Moreover, one of Taiwan's flagship platforms, *vTaiwan*, has brought citizens and government together to shape policy through blended online and offline engagement. Using AI tools like Pol.is, which cluster comments around areas of consensus – rather than polarization – the platform has helped inform legislation on complex issues ranging from ridesharing to AI regulation. This approach demonstrates how transparency and participation can reinforce each other in practice. By making deliberation visible and inclusive, Taiwan has fostered a more collaborative – and more accountable – form of policymaking (Chen and Wang, 2024; Sieker, 2024).

Importantly, Taiwan's model of open governance has also been an important defence against misinformation and democratic erosion. In response to coordinated disinformation campaigns, particularly around elections, the government has developed rapid-response strategies that combine civic technology, fact checking and citizen engagement. Projects like Cofacts – a collaborative, AI-supported fact-checking platform – and 'prebunking' efforts to counter false narratives before they spread have helped protect public discourse and reinforce trust in institutions (Hattenstone, 2024; Tang, 2024). These innovations reflect an understanding that transparency is not just about sharing information openly, but also about ensuring its accuracy and reliability so that citizens can make well-informed judgements about government action.

Taiwan's innovative approach illustrates how digital tools and open information can strengthen transparency and participation in governance. It is part of a wider global movement towards open government data (OGD), which has expanded access to public information and enabled new forms of oversight and civic innovation. Platforms like the UK's data.gov.uk and similar initiatives in over forty countries have made vast amounts of government data publicly available. Estonia, often cited as a leader in digital government, combines user-friendly data portals with strong legal frameworks to ensure transparency. Challenges remain, such as uneven data quality and slower adoption at local government levels, highlighting the need for clear standards and institutional capacity to ensure open data truly supports accountability (Lourenço, 2015; Rajamäe-Soosaar and Nikiforova, 2024).

Transparency is thus vital for supporting the exercise of rules, strengthening institutional capacity and empowering the public to participate in shaping outcomes. But to fulfil this promise, transparency must be backed by accountability: mechanisms that ensure information is not only available but also used. Transparency without accountability risks becoming performative, while accountability without transparency lacks legitimacy and effectiveness. As governments, civil society and citizens continue to grapple with complex, intersecting challenges – from climate change to digital transformation – transparency will only grow more important. When designed well and implemented strategically, transparency enables us to see what is working, what is not and why – and to course-correct in real time. It helps shift power, inform policy and build public trust. Most importantly, it makes visible whether we are actually working to advance the common good.

10.4 Developing the right measurements

Steering an economy towards the common good requires more than good intentions – it demands knowing whether our actions are delivering results. We must therefore be able to measure what we value and track whether progress is genuinely being made. Without the right measures, even well-designed rules, capable institutions and transparent processes may fail to guide us in the right direction. This is where accounting for growth – how we measure and interpret economic activity – becomes essential.

Traditional metrics like GDP reflect deep-seated assumptions about individual behaviour and the relationship between value and prices, often undercounting the activities that reflect how we truly value people and nature (Mazzucato, 2018c). Feminist economists and environmental economists have highlighted these shortcomings for decades (Parvez Butt et al., 2023). For instance, when care work is not measured, it is undervalued, leading to low pay and underinvestment. Conversely, when sectors such as finance are overvalued, we risk misclassifying rent seeking as productive, rewarding activities that extract rather than create value. These distortions are reflected in GDP's structure and, in turn, influence where resources are allocated.

The Stiglitz–Sen–Fitoussi (2009) *Report by the Commission on the*

Measurement of Economic Performance and Social Progress identifies three key shortcomings of GDP: (1) it emphasizes market production, ignoring unpaid work, environmental degradation and income distribution; (2) it fails to capture quality of life, such as health, education and subjective wellbeing; and (3) it overlooks sustainability, or whether current growth compromises future generations. The report recommends moving towards a multidimensional framework of measurement that includes inequality, non-market activities, environmental sustainability and broader indicators of wellbeing, such as quality of life and social connections.

Similarly, the growing movement of 'Beyond GDP' advocates incorporating broader measures of wellbeing and environmental impacts into assessments of economic performance (Coyle et al., 2023). Recent updates to the UK Treasury's Green Book, which is the government's guidance to departments on appraising and evaluating policies, programmes and projects, have begun to consider adding these 'wider' costs and benefits, such as environmental externalities and subjective wellbeing, into cost benefit analyses. However, while official statistics and guidance are gradually shifting towards more socially reflective measures, economic theory has been slower to evolve. One persistent challenge lies in the lack of robust methods for valuing non-market goods. Rather than forcing all activities into price-based frameworks, alternative approaches advocate rethinking how we measure welfare altogether.

Behavioural economists have developed multidimensional indexes based on stated preferences rather than market prices. For instance, Amartya Sen's capabilities approach includes factors like mobility, education, health and the built environment. Happiness economists have also worked to integrate life satisfaction data into cost benefit analyses, leading to tools such as WELLBYs (Well-Being-Adjusted Life-Years), which builds on earlier measures such as QALYs (quality-adjusted life-years) and DALYs (disability-adjusted life-years) (Coyle et al., 2023). Yet the WELLBY remains controversial, particularly in psychology, where reliability and comparability of life satisfaction scales continue to be debated.

A more systematic critique of GDP comes from Kate Raworth's *Doughnut Economics* (2017), which challenges GDP growth as the central policy goal and proposes a new framework based on operating within a 'safe and just space' – bounded by a social foundation, which ensures that basic human needs are met, and an ecological ceiling, which prevents environmental collapse. Raworth advocates regenerative and distributive economic design, with metrics that track wellbeing, equity and planetary health, rather than focusing solely on output or consumption.

In *The Value of Everything* (2018c), I argue that reforming economic measurement is not just about adding new elements to GDP or subtracting harmful activities but about questioning the type of growth we pursue and the activities we choose to value. Modern economies have blurred the distinction between productive and extractive activities, so pollution clean-up or speculative trading is treated as value generating. Why? Because GDP measures only what has a market price, and the costs of addressing pollution increase GDP, while the damage itself is ignored. This demonstrates the importance of assessing not only the rate of growth, but also its *quality* and *direction*, by setting the right measures to ensure that economic activity genuinely contributes to societal wellbeing and the common good.

These measurement frameworks are also essential for helping governments move beyond a narrow 'market-fixing' mindset towards a more proactive, 'market-shaping' approach. Traditional metrics often focus on filling gaps, and any action beyond that is criticized for potentially 'crowding out' the private sector – the so-called value creators. Even when public intervention is clearly beneficial – for example, if it is 'crowding in' business investment – the framing remains negative, emphasizing crowding rather than contribution. Indeed, public administration has historically relied on static metrics such as cost benefit analysis (CBA) and net present value calculations. Had NASA performed a CBA, the moon landing would have never happened! This is not to suggest that governments should not be prudent with public funds. The point is that the logic should be to first set the goal and then ask what metrics are required to evaluate those goals. The dynamic spillovers along the way to the moon – camera phones, home insulation and software – were perhaps the most important outcomes and were the result of big and outcome-oriented thinking, not static measures.

Building on these ideas, the five common good elements offer a framework for measurement that goes beyond GDP to capture a broader picture of economic and societal outcomes while supporting governments in adopting a market-shaping mindset. Purpose and directionality can be measured using tools such as mission maps and SDG indicators, which assess whether economic activity aligns with societal missions and contributes to collective goals. Co-creation and participation can be tracked using collaboration indexes, outcomes from public–private partnerships and social innovation metrics, while also measuring the additionality of high-risk investments.* Collective learning and knowledge sharing can be captured through indicators on open data, public R&D outputs, collaborative networks, and policies such as patent pools and licensing that encourage knowledge diffusion. Access for all and reward sharing can be assessed using measures such as Gini and Palma ratios, labour's share of income, inclusive wealth and value chain analyses, which reveal how risks and rewards are distributed across society. Finally, transparency and accountability can be monitored through institutional quality indexes, open government initiatives, fiscal transparency and stakeholder governance indicators, while minimizing unnecessary intermediation or outsourcing. Together, these complementary measurements provide a more comprehensive view of economic and social performance, supporting policymakers in evaluating progress across multiple dimensions of the common good. Table 5 summarizes how each element addresses long-standing critiques of GDP and illustrates corresponding alternative metrics.

* 'Additionality' refers to the idea that an intervention, project or policy should create benefits that would not have happened without it. In finance it means that public or blended finance mobilizes private investment that wouldn't have been made otherwise.

Table 5 Critiques of GDP and alternative metrics derived from the common good compass

Element	Critique of GDP	Alternative Metrics
Purpose and directionality	GDP is agnostic to the quality or direction of growth. It treats all market activity as equal, including harmful or unsustainable ones (e.g. fossil fuels). See Stiglitz, Sen and Fitoussi (2009); Raworth (2017); Mazzucato (2018c; 2021).	Measurement should capture whether growth is aligned with societal missions. Use mission maps and SDG indicators.
Co-creation and participation	GDP records only market transactions and ignores non-market collaborative efforts in public, civic and private sectors. It misses collective processes and especially undervalues the role of state actors and civil society. See Mazzucato (2013; 2018c); Ostrom (1990); Fleurbaey (2009).	Metrics should value multi-actor contributions. Include collaboration indexes, outcomes from public–private partnerships and social innovation indicators. Also useful to be clear on which investments are the highest risk and create 'additionality'.
Collective learning and knowledge sharing	GDP rewards privatized knowledge (e.g. IP rents), not open, shared innovation systems or the spillovers of public R&D. See Arrow (1962); David (1993); Nelson and Winter (1982); Lazonick and Mazzucato (2013).	Track open data, public R&D outputs and knowledge commons. Include indicators for accessibility of innovation and collaborative networks. Govern intellectual property rights so to maximize diffusion (e.g. patent pools and licensing).

Access for all and reward sharing	GDP aggregates income/ output but is distribution blind. It does not reflect who benefits from growth – labour vs capital, or by income group. See Mazzucato (2013); Piketty (2014); Atkinson (2015); Stiglitz (2012).	Use indicators for inequality (Gini, Palma ratios), labour share of income and inclusive wealth. Consider value chain analysis for distributive impacts. Map how risks are shared, so that rewards can be proportional.
Transparency and accountability	GDP does not reveal the governance structures, decision-making processes or institutional accountability behind economic activity. See Sen (1999); Rodrik (2007); Standing (2011); Collington and Mazzucato (2024)	Include institutional quality indexes, open government measures, fiscal transparency and stakeholder governance indicators in corporate and public sectors. Limit the use of unnecessary intermediation and outsourcing.

Source: Author's creation

More complex evaluation frameworks like the ones proposed above not only make performance visible and measurable, but also help prevent 'common good washing'. By incorporating multiple indicators and considering systemic interactions, these frameworks can capture spillovers – both positive and negative – across communities, sectors and the environment, revealing impacts that traditional metrics often miss. For example, if a company appears at the World Economic Forum in Davos to promote its 'purpose' or endorse B Team-style principles, new measures could test whether these claims hold up by examining: (1) whether the organization operates in an outcomes-oriented way, setting clear goals aligned with societal purpose; (2) whether it shares knowledge for public benefit rather than keeping the gains of the knowledge economy private; and (3) how it contributes back to society – through paying fair taxes, investing in public funds or supporting collective initiatives – reflecting the broader social and economic spillovers from its activities.

Better metrics, then, are critical to align measurement with values and to hold institutions accountable to broader societal goals. Without them, even the most capable institutions with well-designed rules risk serving narrow interests, guided by flawed measures of progress. With the right measurements – grounded in transparency and enforced with public accountability – we can begin to build an economic system that recognizes and rewards what truly matters.

Conclusion

Transparency and accountability are often treated as technical fixes or procedural requirements. But as we have seen, they are far more than that: they are essential to determining whether and how societies can orient themselves towards the common good.

The law is the foundation of transparency and accountability: the rules of the game that define responsibilities, determine rights and set enforceable standards. These rules embed a society's core values in political and economic life. But rules alone are not enough. Without the capacity to implement them, they remain aspirational.

Equally critical are transparency mechanisms, which make power visible by documenting actions and opening institutions to public scrutiny. Yet transparency alone is insufficient without the right metrics and evaluation systems to track the right kind of progress. Truly accountable governance requires measures that reflect what we collectively value. Dynamic evaluation methods are particularly valuable because they capture complex systemic relationships, including additionalities and spillovers from public and private sector activity.

Taken together, these four layers – rules, capacities, mechanisms and measures – form an integrated system. When any layer is missing or weak, transparency and accountability falter. When all are aligned, they create a robust foundation for mission-oriented governance to promote the common good.

PART III
Local and Global Flourishing

'People forge bonds in places that have healthy social infrastructures – not because they set out to build community, but because when people engage in sustained, recurrent interaction, particularly while doing things they enjoy, relationships inevitably grow.'

– Eric Klinenberg (1970–), *Palaces for the People*

11.
Reimagining places and welfare

Making the common good the driving force of the economy requires more than just policy, it demands renewed attention to the *places* where people meet. *How* individuals and organizations interact, negotiate, design and implement the principles of the common good matters as much as *what* they are trying to do together. As Eric Klinenberg (2018) emphasizes in the quote that begins Part III, taken from his book *Palaces for the People: How to Build a More Equal and United Society*, shared spaces such as libraries, parks, community centres, youth clubs and public pools are as important as roads, bridges and utilities. They are the places where we forge community, where relationships are formed and where people feel a sense of purpose and feel valued. Evidence shows that areas with strong social infrastructure have not only stronger social cohesion but also better health outcomes, lower crime rates and greater resilience during crises (like natural disasters or pandemics). In this chapter we look at how the common good requires investing in our physical and social infrastructures, and the need to design such infrastructure so that it nurtures community interaction, dignity and wellbeing.

John Maynard Keynes is not only remembered for being the father of macroeconomics and the key role of public investment in economies, but also for his vision of a society in which economic prosperity, social stability and cultural life are intertwined to support human flourishing. His experiences after the First World War – particularly his observations of the harsh economic conditions imposed on Germany and the devastation of the Great Depression – shaped his understanding of the social consequences of economic hardship. Keynes argued that widespread poverty and unemployment could fuel social unrest, political extremism and even future conflicts. He believed that government intervention through public spending, job creation and social programmes was essential to prevent such tragedies and create the conditions in which societies could live peacefully, securely and in culturally enriching ways (Carter, 2021).

This vision found clear expression in his support for the creation of the British welfare state as part of the post-war reconstruction that followed the Second World War. Keynes regarded the 1942 Beveridge Report, properly titled *Social Insurance and Allied Services*, written by fellow economist William (Lord) Beveridge (1879–1963), as a 'grand document' charting a new course for British life. Its proposals for social insurance, unemployment support and expanded public services aligned closely with Keynes's belief that government action was essential to prevent poverty, stabilize society and sustain economic demand. Keynes contributed intellectually to the report and endorsed it publicly, playing an important part in making Beveridge's vision a cornerstone of post-war Britain. The welfare state they designed remains one of the most ambitious projects ever undertaken to place the common good at the centre of economic and political life, so enduring that even decades of austerity policies have not been able to dismantle it.

Keynes's commitment to the common good extended beyond economics and social policy. He believed that the elements which make life truly rewarding – beauty, community and a vibrant cultural life – could only flourish through collective effort. These pursuits, he argued, could not be sustained if left solely to the demands of profit or private financial success. For him, economic security and cultural vitality were inseparable: a society that protected its citizens from poverty and insecurity was also one in which art, literature, theatre and intellectual life could thrive. His own life reflected this conviction. He was an avid art collector, a patron of the theatre and a driving force behind the establishment of institutions such as the Arts Council of Great Britain, founded in 1946 in part due to his influence. In this way, Keynes's vision for the economy went beyond material wealth to embrace the enrichment of human life, with welfare and culture together forming the foundations of a flourishing society (Carter, 2021). And from across the Atlantic in Brazil, a similar point was being made by Celso Furtado (1920–2004), an important economist in the Latin American school of development who was the Brazilian Minister of Planning (1962–4) and later Minister of Culture (1986–8). He claimed 'culture is the foundation of the development process' (Furtado, 1984, p. 33). Furtado connected to the view of collective value creation as the way that culture can promote everyone's participation in society and the economy. As Minister of Culture, he claimed that investing in cultural policies 'should liberate the creative forces of society' (Furtado, 2012, p. 101).

Today, the lessons from Furtado and Keynes are more important than ever, offering a vision for societies still grappling with inequality, instability and the search for a fulfilling life. After decades of austerity and underinvestment, many public services have become run down, falling short of the vision proposed during the post-war welfare state and of the cultural vitality that remains essential for human flourishing. This matters greatly because vibrant public spaces that foster community and cultural life are critical for the type of co-creation and participation that is required to make the common good possible.

I experienced the power of public spaces while working with Camden Council (see Chapter 7), where residents came together in community halls to debate and shape missions through the *We Make Camden* initiative, and later working with residents of low-income housing estates to discuss, for example, the green agenda for their community, their role in building community gardens and the transformation of food banks into green food cooperatives, where a sense of pride and real ownership thrived. It is critical to build public places where people feel valued and community is formed, while services are delivered at the local level. To do so, we must take these places seriously, moving them from the periphery to the centre of our economic, social and political life. This means that governments need to fund and prioritize them as much as they prioritize economic growth – the idea that we can only have one or the other is a false dichotomy.

To value places like community centres or public housing, we must care about their design and, yes, their beauty. Art curator Kieran Long's Public Luxury exhibition (ArkDes, 2019) explored the impact of beauty on public spaces. Long's exhibition, which showcased twenty-eight design projects in Sweden, acknowledged that everything in the public realm exists for more than merely functional reasons. Beauty in public spaces is not frivolous but necessary for healthy human life, and has an innate discursive power on 'how we tell our stories about ourselves, who we are, who we have been and who we hope to be' (Bednar, 2023, p. 35). Beauty can inspire a renewed sense of egalitarianism, justice and belonging.

The idea is far from idealistic. In the economic recovery following the 1929 crash, President Roosevelt (who received extensive advice from Keynes) brought artists, designers and architects to work on public recovery projects. He wanted the public financing of the New Deal to be informed by big thinking on how we can live together differently; for example, by investing in national parks and paying explicit attention to the design of social housing, not just its existence.

While beauty is, to some degree, in the eye of the beholder, it is also clear that people value social infrastructures that are functional *and* beautiful the most. Beautiful public spaces invoke civic pride by conveying that beauty is available to all citizens, not just the wealthy. It is telling that in an era in which we value public goods less, there are fewer artists, architects and designers helping to design public infrastructure. Public Practice, an organization dedicated to bringing back designers and architects into the UK's city councils, has found that forty years ago, a top architecture or planning graduate would have been as likely to go into public service as private practice. In 1976, 49 per cent of all architects in the UK worked for the public sector. Today it is 0.9 per cent, and only 0.2 per cent in London, as most work for the private sector (Williams, 2018).

As we will explore in this chapter, our commitment to the common good must therefore begin with recognizing the true value of public places, and how their governance, design and funding shape a flourishing society. This includes investing in public infrastructure, adopting people-centred design and placing arts and culture at the heart of our economy (Mazzucato, 2025e). By supporting the places where people come together, we can not only strengthen the foundations of civic life but also promote *good growth* – growth that enables everyone to live a good life by building an economy that is genuinely inclusive and sustainable.

11.1 Investing in public infrastructure: housing, health and community centres

Governments are generally not very good at valuing public investment or differentiating it from day-to-day spending. Too often, public infrastructure – whether housing, healthcare or community spaces – is treated as a cost rather than an investment that generates long-term social and economic returns. This narrow accounting approach undervalues the multiplier effects and intangible benefits that well-funded public infrastructure provides: healthier populations, more resilient communities and a stronger social fabric. When investment is neglected, public infrastructure deteriorates and societies end up paying a much higher price in the form of inequality, social fragmentation and lost economic potential.

Housing

Few areas illustrate this failure more clearly than housing. In the UK, one study estimated that building 90,000 social homes would yield an economic value of £51.2 billion (CEBR, 2024). This figure captures not only the direct economic impact of construction, management and lower spending on housing support, but also the indirect benefits such as reduced homelessness and healthcare costs, and higher tax receipts from employment. Yet, despite these substantial and well-documented benefits, the UK has experienced a steady and severe erosion of its social housing stock. In 1980, social housing accounted for nearly one third of all homes in England, around 6.5 million in total. Today, it represents barely 17 per cent, with 4.5 million units remaining, of which 2.9 million are owned by private registered providers and 1.6 million by local authorities. The decline is largely the result of decades of insufficient construction, large-scale privatization under Right to Buy, and the demolition of ageing council estates without adequate replacement (Shelter, n.d.; Hanley, 2022; Regulator of Social Housing, 2025).

Over the same period, the private rented sector has more than doubled in size, and public expenditure has shifted accordingly. Instead of building new social housing that remains in public hands, governments have increasingly subsidized private landlords through housing benefit, spending that has risen by 83 per cent in real terms since 1994 (Shelter, n.d.). The result has been a steady transfer of public wealth to private property owners while failing to address the underlying shortage of affordable homes. The consequences are severe, with more than 1.3 million households on waiting lists for social housing and homelessness, including among children, reaching record levels (Shelter, n.d.). Much of this rise stems from families reaching the end of private tenancies and being unable to pay increasing housing costs or secure alternative accommodation (MacInnes et al., 2015). The social costs are profound, as children growing up in temporary or insecure housing experience worse health and educational outcomes, while adults face heightened financial stress, instability and mental health risks.

Similar trends are evident in other high-income countries such as Canada, Sweden and the Netherlands, where privatization, reduced public investment and a shift towards subsidizing private rentals have eroded the share of social housing (Gurstein, Patten and Rao, 2015). Across the OECD, the average share of social rental housing amounts to only about 7 per cent of total housing stock, and approximately 8 per cent across the EU (OECD, 2024d). The result has been deepening inequality, speculative real estate bubbles and the displacement of low- and middle-income households to city peripheries, undermining access to jobs, education and community infrastructure.

Addressing these challenges requires rethinking how housing is designed and valued. As we saw in Chapter 10, Leilani Farha and I (Mazzucato and Farha, 2023) argue that a human-rights-based approach to housing is needed to ensure access to adequate, safe and affordable homes for all. This can be achieved by applying specific criteria, including affordability, habitability, location, accessibility, availability of services, security of tenure, sustainability and cultural adequacy (recall Figure 11 in section 10.1). The key point here is that how people live is fundamentally intertwined with broader factors like health, access to education and community. Too often, housing has been treated as a numbers game (focused narrowly on targets for units built) rather than on the broader question of how housing contributes to community resilience and social flourishing. Therefore, the question must not be 'What is the cheapest way to deliver it?' but rather 'What kind of society do we want to build?'

Healthcare

The same applies to health. Human flourishing depends on how we invest in healthcare, but also on the places where it is delivered. Public health is fundamental to people's ability to prosper, yet chronic underinvestment in physical health infrastructure, preventative care and workforce capacity has left many countries ill prepared for health emergencies, widened inequalities and weakened long-term health outcomes. Even before COVID-19, public health accounted for only a small share of national health spending in most countries. And, as with other areas of policy shaped by a short-term, market-fixing mentality, spending is overwhelmingly directed towards treating illnesses after they occur rather than investing in preventative care or social and economic determinants of health that make people healthy in the first place (Marmot, 1999). On average, OECD countries dedicate only 2.8 per cent of their total healthcare spending to health promotion and disease prevention, compared to around 80 per cent devoted to curative and rehabilitative care (Gmeinder, Morgan and Mueller, 2017).

In the US, this imbalance is especially stark. Only 2.5 per cent of the nation's US$4.5 trillion healthcare expenditures goes towards public health and prevention (Trust for America's Health, 2024), with the pervasive privatization of health services making healthcare exorbitantly expensive in the country. The country has also been making deep and sustained cuts to its healthcare budgets, undermining its capacity to prevent disease and respond to crises. Between 2008 and 2017, more than 55,000 local public health jobs were lost due to federal and state budget reductions, and further cuts to Medicare, Medicaid and the National Institutes of Health under Donald Trump have compounded the problem. The consequences are clear. The US spends far more on healthcare than its peers yet achieves worse outcomes. Life expectancy, at 76.4 years, is well below the OECD average of 80.3 (OECD, 2024c), while chronic diseases and mental health conditions account for 90 per cent of all healthcare costs (Trust for America's Health, 2024).

Even in countries with universal systems, such as the UK, sustained cuts have weakened healthcare infrastructure and services. Between 2015 and 2025, the public health grant to local authorities in England was reduced by 26 per cent in real terms (Finch, Gazzillo and Vriend, 2025). While the creation of the UK Health Security Agency (UKHSA) after COVID-19 signals some reform, persistent underfunding has eroded local capacity, particularly in deprived areas. Without renewed investment in prevention and public health infrastructure, gains in life expectancy are likely to stall, and health inequalities will continue to grow (NHS, 2014).

Globally, the disparities are even more pronounced. Health ministries in the Global South spend an average of only US$40 per person per year, compared to over US$4,000 in the Global North (WHO, 2023). Health expenditure as a share of GDP is also roughly three times higher in OECD countries than in sub-Saharan Africa or South Asia (Wang et al., 2021; Rahman, Khanam and Rahman,

2018). Moreover, in many Global South countries, high out-of-pocket expenses push millions into poverty each year (WHO, 2023). Donor aid and vertical funding streams targeting specific diseases (e.g. HIV or malaria), though sometimes very generous, often bypass national health systems, reinforcing fragmentation rather than building comprehensive and resilient public health infrastructure. Colonial legacies and debt burdens further restrict fiscal space, with many governments spending more on interest payments than on health or education.

As public systems come under pressure from funding shortfalls, more and more people turn to private insurance, further eroding confidence in the public model. In Catalonia, Spain, a survey of 15,000 individuals found that those who purchased private health insurance were less likely to support the national health system (Costa-Font and Jofre-Bonet, 2008). Similarly, in the UK, private insurance uptake was associated with reduced support for public sector health spending (Hall and Preston, 1998). Robert Reich warned about this in a 1991 *New York Times Magazine* article, describing what he called 'the secession of the successful', whereby the more well-off increasingly withdraw from public life by using private alternatives – clubs, security, healthcare, transport and more – and become less inclined to support public services they no longer depend on. This withdrawal contributes to a gradual decline in the quality of public provision, leaving fewer people willing to defend or invest in it. Meanwhile, the affluent remain insulated by their private services, while those with fewer resources depend on underfunded services. Over time, this cycle widens social and economic divides and fragments the collective social contract.

Tackling these challenges therefore requires more than higher healthcare spending – it requires rethinking what health truly means. Health depends not only on medical care after illness but also on prevention and, critically, on the social and economic determinants of health, such as quality housing, education, secure work and strong communities. Reinvesting in public health infrastructure and services, alongside stronger investment in prevention and these broader determinants, is essential to reduce inequalities and build more thriving societies.

Community spaces

Public infrastructure extends beyond housing and healthcare to the local institutions that sustain civic life – community centres, schools, youth clubs, parks, church halls, libraries, pools and more. These are the spaces where communities form, identities are shaped and civic participation flourishes. In difficult times, they offer refuge and uphold social cohesion, while in more stable periods they strengthen our social fabric and allow us to imagine and build the future together. Yet their benefits are often intangible and difficult to measure, so these spaces are routinely undervalued. Traditional evaluation frameworks focus narrowly on service metrics and cost efficiency, overlooking the broader social value they provide (McShane and Coffey, 2022). Libraries illustrate this point. Beyond book lending, vitally important though that is, they function 'as a network of integrated, mutually reinforcing, evolving infrastructures' that are simultaneously platforms, social infrastructures and technological-intellectual hubs (Mattern, 2014). As platforms, they provide access to information, media and production materials. As social infrastructures, they offer spaces to connect, learn and seek guidance. As technological-intellectual hubs, they enable access to knowledge and cultural resources that empower citizens. Above all, libraries stand as spaces of values and ethics, fostering openness, egalitarianism and freedom in an otherwise commercialized and surveilled landscape (Mattern, 2014).* Yet despite their value, librar-

* Arup Digital Studios (2019) evaluate the public value delivered by the Sheffield Library, UK, making a range of design-informed recommendations for its upgrade. They argue that Sheffield Library delivers wide economic and social benefits to the region despite the 'parlous state of the building' (Arup, 2019). The library performs an enormous range of functions such as providing a sense of belonging to

ies have been repeatedly targeted by austerity cuts. In the UK, for example, net government expenditure on library services fell 30 per cent in real terms between the fiscal years ending in 2015 and 2024 (Woodhouse, Samuel and Zayed, 2025).

Public spaces also play an important role as sites of struggle for justice over class, gender, race and sexuality. Public swimming pools, for instance, promote health, recreation and community life. Designer and urbanist Dan Hill describes pools as part of the green and blue infrastructure that embodies civic sensibility (Hill, 2016). Yet they have also mirrored and contested patterns of exclusion. In Australia, they have been sites of both segregation and activism, such as the 1994 campaign to save Melbourne's Fitzroy Public Baths – a defining moment in the working-class defence of public space (McQueen, 2011). In the US, municipal pools have also reflected shifting racial and class dynamics: initially inclusive working-class facilities in the early twentieth century, they became segregated leisure spaces for wealthier white populations in the 1920s–40s, followed by gradual desegregation in the 1950s–60s (Wiltse, 2007). More recently, these spaces risk losing part of their role as wealthier residents retreat to private pools, reducing opportunities for social mixing and civic dialogue and contributing to broader social fragmentation:

> The proliferation of private swimming pools after the mid-1950s, however, represented a retreat from public life. Millions of Americans abandoned public pools precisely because they preferred to pursue their recreational activities within smaller and more socially selective communities. Instead of swimming, socialising, and fighting with a diverse group of people at municipal pools, private-pool owners fenced themselves into their own backyards. The

---

citizens, aiding the delivery of council services and facilitating democratic political engagement. They then use a dynamic evaluation model to assess the library's value, inspired by the UCL IIPP and British Library 2016–21 programme research on 'Libraries Deliver'. This dynamic evaluation model can help promote policy-making that is more holistic, comprehensive and informed about value.

consequences have been, to a certain extent, atomised recreation and diminished public discourse (Wiltse, 2007, p. 6).

When community spaces such as libraries, pools, and youth centres are neglected, opportunities for social mixing, civic engagement and community building diminish, leading to far-reaching social costs. Isolation, loneliness and anti-social behaviour – including gang activity – rise, costing far more in the long term.

For example, in the United Kingdom, the quiet dismantling of youth clubs is a case study in the long-term damage caused by short-term thinking. As John Harris recently reported in the *Guardian*, over a decade of austerity has seen youth services in England and Wales lose around 70 per cent of their funding, with more than 1,200 youth centres closed and thousands of youth workers laid off. Indeed, more than two thirds (42 per cent) of council-run youth centres in England and Wales closed between 2010 and 2023 (Unison, 2024). What makes this erosion even more striking is the lack of public or political outcry. Youth clubs, once recognized as vital civic spaces where young people could build confidence, access support and develop social bonds, have been treated as expendable in budget decisions. Their absence has contributed to rising loneliness, social alienation and a sense of abandonment among young people – especially those in disadvantaged communities. This is not only a moral failure but a deeply costly one. When youth are denied safe, supportive environments, society pays the price elsewhere: in increased demand for mental health services, higher school dropout rates and ultimately in the criminal justice system. Indeed, young people affected by youth centre closures in the UK experienced worse educational outcomes and were 14 per cent more likely to engage in criminal activity within six years of closure (Villa, 2024). Each reduction in youth centres also corresponded to a rise in knife crime (National Youth Agency, 2023). Preventive investment in youth clubs has a far higher social return, but in their absence, government is left to pick up the pieces through emergency interventions and punitive systems that come too late.

Youth clubs represent precisely the kind of social infrastructure that creates long-term public value. They are not luxuries but essential generative spaces where social trust, solidarity and personal resilience are cultivated. Their loss reveals a systemic undervaluing of non-market goods and a failure to measure value beyond narrow economic terms. Rebuilding the common good demands more than repairing roads and balancing books – it requires restoring the relational institutions that make a healthy, inclusive society possible. Neglecting the young is not only unjust; it is fiscally reckless and socially self-defeating.

Targeted investment in community infrastructure can deliver measurable improvements and quickly. In Chicago, the Scaling Community Violence Intervention for a Safer Chicago initiative combined investments in schools, parks and youth programmes with holistic violence prevention, leading to a 25 per cent drop in fatal shootings and a 33 per cent fall in overall crime within one year. Similarly, Baltimore – long affected by disinvestment and violence – has seen record lows in homicides and violent crime following sustained investment in parks, recreation centres and youth programmes. Baltimore's Mayor, Brandon Scott, says that building healthy and resilient communities requires investment not just in policing but also in the places that nurture social cohesion and support wellbeing (Fowler, 2025). Investment in policing should also mean new training and reform to change those practices in the criminal justice system that perpetuate the marginalization and inequalities that exist by over-policing certain racial and social income groups more than others, including using data in non-democratic ways, such as the 'gang matrix' used in the UK (Cresto-Dina, 2023). Indeed, it is necessary to understand the drivers of crime in terms of the social and economic determinants.

With place-based, collaborative and multi-sectoral approaches, cities can unlock the full social value of community spaces (McShane and Coffey, 2022). For that to happen, we need to stop viewing public infrastructure as a discretionary cost and instead see it as the investment in wellbeing, social resilience and long-term prosperity that it is. When governments fail to distinguish between spending that merely sustains consumption and investment that builds lasting social assets, societies pay the price. Affordable housing, universal healthcare and vibrant community spaces do more than meet immediate needs – they strengthen the bonds that hold communities together and sustain the social contract itself.

11.2 Building people-centred places

Valuing public infrastructure means designing and shaping spaces for and with the people who use them, ensuring they meet their needs and actively support their flourishing. In other words, of course austerity needs to be confronted, with the arguments made above, but this cannot just end up with a drive to build without taking care of 'how we are building', and with whose voices. In *Building and Dwelling: Ethics for the city,* Richard Sennett (2018) provides a key lesson for shaping cities for the common good. He emphasizes the ethical tension between how cities are physically constructed (*building*) and how they are inhabited (*dwelling*), arguing that urban design must be attentive to human behaviour, social interaction and everyday life. For Sennett, it is not enough for cities to function efficiently; they must also foster spaces where people want to live. He stresses that the process of building itself should be participatory, allowing citizens to shape the spaces they inhabit and ensuring that infrastructure reflects democratic and ethical values.

Hilary Cottam (2018), in *Radical Help*, takes these ideas further, proposing the need for a 'relational welfare state'. She critiques the transactional logic of current systems, arguing that meaningful change depends on relationships, co-creation and trust. Drawing on design thinking and her vast experience with community engagement, her approach seeks to create ecosystems of support that enable people to participate in shaping their own lives. Together, these perspectives suggest a relational paradigm of flourishing – one that recognizes human interdependence and the essential role of institutions, values and care infrastructures.

This approach transforms how we think about public spaces. A youth centre, for instance, is not just a place to keep children off the streets, but when co-designed by and for young people, it becomes a site where they feel valued and empowered to contribute to their community. Similarly, parks and public squares can cultivate social cohesion, nurture civic pride and strengthen democratic engagement.

Public libraries can be seen not merely as places to access books, but as hubs for innovation that bring a wide range of knowledge into communities. Connecting community libraries to central institutions – such as the British Library in London, from which they are currently quite disconnected – would allow local branches to offer advanced resources while remaining locally relevant. Of course, the British Library does have its own digitization programme, but the point here is that given that it is public, it could be more connected to the community libraries through a hub-and-spoke model that enables residents to create podcasts, music or art using archives and other resources through the lens of a 'data commons'. While some may assume that everything is already online, many valuable materials remain inaccessible. Access alone, however, is not enough. People also need the skills, training and confidence to turn these resources into meaningful value, transforming public libraries into vibrant centres of social and creative innovation.

Infrastructure designed for and by the people also bridges the gap between welfare and innovation, fostering communities where knowledge is shared and everyone can contribute. The question then arises: how do we build places where people feel valued and part of a community? And what does it mean to invest in social spaces like community centres and public parks in ways that nurture wellbeing and community? Addressing these questions requires us to see these spaces as investments in an economy that truly values all people and especially the ways they come together. If public spaces are drab and grey, it is not so surprising that people living in them might neither care for the buildings nor feel cared for themselves.

Three examples of how thoughtful design and investment in public spaces can transform not just the built environment, but also social life and wellbeing for entire communities, are Robin Hood Gardens in London, 'care blocks' in Bogotá and *UTOPÍAS* in Mexico City.

Robin Hood Gardens

The story of the Robin Hood Gardens estate in the Tower Hamlets area of East London is an illustration both of how to build people-centred housing and of how bad we are at holistically valuing the social infrastructure that such an investment requires. Designed in 1968 by Alison and Peter Smithson, Robin Hood Gardens was more than a housing project. It was a creative experiment in building community through architecture. Its 'streets in the sky', generous internal layouts and the large communal green at its centre were a conscious attempt to create spaces that fostered dignity, safety and solidarity among working-class residents (Gillard, 2016). At a time when the UK faced a housing shortage, it represented the idea that public housing could also be visionary and be designed not for profit, but for people. Kids played together not only in the youth centre but also on a purpose-built hill in the middle of the estate in a way that meant their parents could keep them in view from their balconies, while pensioners met at the community club. The apartments were spacious, bright and well designed.

And yet, despite this bold vision, Robin Hood Gardens was demolished in 2017. Not because its design failed, but because society failed to maintain, invest and believe in the long-term public value of such projects. This is not a market failure; it is a failure of imagination and governance.

What Robin Hood Gardens offered was a framework for inclusive design: not just housing units, but infrastructure for community. In fact, empirical research backs this up. According to the Social Life and Joseph Rowntree Foundation study (2015), social housing estates that support informal interaction and have shared, well-designed spaces show higher levels of trust and wellbeing. Furthermore, the Building Better, Building Beautiful Commission in the UK acknowledged in 2020 that design quality in housing is directly correlated with mental health, social cohesion and community resilience.

Ultimately, we must stop seeing housing as a cost and start seeing it as an investment in collective capability. This requires shaping communities, spaces and housing to produce outcomes that align with public purpose – like affordable, sustainable, community-oriented housing (Mazzucato and Farha, 2023). When we build youth centres, public pools or new housing, the question, as mentioned before, must not be 'What is the cheapest way to deliver it?' but rather 'What kind of society do we want to build?' Robin Hood Gardens was a bold answer to that question. It demonstrated that the architecture of care is not a luxury – it is a common good. We would do well to recover that spirit, and to embed it in how we finance, design and govern the spaces we call home.

Care blocks in Bogotá

Bogotá, one of Latin America's largest cities, faces deep inequality and urban development challenges. Many residents live in informal settlements with limited economic opportunities and entrenched gender norms that restrict women's participation in education and work. Much of the city's female population are full-time unpaid caregivers, 90 per cent of whom are low income, a third report having no time for self-care and 70 per cent cannot pursue education (Burdett and Mazzucato, 2025).

To address these challenges, Claudia López, Mayor of Bogotá between 2020 and 2023, tasked the Bogotá Secretariat for Women with designing a care system for unpaid caregivers. Based on extensive engagement with government, funders, caregivers and care recipients, the city developed *manzanas del cuidado* or care blocks (Secretaría de la Mujer, 2023).

Care blocks are neighbourhood hubs bringing services – daycare, education, healthcare, legal advice, laundry facilities and psychological support – within a thirty-minute walk of caregivers' homes. They also provide door-to-door care and mobile services in underserved areas. Currently, twenty-three care blocks operate across the city, with plans to expand to forty-five by 2035 (Alcaldía de Bogotá, 2023).

Guided by the principle, *Quien cuida, también merece cuidado* – 'Those who care also deserve care' – Bogotá is reframing caregiving as a shared social responsibility, addressing caregivers' immediate needs while challenging social norms around gender, labour and the value of care.

*Mexico City's UTOPÍAS**

Iztapalapa, Mexico City's most populous borough, has long struggled with severe socio-economic inequalities. Located in the city's southeast, it is home to millions of residents, many living in areas marked by high levels of violence, poor public services and limited access to basic infrastructure. Decades of neglect by city authorities and the wider metropolitan region have deepened residents' sense of social exclusion.

Determined to change these conditions, Clara Brugada, elected as Iztapalapa's borough mayor in 2018, made urban transformation a central priority of her administration. One of her most ambitious initiatives was the creation of Units of Transformation and Organisation for Inclusion and Social Harmony – known as *UTOPÍAS*, its acronym in Spanish.† This innovative strategy seeks to tackle structural inequalities by revitalizing neglected public spaces and creating a network of large, well-designed, multifunctional facilities that foster civic participation, social engagement and community development.

During her time as borough mayor, Brugada oversaw the construction of twelve *UTOPÍAS*, providing high-quality cultural,

* This section on the UTOPÍAS in Mexico City is a summary of my experience visiting one in Iztapalapa with the Mayor's team in May 2025, as well as how it is described in the website publication, which can be found at: https://mexicocity.cdmx.gob.mx/tag/iztapalapa-utopias/.

† Unidades de Transformación y Organización Para la Inclusión y la Armonía Social.

recreational, social and sports amenities to strengthen community ties and expand local opportunities. These facilities include swimming pools, ice rinks, libraries, film and photography schools, butterfly sanctuaries, and spaces for dance, theatre and support groups serving youth, the elderly and other vulnerable populations. Since becoming Mayor of Mexico City in 2024, Brugada has expanded the programme beyond Iztapalapa, with plans to establish 100 such centres citywide by 2030.

UTOPÍAS go beyond infrastructure, offering a vision of social regeneration that rebuilds social bonds and fosters collective well-being. Through co-creation, residents participate in the design, governance and maintenance of these community spaces, cultivating a sense of ownership and empowerment among traditionally marginalized populations. The centres also provide safe, inclusive environments that reduce violence by engaging youth in cultural, educational and recreational activities, offering alternatives to gang involvement and street crime. By promoting creativity, self-expression and social connection, the *UTOPÍAS* break cycles of exclusion and strengthen community ties, demonstrating how investment in shared public spaces can enhance safety, dignity and social integration.

11.3 Valuing culture and the arts

Brazilian economist and former Minister of Culture Celso Furtado argued that cultural policy should aim to give all the access to being a productive and creative member of society. In this sense, he argued that cultural policy is development policy (Furtado, 1984, 2012). While the social value of culture and the arts is increasingly recognized, methods for robustly measuring this value in standard policy appraisals remain underdeveloped. As a result, arts and culture are often treated solely as a sector to be supported for its economic prospects or as assets to be preserved (which are considerable, as shown below), rather than as tools reimagining and achieving societal goals (Potts and Cunningham, 2008).

All forms of arts and culture – including music, museums, theatre, cinema and design – are not just entertainment. They profoundly shape civic identity, dialogue, shared values and narratives. Cultural experiences help communities understand other perspectives and experience empathy or 'felt knowledge' (Eliasson, 2017), and to drive social change. Yet conventional cost benefit analyses consistently undervalue our collective capacity to imagine alternative futures through arts and culture. In a recent paper, I argue that we must rethink how arts and culture can (1) help us reimagine what society we want to live in; (2) can go to the centre of economic policy, not just in the Ministry of Culture; and (3) we must learn to value the impact of such investments on the long-run health of an economy focused on human flourishing (Mazzucato, 2025e).

For instance, artists and actors are often judged by the popularity of their work, while many museums and theatres are evaluated primarily on ticket sales. Frances Morris, former head of the Tate Modern, once told me that what she was most proud of during her tenure was bringing people into a museum who have never set foot in one before and showcasing artists who are often marginalized in this type of institution. She managed to achieve this despite the incentives favouring what she called the 'blockbuster' model.

Cultural production is an inherently collective process. A successful film, for instance, is not the product of a lone genius but the outcome of the joint efforts of writers, actors, cinematographers, editors, set designers, costume makers, sound engineers and more. And beyond the studio, it also draws on public infrastructure (such as national film boards, state subsidies, education systems, and even transport or location access), as well as the cultural commons – shared narratives, histories and languages that shape storytelling itself (Cresto-Dina, 2026). The collective nature of the arts is also why they have such a high economic value. Globally, the arts are a significant sector, accounting for 3.1 per cent of GDP and 6.2 per cent of employment (UNESCO, 2022), with investments in these industries generating a higher multiplier effect than many other sectors. In the UK, every £1 invested in arts and culture generates £2.24 of GDP. The multiplier effect is high due to the ways in which culture creates jobs and supports supply chains across tourism, education, retail and more (Centre for Economics and Business Research, 2019).

But art is not just an industry (the 'cultural sector') with a high multiplier effect; it is also a way for a society to question what it values and in so doing has the ability to transform society (Mazzucato, 2025e; O'Connor, 2024). The current Minister of Culture in Brazil, Margareth Menezes, argues that we must move from the cultural sector to the creative economy (Government of Brazil, 2024). There is a long history of bringing the arts to the centre of the economy. The Bauhaus school, founded in Germany in 1919 with public funding, exemplifies how purposeful, state-backed investment can create transformative societal impact. By bringing together artists, architects and designers around a mission to integrate aesthetics, craft and social utility, Bauhaus did more than produce objects – it reimagined how people inhabit, connect with and experience the world, leaving a legacy of innovative design and socially conscious architecture that endures today. Similarly, during the Great Depression, President Franklin D. Roosevelt's Works Progress Administration (WPA), as part of the New Deal, recognized culture itself as a public asset. By employing thousands of artists, writers, musicians and architects, the WPA not only generated employment but also made strategic investments in community, resilience and the collective imagination, embedding public value in the very fabric of American life (Naylor, 2014; Schulz-Keil, 1979).

But it is not enough to recognize the role of the arts; how they are financed and who captures the profits are key. The history of blues, jazz, reggae and rap provides a striking example of both the transformative potential of culture and the inequities in how its value is captured. As George Mpanga (known as 'George the Poet') notes in his Peabody Award-winning podcast, Black artists have collectively preserved and amplified the history of Black music – from blues to modern hip hop – but these contributions are often unrewarded (Mpanga, 2021). Profits are concentrated in a few hands, while little is reinvested in the communities that created it. This 'lottery model' of creativity means that only a tiny few succeed, while many are excluded or marginalized (Mpanga, 2021). George the Poet emphasizes that Black music could drive substantial job creation, wealth creation and ultimately liberation for Black communities, but systemic change is required. Production companies and major labels could rectify inequitable practices like unfair contracts and share profits in such a way that the communities which produce the ecosystem of artists benefit as well. Mpanga notes that black artists must be recognized not just as individual entrepreneurs but as stewards of a shared heritage, whose work is critical for shaping broader social and economic change (Mpanga, 2024).

Countries that recognize the potential of arts and culture are beginning to harness it intentionally. During our work with Barbados on its mission-oriented approach to industrial strategy between 2022 and 2024, I was struck by Prime Minister Mia Mottley's decision to make culture both a mission in itself and a 'beacon' cutting across all missions. The culture mission aims to invest in shared local heritage and the creative industries, while the cross-cutting dimension seeks to foster confidence, dignity and value for all Barbadians in their 'large ocean state' (not small island state) – against the tragic effects of the legacies of slavery and colonialism on wellbeing and mental health. This approach illustrates how a country can harness culture to strengthen identity, empowerment and social cohesion.

Barbados's many music traditions – Calypso, Soca, Reggae, Spouge and Tuk – are not only central to its national identity but also contribute to its economic growth. Crop Over, the country's flagship festival, contributes an estimated US$80–100 million annually, resulting in a 3.9 per cent boost to GDP in 2022 (*Barbados Today*, 2021; Madden, 2022). The festival season creates a surge of employment with scores of opportunities in costume design, event production and hospitality, leading to a multiplier effect that ripples across the economy. Other festivals, such as the National Independence Festival of Creative Arts (NIFCA) or the Food and Rum Festival, similarly boost tourism, create jobs and showcase local culture. In Barbados, arts and culture are both an end in themselves – a flourishing creative sector that enriches the social fabric and empowers citizens – and a means to achieving broader goals like sustainable development and local economic growth.

Carnival and Bem Viver

The connection between arts, social justice and historical memory is evident in carnivals around the world, from Rio de Janeiro in Brazil to Notting Hill in London. Brazil's Carnival is a powerful expression of collective creativity, participation and community-based cultural production, where music, dance, visual arts, costume design and performance transform entire cities into shared artistic spaces. Carnival in Brazil dates back to the era of slavery, when enslaved Africans blended their cultural traditions, music and dance with European festivals brought by Portuguese colonizers. Over time, these Afro-Brazilian expressions, especially samba, became central to the country's carnivals, transforming them into a powerful celebration of cultural resilience and identity. The carnival in Rio de Janeiro involves more than 400 street *blocos* and approximately thirty samba schools, engaging hundreds of thousands of participants each year, including musicians, dancers, choreographers, costume designers, set builders and local residents who work year-round to produce the parades and celebrations. The carnival in Salvador, Bahia attracts around 2.5 million people annually, driven by Afro-Brazilian musical traditions such as axé and bloco afro performances, with thousands of artists and cultural workers contributing to parades, sound systems, costumes and street performances that reinforce community identity and cultural heritage (Governo da Bahia, 2010). The carnival in Recife and Olinda is rooted in local traditions like frevo and maracatu, with the Galo da Madrugada alone drawing over 2 million participants, making it one of the largest street parades in the world; here, neighbourhood groups, musicians and artisans collaboratively create giant puppets, costumes and performances that reflect local history and social life.

Across these cities, carnivals function as living cultural ecosystems, generating large-scale artistic collaboration, sustaining traditional and contemporary art forms, and strengthening social bonds through shared creative practices. Within this ecosystem, organizations such as samba schools offer a powerful example of how cultural institutions can function as spaces of education, inclusion and social development: they provide year-round training in music, dance, costume design and collective organization, creating opportunities for community members to develop artistic and transferable skills (Giglio, Silva and Cruz, 2020). These schools also act as community hubs, anchoring family networks and neighbourhood engagement, and many extend their role into social support by facilitating access to health outreach, sport and recreational activities. Participation often spans generations, strengthening social bonds and pathways for social mobility by connecting young people and adults to mentors, informal economies and civic networks that extend beyond the carnival itself.

And across the Atlantic is the Notting Hill Carnival in London. Conceived by descendants of formerly enslaved Africans, the Carnival draws on music and street performance traditions to celebrate diversity, cultural identity and resilience in the face of historical oppression (Mazzucato and Barrington, 2024). Its origins are a cultural response to racial exclusion, violence and social marginalization emerging from the struggles of the Caribbean diaspora in Britain. In the late 1950s and early 1960s tens of thousands of Caribbean migrants, part of the 'Windrush generation', settled in the working-class neighbourhood of Notting Hill, where they often faced discrimination, poor housing conditions and racially motivated attacks, including the murder of Antiguan carpenter Kelso Cochrane in 1959. In reaction to these hostilities and seeking to build unity and visibility for Black Britons, Trinidadian activist and journalist Claudia Jones organized an indoor Caribbean carnival in St Pancras Town Hall in January 1959 to celebrate Caribbean culture through music, dance and community – a precursor to the street carnival that would follow. From the mid-sixties, the carnival moved outdoors when local community organizer Rhaune Lasletts staged a multicultural street fair in Notting Hill in 1966. With the participation of steel pan bands, the event quickly transformed into the outdoor parade and celebration of Caribbean traditions that it has been ever since. It is not just a festive display of calypso, soca, costumes and food, but also a symbol of Black British identity and resistance. It weaves together resistance and reclamation with exuberant cultural celebration.

Both the Brazilian carnivals (across its major cities) and the Notting Hill carnival have a high multiplier effect. The Brazilian government estimates that the direct economic impact (through tourism, food and beverages) is more than US$1 billion, though the indirect impact is even greater given its role in job creation, network formation, social cohesion, skills and so much more. Similarly, the Notting Hill carnival, attended by about two million people over the two days in late August, attracts around 160,000 international tourists annually and is estimated to generate nearly £400 million a year when factoring in spending on accommodation, food, shopping, entertainment and travel (Motune, 2024). But the greater impact is the way it supports the equivalent of 3,000 full-time jobs, and provides entrepreneurs and minority-owned businesses with access to broader markets, the skills needed for steel drums, costume design, and the social cohesion it creates in the community.

Carnivals can help us understand not only the importance of the cultural sector but how to build a *more creative economy*: generating employment, income and long-term skills development across music, fashion, design, event production, tourism and media. Carnivals sustain thousands of formal and informal jobs each year – from costume makers and instrument builders to sound engineers, dancers and cultural producers – while attracting domestic and international visitors who contribute significantly to local economies. Beyond short-term revenue, the knowledge, networks and artistic innovation developed through the carnivals circulate year round, reinforcing culture as an economic asset and demonstrating how community-led creativity can drive inclusive and resilient urban economies, and in the process help create stronger democracy. Investing in Carnival's broader ecosystem, including community organizations, year-round training programmes and social support structures, means supporting not just a cultural event but the ongoing social infrastructure that nurtures learning, builds resilience and expands opportunities across communities (Rosini et al., 2024).

Indeed, there is a growing body of Latin American social, philosophical and cultural thought that brings notions of the common good to the heart of understanding society: *bem comum* (the common good), *bem viver/buen vivir* (living well) and *alegría* (joy) as interdependent values. *Bem viver* is rooted in Indigenous Andean and Afro-Latin worldviews and emphasizes collective wellbeing, harmony with nature, cultural continuity and relational life over individual accumulation. Within this framework, the *bem comum* is not merely shared resources or public goods, but the conditions that allow communities to flourish together: mutual care, cultural expression, dignity and participation. *Alegría* plays a crucial role here – not as superficial happiness, but as a collective, embodied expression of social health, resistance and belonging. Gudynas (2011) argues that joy, ritual, celebration and creativity are indicators of a society aligned with *bem viver*, because they signal balanced relationships between people, culture and environment.

In this sense, practices like carnivals can be understood as lived expressions of *bem comum* and *bem viver*: they generate *alegría* through shared creativity, temporarily suspend hierarchies, reinforce community bonds and affirm cultural identities. Joy becomes political and economic not escapist – and a form of social reproduction, cultural resilience and collective meaning making.

Yet, like many cultural initiatives, carnivals face growing funding challenges. Public and private sectors alike tend to view cultural activities as costs rather than transformative investments, largely because their immense value cannot be captured through conventional economic metrics. This is a serious oversight. The carnivals' co-creative nature not only generates an economic multiplier but also fosters social cohesion, civic pride and community empowerment – elements essential for a flourishing society. Moreover, it highlights that art continues to serve as a tool for struggle and social justice, as seen in places like Cali, Colombia, where creative expression remains a powerful means of contesting inequality and oppression.

*Cali's Estallido Social: painting resistance through street art**

In 2021, Cali became the stage for a national uprising known as the *Estallido Social* (Social Outburst). Sparked by a proposed tax reform perceived to deepen poverty and inequality, the protests quickly grew to address a far wider set of injustices: lack of access to education, healthcare and housing; chronic youth unemployment; and the violent repression of marginalized communities. The proposed tax reform fanned a fire that had been smouldering for years in the hearts and minds of Cali's most vulnerable residents.†

As protests spread, public spaces like Calle Quinta and Siloé were transformed through a powerful movement of co-creation and collective action. Artists, musicians, youth, mothers and community organizers turned their neighbourhoods into canvases of resistance, hope and solidarity. Massive murals, graffiti and public art sprang up as testaments to the struggle for justice. In Puerto Resistencia, formerly known as Puerto Rellena, street artists and neighbours collectively renamed and reclaimed the space, honouring the people who had died during the protests and transforming grief into collective memory.

Community centres and safe spaces along Calle Quinta became

* This section is based on my visit to Cali in October 2024. The story was shared with me by the young people who took part in the national protests of 2021, as well as by mothers who lost their children due to police violence during those protests. These courageous women are known as *Mamás de la Primera Línea*. For more information on the 2021 protests in Cali, I recommend a book written by young people who participated in these protests: Juntanza Popular por la Transformación Social, *El Gran Estallido: Cali La Sucursal de la Resistencia* (2024), https://juntanza-popular.org/wp-content/uploads/2024/02/20240201_El_gran_estallido.pdf.

† In 2021, President Iván Duque proposed the Sustainable Solidarity Bill to raise state revenues amid COVID-19 costs. It sparked widespread protests as many feared higher living costs, particularly due to the removal of VAT exemptions on essential goods. While the bill offered compensation for poorer Colombians, middle-class households were excluded. Facing intense backlash, the government withdrew the bill, and the finance minister resigned.

gathering points for dialogue and cultural exchange, where people could engage in conversations about their shared past and envision a different future. Young people were deeply involved in creating street art, and this artistic engagement was supported by educational programmes, job training and mentorship, empowering them as active agents of change within their communities. These combined efforts brought the ideal of the common good to life – not as a distant concept but as everyday actions rooted in collaboration and collective care.

As I experienced, guided by local youth in Cali, it was clear that this participatory, grassroots co-creation gave people a renewed sense of pride, worth and dignity, in a society where the broader social and economic system often seemed determined to do the opposite. These acts of collective reclamation repurposed physical space and redefined the social meaning of the street. Through art, music and storytelling, the community began to reclaim a narrative of unity, healing and collaboration.

While Cali continues to face growing violence and social challenges today, the 2021 protests demonstrated the power of communities to push for change and the importance of art and culture that support these movements. The spirit of solidarity and co-creation that emerged in the city, expressed vividly through murals, graffiti and street art, remains a vital reminder that, despite ongoing struggles, people coming together can reshape a city's future.

Conclusion

Investing in the common good begins with the spaces where it is most directly experienced, the buildings, centres and services that shape daily life. These spaces deserve to be designed and maintained with the people who use them in mind. Public spaces are not just functional: they express a society's values. Through thoughtful design, culture and the arts, they can spark creativity, foster civic pride and strengthen democratic engagement. Klinenberg's notion of 'palaces for the people' captures this idea, showing that well-designed public infrastructure, with places for people to build relationships and meaning, is foundational to people feeling valued, and eventually, as Furtado argued, to becoming more creative members of society.

The common good compass provides a practical guide for funding and designing infrastructure that truly serves the common good. It calls for clarity of direction, genuine co-creation and participation to bring users into the design process, knowledge sharing to make public spaces sites of learning and collaboration, reward sharing to ensure benefits are widely distributed, and transparency so ownership and decision making are clear and fair.

It is critical to integrate all five elements holistically. Projects such as New York's High Line, a 2.33 km elevated park built on a former railway line in the West End of Manhattan, illustrate both the potential and the pitfalls of public infrastructure. While the High Line provides a beautiful urban garden, walking paths and public art above the busy streets of Manhattan, many of the financial rewards flowed primarily to surrounding real estate owners rather than being reinvested into the High Line itself or the local community. Without careful attention to co-creation and reward sharing, such projects can drive gentrification and undermine their broader social, cultural and artistic purpose.

The economics of the common good is inseparable from the places and structures that sustain community life. A society where people feel valued and have a voice in shaping the economy depends on these investments. Beauty, culture and participatory design are not luxuries: they are essential for fostering equity, social trust and human flourishing. Without them, the social fabric frays and the promise of inclusive, sustainable growth is not possible. Carnival is a perfect example of the common good in action: uniting people across social, racial and economic divisions in a shared celebration that preserves cultural heritage, encourages social inclusion, and fosters collective joy and community identity. Looking ahead, the challenge is to extend this vision to global governance, ensuring that the principles of the common good guide not only local communities but also the broader structures that shape our collective future.

12.

Global governance and voice

Many of humanity's most serious challenges cannot be solved by a single country. Cleaning the oceans of plastic requires global cooperation, as currents carry waste across national boundaries. Pollution drifts from one state to another. And deforestation of the Amazon has been found to cause floods and droughts in different parts of the world, making biodiversity loss our common problem. In all these cases, a global solution is essential – but too often countries resort to nationalistic policies instead. This tension is perhaps the ultimate challenge to the common good.

International financial institutions such as the World Bank and the International Monetary Fund carry words like 'world' and 'international' in their names, but they are largely dominated by a few Global North countries. Similarly, while G20 countries produce 80 per cent of carbon emissions, countries in the Global South bear the brunt of climate change but have little voice in determining solutions.

Health is another area where global action should be coordinated, yet nationalism is pervasive. As Chair of the World Health Organization Council on the Economics of Health for All, I sought to apply common good principles to help countries work together to prepare for the next global pandemic, which COVID-19 showed the world was very unprepared for. We identified five central principles to make this possible: inclusivity, universality, transparency and accountability, complementarity and local ownership (WHO, 2023). Unfortunately, I cannot say, at least so far, that we have been successful. While our recommendations were adopted and even passed in a World Health Assembly resolution in May 2023, vaccine nationalism and inequitable health access remain pervasive. Still, there are signs of hope. The establishment of the international mRNA hub in South Africa represents a concrete step towards reversing the structural dependencies between Global North and Global South countries, empowering low-income nations to produce vaccines independently rather than rely on handouts (Dutt et al., 2024).

So, what do the common good principles explored in this book mean for building solidarity in the global arena? How can nations come together in ways that respect their dignity and provide them with a meaningful voice rather than tokenistic participation? What does this mean for the structure of global finance or the ways we foster international collaboration to manage global common goods and address crises in biodiversity, water and climate? These questions are critical because the places where countries meet to address collective challenges shape our ability to act jointly and realize the common good at a global scale. This chapter examines what the common good means for global financial institutions and the governance of global problems from health pandemics to climate action, both essential levers for meaningful change.

12.1 *From global public goods to global common goods*

As discussed in Chapter 2, the traditional literature on public goods frames them largely as corrective mechanisms for market or system failures. This same logic extends to the global level, with the concept of *global public goods*, where multilateral institutions such as the United Nations or the World Bank are seen as entities that should fill the gaps left by failing markets or inadequate governance. The 'global public goods framework' has played an important role in highlighting the need for international cooperation around shared challenges such as climate change, pandemic prevention and financial stability (Kaul, 2016). However, by accepting that the problem is market failures, it has overlooked a crucial dimension by neglecting the need to transform the behaviour of corporations and governments – the very actors whose behaviours create the dysfunctions global institutions seek to correct. In other words, it tends to over-rely on international organizations or philanthropies to 'fill in the gaps' without changing the structures of capitalism that produce inequality and environmental harm in the first place.

By contrast, a *global common good* perspective shifts the emphasis from fixing failures to shaping systems proactively towards shared global objectives, such as ensuring that essential resources like water and energy are governed equitably and preserved for both present and future generations. Governing global common goods builds on the Polanyian understanding, reviewed in Chapter 4, of how markets are embedded in society and shaped by political choices. Effective global common good governance therefore requires global rules and incentives to be transformed so they foster better relationships that align with the common good.

*Global water governance**

Global water governance faces significant challenges. Countries and communities are deeply interdependent through the hydrological cycle – not only via trans-boundary rivers and lakes but also through atmospheric 'green water' flows, which extend far beyond traditional watershed boundaries. Moisture travels great distances, linking regions and countries beyond visible water bodies. For example, deforestation in the Congo Basin reduces rainfall in neighbouring countries and even across the Atlantic in the Amazon (GCEW, 2024).

Water scarcity is not just an environmental issue – it affects nearly all the SDGs and has profound social and economic impacts. Women and girls spend 200 million hours each day collecting water,

* This section draws on my work as co-chair of the Global Commission on the Economics of Water (GCEW), alongside Tharman Shanmugaratnam, President of Singapore; Ngozi Okonjo-Iweala, Director-General of the WTO; and Johan Rockström, professor at the University of Potsdam and Director of the Potsdam Institute for Climate Impact Research (GCEW, 2024).

which limits education and economic opportunities (SDG5). Nearly 3 billion people – and more than half of global food production – reside in areas where total water supply is projected to decline (SDG1). With agriculture consuming 70 per cent of freshwater globally, water scarcity threatens up to 55 per cent of food systems and 15 per cent of global GDP (GCEW, 2024).

The water crisis is closely linked to other global challenges such as climate change and biodiversity loss. Wetlands, forests and other ecosystems store vast amounts of carbon but depend on stable water cycles to do this (GCEW, 2024). At the same time, water-intensive industries such as lithium mining, essential for batteries and electric vehicles, illustrate how competing demands across sectors can amplify environmental and social risks.

These challenges are compounded by structural inequities in global governance. Just as global financial institutions have historically prioritized the interests of the Global North, water management often favours wealthier countries and industrial users, leaving low-income communities – particularly in the Global South – disproportionately exposed to water risks. Actions in one country or sector can also generate unintended consequences elsewhere, underscoring the need for systemic, cross-border solutions.

The common good framework offers practical guidance for managing water as a global common good. Its first element, **purpose and directionality**, emphasizes setting clear missions to preserve the global hydrological cycle. To put this into practice, the Global Commission on the Economics of Water, established in 2022 to redefine how water is valued and governed globally, has identified five interrelated missions: launching a revolution in food systems, conserving and restoring natural habitats, establishing a circular water economy, enabling a clean-energy and AI-rich era, and ensuring that no child dies from unsafe water by 2030. These missions illustrate the importance of aligning local and global priorities while fostering cross-sectoral collaboration, ensuring that efforts in sectors like agriculture, energy, health, technology and urban development reinforce rather than undermine sustainable water management.

The second element, **co-creation and participation**, emphasizes the critical value of local and Indigenous knowledge in shaping sustainable water management. Communities that have lived in close relationship with water for generations possess unique insights into seasonal cycles, ecosystem dynamics and resource conservation practices that modern science alone cannot replicate. Incorporating these perspectives can lead to solutions that are more culturally appropriate, resilient and locally supported. Co-creation and participation also extend to trans-boundary water resources, such as the Rio Bravo shared by the USA and Mexico, where equitable and effective management requires dialogue, negotiation and joint planning. By involving all stakeholders – communities, governments and private actors – co-creation ensures that policies and interventions reflect both local realities and broader regional priorities, fostering legitimacy and long-term sustainability.

The third element, **collective learning and knowledge sharing**, complements co-creation by ensuring that scientific insights and technological innovations are widely accessible rather than concentrated in private hands. Open access to knowledge allows countries and communities to implement evidence-based solutions and prevents the reinforcement of existing inequalities. Lessons from Europe's Carbon Border Adjustment Mechanism illustrate how failing to share knowledge can inadvertently penalize developing countries, slowing progress and deepening disparities. By contrast, structured knowledge sharing enables treaties, agreements and technologies to support global water security in a manner that is both sustainable and equitable.

The fourth element, **access for all and reward sharing**, is equally critical. In a water-conscious economy, household and community access must take precedence over industrial consumption, particularly as sectors such as data centres increasingly compete for limited resources. Both companies and governments must be accountable for managing water sustainably, ensuring that vulnerable populations are not disproportionately affected.

Finally, the fifth element, **transparency and accountability**, emphasizes the importance of clear and accessible information on water use, costs and allocation. Transparency enables informed decision making, holds stakeholders accountable and builds trust between governments, companies and communities. Digital tools and artificial intelligence can enhance monitoring, detect leakages, optimize distribution and support more efficient resource management. By making data open and actionable, transparency and accountability ensure that water governance decisions are not only effective but also equitable, reinforcing the broader principles of the global common good.

Implementing this framework can help reshape economic systems that currently encourage unsustainable water use. For example, in 2023, direct and indirect subsidies to water users in agriculture and in water, sanitation and hygiene alone totalled over US$700 billion (GCEW, 2024). Many of these subsidies incentivize water-intensive crops in arid regions, drive deforestation and contribute to nitrogen pollution. Governments should redirect these subsidies from water-extractive to water-saving practices, prioritizing those who need water most.

Similarly, trade must reflect the true value of water. As noted in the Global Commission on the Economics of Water report, 'trade distortions emerge when the opportunity costs of using water in one country are not reflected in the price of traded goods, such as when water is undervalued and is not properly priced and subsidies weaken the price signal' (GCEW, 2024, p. 194). Trade agreements can embed conditionalities for equitable and sustainable water productivity, reducing pressure on scarce resources while allowing trade flows to reflect countries' comparative advantages.

Addressing the water crisis also requires innovation and collaboration across borders and sectors. Shared knowledge on drought-resistant seeds, AI systems that use less water for data centre cooling – as seen in early comparisons between China's DeepSeek and the US's ChatGPT (Greenly, 2025) – and technologies that reduce the water intensity of extracting raw materials such as lithium, copper and nickel all support a more efficient and resilient water economy. Countries like Denmark illustrate the benefits of linking cleantech, digital innovation and sustainable policy, fostering circular water systems alongside industrial growth.

To conclude, water must be governed as a global common good, since the hydrological cycle knows no borders and national approaches alone cannot ensure sustainability or equity. Applying the principles of the common good compass can help guide the design of water markets, finance and innovation systems in ways that support both human wellbeing and environmental stability. Coordinated global action is essential to address these challenges effectively.

So what does this mean for changing our perspective from financial 'gaps' to asking how global finance is structured?

12.2 Redesigning global financial institutions

The Bretton Woods system, created in 1944 in the aftermath of the Second World War, established institutions such as the World Bank and the IMF to protect and promote peace, stability and development. But their design was skewed towards the interests and the voices of a small group of Global North countries, especially the US. Keynes, who led the British delegation at the Bretton Woods negotiations, was deeply dissatisfied with the system's final structure. He foresaw that making the US dollar the central currency of the international monetary system would grant the US disproportionate economic and geopolitical power. He also warned that the proposed system would result in persistent global imbalances, unfairly placing the burden of adjustment on debtor countries while allowing surplus nations to evade responsibility (Carter, 2021).

As an alternative, Keynes proposed a more balanced and multilateral system based on a supranational currency (the Bancor), which would be managed by a new institution, the International Clearing Union (ICU). His proposal aimed to make debtor and creditor countries jointly responsible for correcting trade imbalances. The

ICU would impose penalties on countries with persistent deficits and, critically, on those with chronic surpluses, recognizing that imbalances are a shared problem. The intention was to promote global economic stability while preventing the kind of structural asymmetries that continue to plague the international monetary system today. However, as the US had funded most of the Allied war effort, and European countries were heavily indebted, the balance of power was clearly tilted. The US delegation prevailed and Keynes's more equitable vision was rejected in favour of a dollar-dominated system that entrenched American dominance in global finance (Carter, 2021). The result is a set of institutions that aspire to serve the global common good, yet whose structures continue to reflect significant imbalances of power and influence.

It is important to recognize that there has been a recent shift by new IMF and World Bank leadership towards greater decentralization within these institutions, with efforts to strengthen country-level leadership, operational capacity and responsiveness to local contexts. While still limited in scope, these steps reflect growing recognition that legitimacy and effectiveness depend increasingly on proximity to the realities and priorities of borrowing countries rather than on decisions concentrated in Washington or other headquarters.

Nonetheless, inequitable governance structures continue to prevent deep and transformative reforms from taking place. In both the IMF and the World Bank, voting power is based on financial contributions, not democratic representation, giving disproportionate influence to wealthy nations, especially the US, which maintains de facto veto power in the IMF. Meanwhile, most countries in the Global South, despite representing the majority of the world's population and often being the main recipients of IMF and World Bank programmes, have minimal say in shaping their priorities or policies. They also frequently pay higher borrowing costs and must comply with conditions that can undermine domestic policy space and development goals.

The consequences have been severe. Between 1970 and 2023, Global South countries paid a staggering US$2.2 trillion in interest to Western creditors (Debt Justice, 2023). Heavy debt burdens have drained resources from essential public services, while austerity-driven structural adjustment programmes have curtailed government spending, restricted taxation of transnational corporations and hindered domestic industrial development. As a result, Global South nations have become increasingly dependent on foreign borrowing. Today, over 2 billion people – including roughly 57 per cent of Africa's 751 million residents – live in countries that spend more on debt servicing than on education or healthcare (PASS and IPD, 2025).

It is therefore essential to acknowledge that many problems in the Global South are rooted in the historical development of the Global North, which must take responsibility for providing solutions. This includes financing climate mitigation and development through grants and official development assistance, rather than relying primarily on loans. Philanthropy, while often well-intentioned, is also not sufficient, as it obscures the deeper structural issues it claims to address. In fact, much of the wealth behind these initiatives is generated through practices such as tax avoidance, labour exploitation and restrictive intellectual property regimes, causing more harm than good.

For instance, the Bezos Earth Fund, established by Jeff Bezos, has made important investments in climate adaptation. Yet the fund is funded by wealth generated through deeply problematic business practices. Amazon, the company Bezos owns, has relied on tax avoidance and labour exploitation to accumulate massive profits, while also producing 68.25 million metric tonnes of CO_2 in 2024 – comparable to a mid-sized European country – and its carbon footprint is expected to grow further due to its expansion in AI data centres (Crippa et al., 2024; Amazon, 2024). While philanthropic initiatives like the Bezos Earth Fund provide some support for addressing climate change, they cannot offset the harm caused by the company's core business practices.

Similarly, the Gates Foundation has played a significant role in global health, contributing over US$100 billion since 1994 and supporting lifesaving vaccines for diseases such as HIV and malaria (Park, 2025). While vaccines can reduce child deaths, a broader public health approach – ensuring universal access to clean water and sanitation – would address the root causes of these diseases (McCoy et al., 2009). It is true that governments are responsible for building these systems, but corporate tax avoidance and the use of restrictive intellectual property rights by companies including Microsoft (the source of the Gates Foundation's wealth) have exacerbated gaps in public health infrastructure (see discussion in Chapter 8).

Real development requires countries to invest in local and national capacity, including building a capable civil service and moving up the value chain by diversifying beyond natural resources into sectors such as digital services as well as manufacturing. In other words, development demands that actors in the Global North, even philanthropic ones, engage in well-designed partnerships that reflect the principles of the common good and support a degree of autonomy, enabling Global South countries to lead their own development agendas.

Unfortunately, many of the solutions proposed to address development challenges in the Global South have been ineffective attempts to patch over problems rooted in a deeply inequitable financial system, without reforming the system itself. One such approach is 'blended finance' – the strategic use of public funding to attract private investment – which gained recognition in the 2000s as a tool to mobilize additional resources to address the lack of progress on the SDGs. The logic was that public resources could 'crowd in' private capital, turning 'billions into trillions'. Yet the lack of progress over the past decade suggests that the problem lies not only in the scale of finance but in the system's design and incentives.

At its peak, blended finance has mobilized only around US$15 billion per year – less than 0.4 per cent of SDG financing needs (Mazzucato, 2025b). Moreover, the majority of these funds originate from public or concessional sources rather than new private investment, while the projects that do attract private participation are often concentrated in already profitable sectors or middle-income countries. As a result, blended finance has produced little true additionality and a low multiplier effect, meaning that the risks continue to be socialized while the rewards are privatized, leaving the public sector to shoulder greater liabilities and debt. These outcomes highlight the need for a deeper transformation in how development finance is structured and governed (Attridge and Engen, 2019; Convergence, 2024; OECD and UNCDF, 2020).

The World Bank and other development banks have recently begun to move away from the 'billions to trillions' narrative towards

Table 6 The limitations of blended finance

1. **Scale:** Turns billions into trillions for development	The blended-finance market has averaged only US$15 billion per year (2014–24) – less than 0.4 per cent of SDG financing needs.
2. **Additionality:** High leverage potential for concessional finance	Public and concessional finance makes up 61 per cent of total blended-finance flows; only 39 per cent of blended finance is genuine private, market rate finance (2018–24).
3. **Impact:** Steers private capital towards development	There are no agreed standards to verify development impact of blended-finance deals.
4. **Distribution:** Benefits the poorest and hardest to reach	Most blended finance goes to middle-income countries (74 per cent of private flows between 2012 and 2018), bankable sectors (88 per cent), and larger investors (83 per cent between 2022 and 2024).
5. **Risk sharing:** Fair risk allocation between public and private sectors	Risk is heavily borne by the public through senior debt, guarantees and PPPs, creating hidden liabilities and fiscal risks.

Source: Adaptation from Mazzucato (2025b) with data from Attridge and Engen (2019); Convergence (2024, 2025); OECD and UNCDF (2020)

a catalytic approach, using innovative financial instruments and updated policies to mobilize investment. The Bank has begun optimizing its balance sheet and revising capital adequacy frameworks to expand lending capacity without compromising financial integrity. It is also experimenting with new risk-sharing tools, such as the International Finance Corporation's first collateralized-loan obligation and developing mechanisms such as Hybrid Capital and the Livable Planet Fund to support climate resilience, food security and pandemic preparedness. These efforts reflect a move towards 'more, but better, debt', accompanied by transparent reporting and mutually agreed conditionalities that protect fiscal sustainability.

While this progress is encouraging, the challenge ahead is to ensure that these reforms contribute to a deeper transformation of the international financial architecture. This is not only a matter of finance but also of governance and power. Genuine reform requires a shift from a system dominated by a handful of wealthy nations to one that grants all countries meaningful power and true ownership of global priorities.

To achieve this, reforms must be guided with the common good at the centre. This includes aligning development and industrial strategies so that growth is inclusive and sustainable. It also means creating governance structures that bring all countries – especially those in the Global South – to the table, instead of perpetuating a system where the richest nations make decisions that often come at the expense of poorer ones. Tackling global challenges such as pandemics and climate change also demands structured collaboration and knowledge sharing: for example, through patent pools – agreements between organizations or states to license patents collectively. Such mechanisms have proven especially valuable during health crises and could also help develop solutions to pressing issues like clean energy and technology access.

Equally important is the fair distribution of the rewards from collective investments. The benefits derived from the extraction of natural resources in the Global South should first and foremost support development in that region, rather than enriching external actors. Ensuring that these rewards are shared equitably would help strengthen domestic finances and reduce dependency on external loans, which often come with restrictive or harmful conditions that erode fiscal space. A global financial transaction tax could play a central role in this effort, generating funds from cross-border financial trades and flows that could be reinvested in global public goods, social infrastructure and sustainable development initiatives.

The common good compass offers a practical guide for reforming the international financial system in ways that truly serve people and communities. Direction matters because investments and finance must create real, measurable impact rather than simply circulating through global markets. Global South countries must have a meaningful voice at the table of institutions such as the World Bank and IMF, ensuring their priorities shape global decision making. Knowledge and rewards should be shared fairly, with protections in place to prevent further debt burdens from undermining development. Transparency is essential to reveal hidden liabilities and fiscal risks that could destabilize economies. Together, these principles provide a roadmap for reform that is not only fair and effective but capable of fostering shared prosperity, resilience and a more equitable global order.

These ideas are not utopian. Several movements are already advancing them. The Bridgetown Initiative, launched by Prime Minister Mia Mottley of Barbados in 2022, aims to redesign the international financial architecture to provide low- and middle-income countries with debt relief and affordable access to green finance. Its key policy proposals include expanding liquidity through the International Monetary Fund (IMF) by suspending surcharges and improving access to rapid-financing facilities, as well as redirecting at least 100 billion US dollars' worth of unused Special Drawing Rights (SDRs) – international reserve assets created by the IMF to supplement countries' official reserves – to low-income and climate-vulnerable nations. The initiative also calls for sovereign debt restructuring through the inclusion of natural disaster and pandemic clauses, scaling up concessional lending from multilateral development banks, and reforming global financial governance to amplify the voices of developing countries. For example, Barbados has already introduced natural disaster clauses in its sovereign bonds that pause debt repayments for two years following a major disaster (Bridgetown Initiative, n.d.). It has also influenced major international discussions, leading to the COP27 loss and damage fund in 2022 – and the 2023 Paris Summit, which produced the Paris Pact for People and the Planet.

Similarly, efforts such as the Vatican's Jubilee Commission,* which advocates reducing the debt burdens of developing countries, point to the growing recognition that the global financial system must evolve. Yet for these initiatives to succeed, they must form part of a more coherent and transformative strategy – one that empowers Global South countries with genuine voice, agency and control over their own development paths. High levels of public debt, for which the global financial system bears substantial responsibility, currently constrain this possibility. They confine Global South countries to narrow negotiations over the cost of capital or mechanisms such as loss and damage funds, instead of enabling them to participate in shaping a fairer and more sustainable international order.

Meanwhile, the BRICS bloc – originally composed of Brazil, Russia, India, China and South Africa and now including Egypt, Ethiopia, Indonesia, Iran and the United Arab Emirates – is set to play an increasingly influential role. Over the past two decades, it has grown to represent more than a third of the global economy and half of the world's population. BRICS aims to provide a counterbalance to Western dominance in international institutions, a shift highlighted by the recent handover of G20 leadership from

* The Jubilee Commission, of which I am a member, is a Vatican-backed expert panel convened in 2025 to address the global sovereign debt and development crises, especially across the Global South. Appointed by Pope Francis and chaired by economist Joseph Stiglitz, this commission brings together economists, policymakers, and civil society figures to produce a comprehensive Jubilee Report advocating debt restructuring, economic justice and reforms to the international financial system.

Brazil to South Africa. These changes signal a reorientation of the global financial system, creating greater space for the priorities and voices of Global South countries in shaping debt, development and sustainable finance agendas (Mazzucato, 2025d).

This shift is also evident in the growing emphasis on mission-oriented finance, although the term 'missions' is often used without the institutional transformation needed to make them truly outcome driven. The World Bank's Mission 300, which aims to provide electricity to 300 million people in Africa by 2030, combines public and private investment to expand power generation and transmission, scale up decentralized renewable solutions such as mini-grids, and improve affordability and regional integration. It also emphasizes community empowerment, particularly for women, by enabling access to clean energy and productive uses that foster local enterprise (World Bank Group, n.d.).

In many ways, Mission 300 aligns with several principles of the common good compass. It promotes co-creation through collaboration with governments and local partners, supports collective learning via open data and shared platforms, and seeks fairer reward sharing by linking investment to social outcomes rather than short-term returns. It also emphasizes accountability and transparency through public reporting and feedback mechanisms, indicating a move towards more participatory governance. At the same time, the initiative highlights the need for a more rigorous and explicit framework grounded in the common good to ensure these elements are applied consistently and not left to chance.

As organizations increasingly adopt 'mission' or outcome-driven language, the real challenge lies in ensuring that these missions are designed and implemented effectively, with careful attention to the broader elements of the common good. The success of Mission 300, and similar initiatives, will depend on practical details such as governance structures, accountability mechanisms and sustained financing, factors that determine whether missions can deliver tangible and lasting change. Moreover, while this progress is good given that it is outcomes-oriented, the challenge ahead is to ensure that these new initiatives contribute not just to new projects but, most importantly, to a deeper transformation of the international financial architecture itself. This is not only a matter of finance or new programming, but of governance and power. Genuine reform requires a shift from a system dominated by a handful of wealthy nations to one that grants all countries meaningful power and true ownership of global priorities.

We now turn to examine what can be learned from experiences on the ground in energy access initiatives across sub-Saharan Africa.

Multilateral funding for energy access in sub-Saharan Africa

Multilateral funds are increasingly focused on trying to help countries engage in a sustainable energy transition. This is because energy access remains one of the most pressing development challenges across the Global South, particularly in Africa. More than 550 million people in the region still lack access to electricity, with rural areas disproportionately underserved by central grid systems (IEA, 2022). In response, decentralized energy solutions, particularly solar-powered mini-grids, have emerged as a possible path to electrification. The hope is that these systems can deliver clean, reliable and affordable power to off-grid communities while supporting other development goals in health, education, gender equity and climate action (SEforALL, 2021).

Despite their technical promise, the governance of mini-grid initiatives is fragmented across an array of international policies, donor frameworks and private sector initiatives. Global governance of energy access – through climate finance, development assistance, technology transfer and regulatory standards – affects how mini-grids are built, financed and their benefits distributed (Newell et al., 2021). Initiatives like the UN's Sustainable Energy for All (SEforALL), the World Bank's Scaling Up Renewable Energy Program and the EU's ElectriFI fund have mobilized billions. However, they have shortcomings, including having short project cycles, using evaluation metrics based on static key performance indicators and being in conflict with community-driven energy development projects (WEF, 2021). Moreover, global finance for these initiatives is often channelled through large intermediaries (international firms, development finance institutions or foreign consultants) who may have few incentives to share intellectual property or empower local actors. While donors emphasize 'local ownership' on paper, many mini-grid projects continue to exhibit inequities in the distribution of economic returns (Newell and Phillips, 2016).

The common good compass can provide a valuable lens to address these challenges. It allows us to propose a new model for shaping grid systems that is focused on collective value creation, long-term public missions and democratic accountability. Applying the five principles of the compass invites us to ask guiding questions:

- Are these systems being developed in ways that serve collective missions, not just donor-driven priorities?
- Do international actors support or hinder co-creation and participation of local stakeholders? If it is the latter, how does their approach need to change?
- Is knowledge generated across projects being shared openly or locked in proprietary systems?
- Are economic rewards fairly distributed or are they extracted to only benefit a select group of actors?
- And are donors, financiers and developers accountable to the communities they serve – or just to their own institutions?

Table 7 presents three case studies of African energy projects to illuminate how a collective challenge like energy access can be analysed using the common good compass. The first example, JUMEME Rural Power Supply Ltd, is a public–private initiative in Tanzania funded by the EU and developed in collaboration with European engineering firms and Tanzanian partners to provide solar-hybrid mini-grids to remote island communities on Lake Victoria (JUMEME, 2018;

Best and Garside, 2016). The second example, PowerGen Renewable Energy, operates across Kenya, Nigeria and Sierra Leone with support from international donors and impact investors. Finally, Nuru (Swahili for 'light') operates in eastern Democratic Republic of the Congo, a region marked by post-conflict fragility and governance challenges, and frames its mini-grid systems as tools for peacebuilding, social inclusion and economic renewal.

Most of these examples are national in scope, but they illustrate how international dynamics in the Global South – particularly the influence of large donors and reliance on loans and grants – can shape local energy initiatives. Global governance structures can both enable and constrain energy access programmes, yet current frameworks often reinforce entrenched power dynamics rather than promote the common good. For instance, JUMEME has positive attributes, such as its international collaboration between the EU and

Table 7 Evaluating micro-grid energy models using the common good compass

	JUMEME Rural Power Supply Ltd (Tanzania)	**PowerGen Renewable Energy (Kenya, Nigeria, Sierra Leone)**	**Nuru (Democratic Republic of the Congo)**
Purpose and directionality	Strong directionality given its alignment with both EU energy access goals and Tanzania's rural-development strategies.	Clear directionality towards clean energy transitions through its work around sustainability and development.	Mini-grid systems are framed as tools for peacebuilding, social inclusion and economic renewal – making it a rare example of strong directionality guided by social rather than commercial logics.

Co-creation and participation	Project has made notable progress in co-creation through community engagement and local hiring, yet its reliance on EU funding and foreign contractors means local agency exists primarily within a donor-defined project scope.	The model does not engage in co-creation beyond customer-facing operations and further co-creation remains limited by its corporate governance structure and market-driven incentives.	Nuru has exemplified the principle of co-creation by working with local stakeholders through energy ambassadors and participatory design.
Collective learning and knowledge sharing	Contribution to knowledge sharing is limited as evaluations and training materials are often limited to EU-funded donor reports rather than being part of an open source ecosystem.	As a privately held entity, knowledge – ranging from software platforms to demand management tools – is largely proprietary, thereby limiting knowledge sharing across the sector.	Nuru sets a standard for knowledge sharing by publishing open source tools and contributing to cross-sector learning.
Access for all and reward sharing	Limited in its reward sharing – despite some incremental employment and productive use initiatives as profits and decision-making power is retained by European and some Tanzanian corporate actors.	One could argue that some degree of reward sharing is achieved through enabling small businesses, but there is no shared ownership or reinvestment scheme.	Reward sharing is less explicit but there are emerging discussions around shared ownership.

Transparency and accountability	Accountability remains wedded to EU development policy instruments, which mandate reporting but may lack mechanisms for continuous community feedback.	Activities are shaped by donor expectations and regulatory requirements but there are few mechanisms to hold the company accountable to end users or civil society actors.	While accountability to local communities is high, its ability to scale is constrained by a global financing system that prioritizes 'low-risk' markets and pre-defined success metrics.

Sources: JUMEME (2018); Best and Garside (2016); PowerGen (2023); Nuru (2023); WEF (2021)

local actors, but the transparency and accountability mechanisms may prioritize EU reporting requirements over meaningful local engagement. PowerGen highlights this tension further given that, as global finance increasingly supports 'bankable' private sector models, there is a danger that public governance structures are bypassed and communities reduced to passive recipients. Nuru, while strongly aligned with most common good principles, faces challenges from global governance systems that limit access to concessional finance, reflecting donor reluctance to fund operations in fragile contexts and high transaction costs for international funding. This highlights how misaligned global governance can penalize the very models that best reflect common good principles.

These dynamics underscore the importance of a global common good approach to green transitions, which must encompass the entire economy – not only energy production, but also how we move (sustainable mobility), how we build (sustainable materials) and how we eat (sustainable agriculture). For these transitions to be effective and socially equitable, justice must be embedded at the centre, not treated as an afterthought. This involves fairness between capital and labour, public and private actors, citizens, and particularly between Global North and Global South countries. Workers in fossil-fuel-dependent sectors will need retraining and support as they shift to new industries, and the design of change must be negotiated from the outset. Trade unions around the world have attempted to shape such transitions, often with mixed results, highlighting both the difficulty and the necessity of early, inclusive engagement.

Historical patterns also underscore the need for global governance. As Jean-Baptiste Fressoz (2024) notes, past energy transitions have generally increased overall resource use rather than simply replacing older sources, illustrating that technological shifts alone are insufficient to reduce environmental pressures. Market forces, left to their own devices, are unlikely to deliver sustainable outcomes. Instead, transitions must be guided by the five principles of the common good compass – purpose and directionality, co-creation and participation, collective learning and knowledge sharing, access for all and reward sharing, and transparency and accountability. Applying these principles ensures that the move to clean energy is not only technically effective, but also socially inclusive, economically just and environmentally sustainable, benefiting communities across sectors and regions while protecting the planet for future generations.

Conclusion

Addressing today's most urgent global challenges – from climate change and water scarcity to pandemic preparedness and energy access – demands a fundamental reimagining of how we govern and finance collective action. Persistent inequities embedded within existing international institutions and market structures highlight the urgent need for a new economic paradigm centred on the common good. Initiatives grounded in common good principles demonstrate both the possibilities and complexities of this transformation. Yet progress depends on more than implementing technical solutions and addressing isolated bottlenecks. What is required is a renewed commitment to global solidarity – one that not only inspires collective action but also charts a concrete path towards the reform of global institutions, ensuring they serve the common good rather than entrenched interests.

While this might sound naïve, it is not. Countries commit to policies of this kind every year in innumerable international forums, such as the UN General Assembly or COP conferences. The obstacle is not wishful thinking. It is the lack of a systemic framework that holds countries to account. The five principles of the common good compass provide such a framework, ensuring that innovations in energy, water or finance are socially inclusive, economically just and environmentally sustainable. By applying these principles, we can begin to create coordinated systems where all actors are answerable for outcomes, ensuring that global solutions deliver real benefits for both people and the planet.

13.

Conclusion: governing for the common good

The book's key thesis is that the common good *is* achievable. But only if we develop the right framing. It is a practical, measurable and governable project – if we choose to build the spaces, reimagine the institutions, design the metrics and invest in the capabilities to make it real. In the decisive years ahead, it can form our collective ambition: shaping economies that are sustainable, inclusive and properly democratic, governed by the values and vision of the people they exist to serve.

Of course we need to be realistic, acting in the spirit of 'pessimism of the intellect, optimism of the will', as the Italian Marxist philosopher Antonio Gramsci (1891–1937) put it. While the book's assumption has been that we will all benefit from an economy driven by the common good, we all know there are serious obstacles to overcome that make building a common good society difficult. Some individuals and organizations benefit from a system that rewards them and they hold the power necessary to maintain the status quo. A pharmaceutical company that continues to abuse the patent system and charge excessively high prices, even while benefiting from publicly funded innovation, reaps excessive rewards. The same is true for the tech companies which, while benefiting from the data created by citizens and the technology created by other companies, pay minimal tax, abuse people's privacy and reap colossal rewards from a winner-takes-all economic system. And of course there are many public institutions that are not doing their job but serving the interests of lobbies or the whims of a minister.

But we cannot afford to let such interests continue to steer the economy in the wrong direction. The book offers a compass for a new common good economy that can guide us in the right direction, and in so doing confront those power relationships head on. What kind of structural changes are needed for the common good? What kinds of relationships and places do we need to invest in to make them possible? The compass helps bring us together to work towards finding solutions to some of the greatest challenges we face today, and make sure that we do not in the process use and abuse the concept of 'good'.

13.1 The common good compass: a recap

The compass developed in the book has five key elements.

First, we must embed **purpose and directionality** into the heart of economic governance. Every major policy, investment and institutional reform must align with clear, collective missions – like the achievement of a green economy, health and wellbeing for all, or the narrowing of the digital divide. The compass can tell us much more than just how fast the economy is growing. It can tell us *where* it is going, ensuring that our trajectory reflects the type of society we truly want.

Second, achieving the common good requires **co-creation and participation** at every level. Economic governance cannot be the domain of technocrats or elites alone; it must be a shared endeavour, informed by a rich plurality of voices. Distrust is fed by people feeling talked down to, being told, for example, that green growth is good – instead of having a voice in how to shape sustainable communities. The compass points to not just the outcomes of participation, but its *inclusivity*: measuring whose voices shape decisions, whose knowledge is recognized and whose experiences inform our collective goals.

Third, **collective learning and knowledge sharing** are elements of our economic systems. Knowledge, like clean air and clean water, must be treated as a common good. Our compass gives us the tools to assess how open innovation ecosystems are, how intellectual property rights are structured to promote collaboration rather than exclusion, and whether learning institutions are resourced to cultivate collective intelligence across societies.

Fourth, **access for all and reward sharing** must govern how the fruits of innovation and investment are distributed. The risks of building a better future are collective; so too must be the rewards. Our compass can indicate who profits and how wealth and opportunity are pre-distributed – generating fair returns to collective investments and embedding equity into value creation itself, not merely through redistribution after the problem has arisen.

Fifth, none of this can be sustained without **transparency and accountability**. Trust is the cornerstone of collective action. The compass illuminates the processes and impacts of governance: from open contracting and conditionalities on private partners, to dynamic evaluation metrics that hold public and private actors accountable to the common good.

Together, these elements move us from a passive state that corrects mistakes to an active state that co-creates shared prosperity. They demand a government not afraid to lead, but willing to listen; not captured by private interests but driven by public purpose. And the common good compass is not just for governments. It prevents 'common good washing' in business. What is the point of aspiring to 'win–win' solutions if the various criteria embodied by the compass are not met. A pharmaceutical company cannot pretend to be purpose oriented if it abuses patents and muddies the data on how much a drug truly costs to produce and which other actors contributed to its creation. A drinks company cannot be 'good' if it refuses to recycle most of its industrial wastewater. And no company is working for the common good if the workers who produce the outputs have no voice, are not being fairly compensated and do not share in the rewards.

Crucially, the compass equips us with a holistic approach to the common good, so that all the elements are seen as equally important for navigation – rather than 'pick and choose'. For example, if a public fund has a clear direction for building public infrastructure, but there is no accountability for that direction because a policymaker has set it without consideration for how it affects local people, then is it for the common good? Equally, even if there *is* co-creation, through genuine participation in decision making, but the financial returns from the infrastructure go to external actors with little reinvestment in the community, we could not say that it was designed for the common good. And if citizens do not understand how a fund in their name serves their interests, then it becomes more difficult to make the case that it is in the common good.

Lastly, a new narrative about growth is integral to common good economics. It is too often assumed that solving problems like climate change stand in opposition to fostering a growing and competitive economy. That could not be farther from the truth. The compass helps us ensure that solutions to the challenges we face are shaped so as to galvanize economy-wide investment and innovation, with collaborations by different types of people and organizations, and that citizens care about the result if they are part of the process and decision making.

The strength of the common good compass is that its combined elements hold accountable what is being designed in the name of the people, rather than picking and choosing an element or two which favour a particular argument.

13.2 *The future of climate, health and artificial intelligence*

To conclude, I consider the implications of a common good economy for the future of our climate, health, and the evolution of data and artificial intelligence.

A sustainable planet

Focusing on emissions reductions alone is not sufficient to address the interconnected layers of the climate crisis, like its impact on biodiversity and water. Unless we govern our solutions to the climate crisis effectively, we may end up with unintended consequences – 'green' is not necessarily 'good' if it is not driven by consideration of the common good. For example, if electrification of private vehicles relies on unsustainable mining practices for critical minerals like lithium and cobalt that lead to the pollution and depletion of water sources, have we really succeeded in mitigating the climate crisis? As we saw in Chapter 12, wetlands and forests, which are vital carbon stores, rely on stable water cycles and thriving biodiversity to function effectively, terrestrial ecosystems currently absorbing 25 per cent of carbon emissions (GCEW, 2024). And biodiversity loss and climate change have mutually reinforcing biophysical dynamics, which means that failing to account for the damage to the latter can lead to underestimations of climate risk (Marsden, 2024; Ranger, Mahul and Monasterolo, 2021; Dunz et al., 2023).

A common good compass can help point us in the direction of a just transition that encompasses the interconnected layers of the climate crisis like emissions, water and biodiversity while also keeping justice and fairness at the centre. Directionality in a green transition would help establish it as a clear societal mission such as the city level net-zero mission discussed in Chapter 6 (element 1). This directionality can also help define the green transition as a systemic, holistic goal that goes beyond just cutting emissions and includes biodiversity and water. Co-creation and participation (element 2) can help ensure that the green transition is co-produced by workers, citizens and trade unions from the start, as well as taking the voice of actors like potentially displaced workers into consideration in the design and implementation of climate-related missions.

Collective learning and knowledge sharing would ensure that clean energy technologies are shared and distributed widely, fostering a mutualistic innovation ecosystem (element 3). Access for all and reward sharing (element 4) would facilitate both universal access to affordable clean energy resources and equitable distribution of the rewards from clean energy innovations. As the examples of local energy communities in the last chapter show, even when we have good citizen engagement (as in the case of Nuru), citizens still struggle to benefit when profits from most energy community models are siphoned back into big companies abroad. And as the historic strike of the United Auto Workers (UAW) in the US demonstrated, battery producers for EVs were only incentivized to pay their workers their fair share following strategic collective action (Mazzucato and Silvers, 2023), whereas a just and green transition would include fair wages from the start.

Finally, transparency and accountability (element 5) would integrate the feedback of affected communities into the process of evaluating net-zero missions, allowing policymakers to reorient as needed. Iterative learning, key to any intelligent system, requires feedback from citizens, but it is impossible for that feedback to happen if citizens cannot see what is happening. The future of AI could help create more transparency, but only if structured to do so (Buolamwini and Gebru, 2018). Together, the five elements of the common good compass turn the abstract goal of a green transition into a measurable, collective mission under a transparent and democratic governance framework which shapes it in a direction that advances the common good.

Health for all

In 2020, during the COVID outbreak, I was asked by the Director General of the World Health Organization (WHO), Dr Tedros, to chair the WHO Commission on the Economics of Health for All. We began the work by reminding the world of the immense benefits of health expenditures for economic growth, with the lower health expenditures, the higher productivity of workers and the spillover effects on the entire economy. But we argued that was not enough. What was required was asking: if health for all is the goal, what does it mean for the economy? What does it mean for how we value health workers, for how we innovate around health and formulate symbiotic public–private partnerships, for how we finance health care and health innovation, and how we build the necessary public sector capacity to govern the complex health challenges (WHO, 2023). The common good compass makes the answers to all this much easier.

Many countries spend an enormous amount of public funds on health care, and yet the outcomes can hardly be said to be driven by the common good. Indeed, as we saw in Chapter 11, the US is the country that spends the most public funding on health while having one of the worst records for health outcomes.

A common good compass for health could therefore help to make sure that the goals of the system are clear. It would do so by giving the mission of accessible health care for all (element 1) a clear direction through co-creation and participation by patients, frontline workers, community groups and local authorities to ensure that health services are designed with inclusive input, embedding shared ownership of health goals (element 2).

It would encourage collective learning and knowledge sharing around open research, shared best practices and joint problem solving across institutions to accelerate innovation and equity, preventing strong and wide patents (element 3). It would also design reward sharing and equitable access to public investments through mechanisms that ensure tangible public benefits: for example, lower prices, licensing, reinvestment in communities, reflecting shared risks and rewards (element 4).

Finally, it would embed transparency and accountability through robust metrics and evaluation frameworks, so that stakeholders can track progress, challenge failures and hold public–private partnerships and all institutions accountable for creating public value across the entire health system (element 5). Together, these five elements provide a practical framework for aligning health systems with the common good, ensuring that collective wellbeing, equity and accountability remain at the heart of the health system.

Artificial intelligence for good

The common good compass can also be used to design the future of our digital- and data-driven economies. We often hear, for example, the concept of the data commons or digital 'public' infrastructure (DPI), but what exactly is 'public' about it? Something is public not just because it is used by people, but because of the way it is designed and governed. Unless it is designed for the common good it is not public, and vague invocations of 'public interest' or 'public oversight' may conceal as much as they reveal. These terms often fail to distinguish DPI from private digital platforms that also claim to benefit society or are subject to regulation. We need a clearer understanding of what constitutes public value in the context of DPI and how that value is intentionally created and sustained (Mazzucato, Eaves and Vasconcellos, 2024). Otherwise, it is impossible to ensure that the most important technological changes of the twenty-first century will be transparent or held to account.

These considerations are important for thinking about how to govern artificial intelligence (AI) around common good principles. A technological breakthrough of epochal proportions, AI could and should be used for the common good. The uncomfortable truth, however, is that it is quickly going in the wrong direction. It depends on access to the gatekeeper's cloud computing platforms. Three companies – Amazon Web Services, Microsoft Azure and Google Cloud – control around 70 per cent of the cloud's market share. This oligopolistic ownership structure has turned AI into a ravenous engine of rent extraction and a drain on knowledge from the public sector, as the private companies use their grossly excessive trillionaire incomes to lure top talent away from public labs, universities and the public service with very high salaries. Meanwhile, data privacy is being breached, misinformation is rampant, and the divide between unskilled and skilled labour is widening. AI platforms also consume enormous amounts of energy, water and minerals, exacerbating climate change, the water crisis and other environmental challenges. For instance, a recent plan to build social housing in Oxford was stalled because the water diverted to cool data centres left too little for the development (Mazzucato, 2024b).

Yet, like previous technological revolutions, today's AI breakthroughs, from voice recognition to large language models, were built on the shoulders of public investments (Mazzucato, 2013). AI models are largely trained on the creative work of writers, singers, artists, journalists, illustrators and more whose creations are used without permission, and who almost always receive no compensation (Mazzucato and Gernone, 2025). Simply tightening copyright protections, as many critics have proposed, will in and of itself be insufficient to correct this dynamic. We should instead treat collective knowledge in the age of generative AI as a common good and collectively fund (and benefit from) its production. Like clean water or vaccines, the creative commons should be accessible to everyone, with risks and rewards equitably distributed among all actors.

AI is still in its infancy, though developing fast. Nobody can truthfully say what direction it will take or what its impact on society will be. We can say, however, that the best approach to AI governance would be to design a public-oriented structure that embodies the five elements of the common good compass to steer AI innovation towards public value creation.

First, AI development should be guided by a clear public mission (element 1) to advance collective wellbeing, social justice and environmental sustainability, rather than serving the short-term profit motives of a few dominant corporations. This mission must be pursued through co-creation and participation (element 2) involving public institutions, universities, civil society, citizens and workers across sectors. Such collaboration would ensure that the design, deployment and regulation of AI reflect diverse perspectives, public needs and democratic accountability, rather than being shaped exclusively by private or commercial interests.

Knowledge sharing and open access to data, models and research (element 3) should replace the current reliance on secrecy and excessive patenting. AI advances funded by public resources should remain open and interoperable, allowing for collective learning and the diffusion of innovation across the public and private sectors. This would also help prevent knowledge extraction from the public domain into private hands, or from Indigenous knowledge to those who monetize it. Moreover, risk and reward sharing (element 4) must be embedded into the AI ecosystem to ensure that value generated from collective inputs benefits society as a whole. For example, imposing a levy on the gross revenues of AI providers could redistribute a portion of profits back into public research, education and cultural production. Just as we pool taxes to fund public infrastructure, the production of creative content in the era of generative AI should be publicly supported with clear conditionalities so that outputs remain in the public domain and serve public purposes.

Finally, transparency and accountability (element 5) must underpin all aspects of AI governance. Independent oversight bodies, open metrics and publicly accessible evaluation frameworks would make it possible to track AI's social, environmental and ethical impacts, challenge failures, and hold both public and private actors to account. By applying these five elements together, we could ensure that AI becomes a genuine driver of shared prosperity and collective flourishing rather than a mechanism for extraction and exclusion.

No time to waste

The immense problems we face as societies and individuals can and must be addressed. Youth movements, climate activism and denouncing the injustices of war inflicted on the most vulnerable show that there is a widespread yearning for a direction, a sense of purpose and participatory models that make sure people are not talked down to but have an active role in their own future. This can only be done by supplanting what has wrongly become 'common sense': outdated assumptions about the role of government, business and finance. *The Common Good Economy* attempts to respond to this yearning, to battle against inertia, and to inspire and inform how economies can be structured for people to flourish, reach their potential and be part of an economy that has been designed with them and for them. This means an economy that cares, values and invests in the ability of local, national and global communities to create a system that prioritizes solutions to concrete problems, sharing the knowledge and the rewards along the way. Because growth depends on investment, and our current global problems require collective intelligence and collective investments, if we can galvanize a common good economy, we can also direct growth, combating the false assumption that we must choose between growth and wellbeing for people and planet.

Crucially, the policies and the places where we plan how to live better, where we build and where we play need to be designed with people at their centre. It is a collective endeavour with colossal potential to build trust, empathy, co-creation and true collaboration. The billions of people in this world and the planet we share deserve it.

Reference list

Adams, R. D., and McCormick, K. (1987). 'Private goods, club goods, and public goods as a continuum', *Review of Social Economy*, 45(2), pp. 192–9. Available at https://www.jstor.org/stable/29769372.

AFL-CIO. (2024). *2024 Executive Paywatch*. Available at https://aflcio.org/paywatch.

Albareda, L., and Sison, A. K. G. (2020). 'Commons Organizing: Embedding Common Good and Institutions in Collective Action. Insights from Ethics and Economics', *Journal of Business Ethics*, 144(4), pp. 727–43. Available at https://doi.org/10.1007/s10551-020-04580-8.

Alcaldía de Bogotá. (2023). *Tiempo y servicios para las mujeres. Manzanas del Cuidado*. Available at https://manzanasdelcuidado.gov.co/.

Alhashel, B. (2015). 'Sovereign Wealth Funds: A literature review', *Journal of Economics and Business*, 78, pp. 1–13. Available at https://doi.org/10.1016/j.jeconbus.2014.10.001.

Amenta, E., Dunleavy, K., and Bernstein, M. (1994). 'Stolen Thunder? Huey Long's "Share Our Wealth," Political Mediation, and the Second New Deal', *American Sociological Review*, 59(5), pp. 678–702. Available at https://doi.org/10.2307/2096443.

Andersen, H. T., and Winther, L. (2010). 'Crisis in the Resurgent City? The Rise of Copenhagen', *International Journal of Urban and Regional Research*, 34(3), pp. 693–700. Available at https://doi.org/10.1111/j.1468-2427.2010.00984.x.

Anderson, S. (2023). *Executive Excess 2023*. Institute for Policy Studies. Available at https://ips-dc.org/wp-content/uploads/2023/08/EE23-FINAL-aug-23-23.pdf.

Andrews, M., Pritchett, L., and Woolcock, M. (2017). *Building State Capability: Evidence, Analysis, Action*. Oxford University Press.

Angell, M. (2004). *The Truth about the Drug Companies: How They Deceive Us and What to Do about It*. Random House.

Aquinas, T. (1981). *Summa Theologica*. Translated by Fathers of the English Dominican Province. Christian Classics.

Aquinas, T. (1993). *Commentary on Aristotle's Nicomachean Ethics*. Translated by C. J. Litzinger. Dumb Ox Books.

Archer, D. (2006). 'The Impact of the World Bank and IMF on Education Rights', *Convergence (Toronto)*, 39(2–3), pp. 7–18.

Aristotle (1984). *Complete Works of Aristotle: The Revised Oxford Translation*, ed. Jonathan Barnes, vol. 2. Princeton University Press.

ArkDes (2019). *Public Luxury: Architecture, Design and the Struggle for the Commons*. Available at https://arkdes.se/en/exhibitions/public-luxury-architecture-design-and-the-struggle-for-the-commons.

Arora, A., Belenzon, S., and Patacconi, A. (2015). *Killing the golden goose? The decline of science in corporate R&D*. NBER Working Paper 20902. Available at http://www.nber.org/papers/w20902.

Arrow, K. J. (1951). 'Alternative Approaches to the Theory of Choice in Risk-Taking Situations', *Econometrica: Journal of the Econometric Society*, 19(4), pp. 404–37. Available at https://doi.org/10.2307/1907465.

Arrow, K. J. (1962). 'The Economic Implications of Learning by Doing', *Review of Economic Studies*, 229(3), pp. 155–73. Available at https://doi.org/10.2307/2295952.

Arup. (2019). *A new vision for the central library in Sheffield*. Available at https://digitalstudio.arup.com/post/a-new-vision-for-the-central-library-in-sheffield.

Atkinson, T. (2015). 'What can be done about inequality?' *Juncture*, 22, pp. 32–41. Available at https://doi.org/10.1111/j.2050-5876.2015.00834.x.

Attridge, S., and Engen, L. (2019). *Blended finance in the poorest countries: the need for a better approach*. ODI. Available at https://odi.org/en/publications/blended-finance-in-the-poorest-countries-the-need-for-a-better-approach/.

Avelino, F., and Wittmayer, J. M. (2016). 'Shifting Power Relations in Sustainability Transitions: A Multi-Actor Perspective', *Journal of Environmental Policy & Planning*, 18(5), pp. 628–49. Available at https://doi.org/10.1080/1523908X.2015.1112259.

B Lab. (n.d.). *Our strategy*. Available at https://bcorporation.uk/about-b-lab-uk/our-strategy/.

B Team. (n.d.). *Our mission*. Available at https://www.bteam.org/who-we-are/mission.

Baasch, S. (2015). 'A local energy transition success story'. In J. Hoff and Q. Gausset, eds., *Community Governance and Citizen-Driven Initiatives in Climate Change Mitigation*. Routledge.

Baggini, J. (2018). *How the World Thinks: A Global History of Philosophy*. Granta Books.

Bahnisch, M. (2001). Social Interests, The Public Good and Contemporary Individualized Discourses of Public Organizations. TASA 2001 Conference, University of Sydney.

Balch, O. (2013). 'Buen vivir: the social philosophy inspiring movements in South America'. *Guardian*. Available at https://www.theguardian.com/sustainable-business/blog/buen-vivir-philosophy-south-america-eduardo-gudynas.

Barbados Today. (2021). *Crop Over 2022 in some form or fashion*. Available at https://barbadostoday.bb/2021/08/06/bteditorial-crop-over-2022-in-some-form-or-fashion/.

Barrett, S. (2007). *Why Cooperate? The Incentive to Supply Global Public Goods*. Oxford University Press.

Batish, A. (2025). *Equilar 100: A Snapshot of the Highest-Paid CEOs in 2024*. Equilar. Available at https://www.equilar.com/reports/116-highest-paid-ceos-2025-equilar-100.html.

Bednar, J. (2023). 'Governance for Human Social Flourishing', *Daedalus*, 152(1), pp. 31–45. Available at https://doi.org/10.1162/daed_a_01958.

BEG Wolfhagen. (n.d.). *Your personal energy transition . . .* BEG Wolfhagen. Available at http://beg-wolfhagen.de/index.php/wir-ueber-uns.

Beinhocker, E. (2007). *The Origin of Wealth: Evolution, Complexity, and the Radical Remaking of Economics*. Random House Business.

Bentham, J. (1776/1891). *A Fragment on Government*. Edited with an introduction by F. C. Montague. Clarendon Press.

Berle, A. A., and Means, G. (1932). *The Modern Corporation and Private Property*. Macmillan Company.

Best, S., and Garside, B. (2016). *JUMEME rural power supply: Remote but productive. Using energy access investments to catalyse enterprises and income in Tanzania's rural communities*. International Institute for Environment and Development. Available at https://www.jstor.org/stable/pdf/resrep02741.10.pdf.

Birnhack, M. (2021). 'A Post-Colonial Framework for Researching Intellectual Property History'. In I. Calboli and M. L. Montagnani (eds.). *Handbook of Intellectual Property Research: Lenses, Methods, and Perspectives*. Oxford University Press, pp. 260–71.

Bivens, J., Gould, E., and Kandra, J. (2024). *CEO pay declined in 2023*. Economic Policy Institute. Available at https://www.epi.org/publication/ceo-pay-in-2023/.

Björkman, M., and Svensson, J. (2009). 'Power to the People: Evidence from a Randomized Field Experiment on Community-Based Monitoring in Uganda', *Quarterly Journal of Economics*, 124(2), pp. 735–69. Available at https://doi.org/10.1162/qjec.2009.124.2.735.

Black, M. S., Liu, A. A., Parry, I. W., and Vernon, N. (2023). *IMF fossil fuel subsidies data: 2023 update*. International Monetary Fund.

BNDES. (2025). *Amazon Fund Portfolio Report March 31, 2025*. Available at https://www.fundoamazonia.gov.br/en/.galleries/documentos/portfolio-report/2025_03_Amazon-Fund-Porfolio-Report.pdf.

Boadway, R. W., and Bruce, N. (1984). *Welfare Economics*. Wiley.

Bohórquez Ramírez, C. (2024). 'Tras tres años del paro, ¿cuál es la realidad de cifras de muertos en las protestas en Cali?' *El Tiempo*. Available at https://www.eltiempo.com/colombia/cali/tras-tres-anos-del-paro-presentan-cifras-de-aquellos-que-murieron-asesinados-en-cali-3342711.

Boldrin, M., and Levine, D. (2013). 'The case against patents', *Journal of Economic Perspectives*, 27(1), pp. 3–22. Available at https://www.aeaweb.org/articles?id=10.1257/jep.27.1.3.

Bonizzi, B., Kaltenbrunner, A., and Powell, J. (2023). 'Uneven development, financialised capitalism and subordination'. In E. Reinert and I. H. Kvangraven (eds.). *A Modern Guide to Uneven Economic Development*. Edward Elgar Publishing, pp. 332–47.

Boonen, C., Brando, N., Cogolati, S., Hagen, R., Vanstappen, N., and Wouters, J. (2019). 'Governing as commons or as global public goods: Two tales of power', *International Journal of the Commons*, 13(1), 553. Available at https://thecommonsjournal.org/articles/10.18352/ijc.907.

Bourdieu, P. (1986). 'The forms of capital'. In J. Richardson (ed.). *Handbook of Theory and Research for the Sociology of Education*. Greenwood, pp. 241–58.

Bowles, S., and Gintis, H. (2013). *A Cooperative Species: Human Reciprocity and Its Evolution*. Princeton University Press.

Bozeman, B. (2002). 'Public-Value Failure: When Efficient Markets May Not Do', *Public Administration Review*, 62(2), pp. 145–61. Available at https://doi.org/10.1111/0033-3352.00165.

Bozeman, B. (2007). *Public Values and Public Interest: Counterbalancing Economic Individualism*. Georgetown University Press.

Bracken, M., Eaves, D., and Wronski, M. (2025). *The Service Gap: Europe's International Digital Strategy 2025*. The Lisbon Council. Available at https://lisboncouncil.net/the-service-gap-europe-international-digital-strategy-2025/.

Brandtner, C., Douglas, G. C. C., and Kornberger, M. (2023). 'Where Relational Commons Take Place: The City and its Social Infrastructure as Sites of Commoning', *Journal of Business Ethics*, pp. 917–32. Available at https://doi.org/10.1007/s10551-023-05361-9.

Bria, F., Blankertz, A., Fernández-Monge, F., Gelhaar, J., von Grafenstein, M., Haase, A., Kattel, R., Otto, B., Sagarra Pascual, O., and Rackow, L. (2023). *Blueprint: Governing Urban Data for the Public Interest*. New Institute. Available at https://thenewhanse.eu/en/blueprint.

Bria, F., Timmers, P., and Gernone, F. (2025). *EuroStack – A European Alternative for Digital Sovereignty*. Bertelsmann Stiftung. Gütersloh. Available at https://www.euro-stack.info/.

Bridgetown Initiative. (n.d.). *The Bridgetown Initiative Rationale*. Available at https://www.bridgetown-initiative.org/rationale/.

Brumfiel, G. (2008). 'Bell Labs Bottoms Out', *Nature News*, 454(7207), p. 927.

Bruns-Berentelg, J., Noring, L., and Grydehøj, A. (2020). 'Developing urban growth and urban quality: Entrepreneurial governance and urban redevelopment projects in Copenhagen and Hamburg', *Urban Studies*, 59(1), pp. 161–77. Available at https://doi.org/10.1177/0042098020951438.

Buchanan, J. M. (1964). 'What should economists do?', *Southern Economic Journal*, 30(3), pp. 213–22. Available at https://doi.org/10.2307/1055931.

Buchanan, J. M. (1975). *The Limits of Liberty: Between Anarchy and Leviathan.* University of Chicago Press.

Buchanan, J. M. (2003). 'Public Choice: The Origins and Development of a Research Program', *Champions of Freedom*, 31, pp. 13–32.

Buchanan, J. M., and Tullock, G. (1962). *The Calculus of Consent: Logical Foundations of Constitutional Democracy*. Liberty Fund, Inc.

Bunn, D., and Bray, S. (2025). *The Latest on the Global Tax Agreement*. Tax Foundation. Available at https://taxfoundation.org/blog/global-tax-agreement/.

Buolamwini, J., and Gebru, T. (2018). 'Gender Shades: Intersectional Accuracy Disparities in Commercial Gender Classification'. *Proceedings of the 1st Conference on Fairnem, Accountability and Transparency*, New York, 23–24 February 2018, pp. 77–91.

Burdett, R., and Mazzucato, M. (2025). *Creating a legacy for just, healthy, and green cities. Council on Urban Initiatives*. UCL Institute for Innovation and Public Purpose Working Paper Series: IIPP WP 2025-07. Available at https://www.ucl.ac.uk/bartlett/publications/2025/apr/creating-legacy-just-healthy-and-green-cities.

Burleigh, E. (2025). 'The world's billionaires now hold more wealth than every country in the world except the U.S. and China – and they'd be even richer if it wasn't for tanking stocks', *Fortune*. Available at https://fortune.com/2025/04/02/world-record-number-of-billionaires-wealth-higher-than-most-gdp-despite-stock-market-bloodbath/.

Burman, L. E., Gale, W. G., Gault, S., Kim, B., Nunns, J., and Rosenthal, S. (2016). 'Financial transaction taxes in theory and practice', *National Tax Journal*, 69(1), pp. 171–216. http://dx.doi.org/10.17310/ntj.2016.1.06.

Camden Community Wealth Fund. (2025). *The Camden Community Wealth Fund*. Available at https://camdencommunitywealthfund.co.uk/.

Camden Council. (2022). *We Make Camden*. Available at https://www.wemakecamden.org.uk/wp-content/uploads/2022/04/We-Make-Camden-Vision.pdf.

Carter, Z. D. (2021). 'Martyr to the Good Life'. In *The Price of Peace: Money, Democracy, and the Life of John Maynard Keynes*. Random House.

Centre for Economics and Business Research (CEBR). (2019). *Contribution of the arts and culture industry to the UK economy*. Report for Arts Council

England. Available at https://www.artscouncil.org.uk/research-and-data/contribution-arts-and-culture-industry-uk-economy.

Centre for Economics and Business Research (CEBR). (2024). *The economic impact of building social housing: A CEBR report for Shelter and the National Housing Federation*. Available at https://assets.ctfassets.net/6sxvmndnpnos/5nQCiTlJiqFDyFCWkvZSYP/5b7418f9cae12d9eae069550c69695cf/Cebr_report.pdf.

Chaddad, F. R., and Cook, M. L. (2004). 'Understanding New Cooperative Models: An Ownership–Control Rights Typology', *Review of Agricultural Economics*, 26(3), pp. 348–60. Available at https://doi.org/10.1111/j.1467-9353.2004.00184.x.

Chandler, D. (2024). *Free and Equal: What Would a Fair Society Look Like?* Penguin Books.

Chapman, P. (2025). 'Plea to drop "absurd" Lake District heritage title', BBC, 11 June. Available at https://www.bbc.co.uk/news/articles/cq85j8wwe1yo.

Chen, F.-Y., and Wang, C. Y. (2024). 'Using AI to Strengthen Democracy: Audrey Tang on Taiwan's Global Role', *CommonWealth Magazine*. Available at https://english.cw.com.tw/article/article.action?id=3795.

Child of the North. (n.d.). *Child of the North 2024/2025 Campaign – Report 12*. Available at https://www.n8research.org.uk/research-focus/child-of-the-north/2024-campaign/arts-creativity/.

Christophers, B. (2020). *Rentier Capitalism: Who Owns the Economy, and Who Pays for It?* Verso Books.

Clark, A. (2007). 'I should pay more tax, says US billionaire Warren Buffett', *Guardian*, 31 October. Available at https://www.theguardian.com/business/2007/oct/31/usnews.

Clark, J. M. (1916). 'The changing basis of economic responsibility', *Journal of Political Economy*, 24(3), pp. 209–312. Available at https://doi.org/10.1086/252799.

Clarkson, M. B. E. (1995). 'A stakeholder framework for analyzing and evaluating corporate social performance', *Academy of Management Review*, 20(1), pp. 92–117. Available at https://doi.org/10.2307/258888.

Coase, R. H. (1960). 'The problem of social cost', *Journal of Law and Economics*, 3, pp. 1–44.

Cogolati, S., and Wouters, J. (eds.). (2018). *The Commons and a New Global Governance*. Edward Elgar Publishing.

Cohen, W. M., and Levinthal, D. A. (1989). 'Innovation and learning: the two faces of R&D', *Economic Journal*, 99(397), pp. 569–96. Available at https://doi.org/10.2307/2233763.

Collington, R., and Mazzucato, M. (2024). 'Beyond outsourcing: Re-embedding the state in public value production', *Organization*, 31(7), pp. 1136–56. Available at https://doi.org/10.1177/13505084231163931.

Convergence. (2024). *State of Blended Finance 2024*. Available at https://www.convergence.finance/resource/state-of-blended-finance-2024/view.

Convergence. (2025). *State of Blended Finance 2025*. Available at https://www.convergence.finance/resource/state-of-blended-finance-2025/view.

Conway, R. (2024). *Citizen engagement. Mutual learning exercise on EU missions implementation at national level: fourth thematic report*. European Commission Publications Office of the European Union. https://data.europa.eu/doi/10.2777/395232.

Cooke, G., and Muir, R. (eds.). (2012). *The relational state: How recognising the importance of human relationships could revolutionise the role of the state*. Institute for Public Policy Research. Available at https://ippr-org.files.svdcdn.com/production/Downloads/relational-state_Nov2012_9888.pdf?dm=1702047310.

Costa-Font, J., and Jofre-Bonet, M. (2008). 'Is there a "secession of the wealthy?" Private health insurance update and National Health System support', *Bulletin of Economic Research*, 60(3), pp. 265–87. https://doi.org/10.1111/j.1467-8586.2008.00285.x.

Cottam, H. (2018). *Radical Help: How We Can Remake the Relationships Between Us and Revolutionise the Welfare State*. Virago.

Coyle, D., Fabian, M., Beinhocker, E., Besley, T., and Stevens, M. (2023). 'Is it time to reboot welfare economics? Overview', *Fiscal Studies*, 44(2), pp. 109–21. Available at https://doi.org/10.1111/1475-5890.12334.

Cresto-Dina, C. (2026). 'E' un'impresa fare un film: il Lavoro collettivo nel cinema e perche ci riguarda'. Einaudi.

Cresto-Dina, L. (2024). *Police Technology and its dangers – The Gangs Matrix as a case study of potential data-driven harms*. Available at https://www.

saunders.co.uk/news/police-technology-and-its-dangers-the-gangs-matrix-as-a-case-study-of-potential-data-driven-harms/.

Crimmins, J. E. (2024). 'Jeremy Bentham'. In E. N. Zalta and U. Nodelman (eds.), *The Stanford Encyclopedia of Philosophy*. Available at https://plato.stanford.edu/entries/bentham/.

Crossick, G., and Kaszynska, P. (2016). *Understanding the value of arts & culture*. AHRC Cultural Value Project. Available at https://www.ukri.org/wp-content/uploads/2021/11/AHRC-291121-UnderstandingTheValueOfArts-CulturalValueProjectReport.pdf.

Cummine, A. (2013). *A citizen's stake in sovereign wealth funds*. PhD Thesis, University of Oxford. Available at https://ora.ox.ac.uk/objects/uuid:5c3b8fa7-768e-445f-b4f1-54297dca9582.

Dahl, A., and Soss, J. (2014). 'Neoliberalism for the Common Good? Public Value Governance and the Downsizing of Democracy', *Public Administration Review*, 74(4), pp. 496–504. Available at https://www.jstor.org/stable/24029432.

Danish Trade Council. (2019). *Insight: Understanding Danish exports*. Ministry of Foreign Affairs of Denmark. Available at https://thetradecouncil.dk/en/services/export/danish-export.

Dardot, P., and Laval, C. (2019). *Common: On revolution in the 21st century*. Bloomsbury Academic.

David, P. A. (1993). 'Intellectual property institutions and the Panda's thumb: patents, copyrights, and trade secrets in economic theory and history', M. B. Wallerstein, M. E. Mogee and R. A. Schoen (eds.), *Global Dimensions of Intellectual Property Rights in Science and Technology*. National Research Council, pp. 19–61.

Davis, M., and Arno, P. (2001). 'Why Don't We Enforce Existing Drug Price Controls? The Unrecognized and Unenforced Reasonable Pricing Requirements Imposed upon Patents Deriving in Whole or in Part from Federally Funded Research', *Tulane Law Review*, 75(3), pp. 631–94. Available at https://www.tulanelawreview.org/pub/volume75/issue3/why-dont-we-enforce-existing-drug-price-controls.

Dawes, R. M. (1980). 'Social Dilemmas', *Annual Review of Psychology*, 31, pp. 169–93. Available at https://doi.org/10.1146/annurev.ps.31.020180.001125.

Debourdeau, A., Schäfer, M., and Buse, C. (2023). *Report on the PESTEL analysis of energy citizenship in Germany*. Energy Prospects. Available at https://www.researchgate.net/publication/370818446_Report_on_the_PESTEL_analysis_of_energy_citizenship_in_Germany.

Debt Justice. (2023). *The colonial roots of global south debt*. Available at https://debtjustice.org.uk/wp-content/uploads/2023/09/The-colonial-roots-of-global-south-debt.pdf.

Deloitte. (2024). *2025 Oil and Gas Industry Outlook*. Available at https://www.deloitte.com/us/en/insights/industry/oil-and-gas/oil-and-gas-industry-outlook.html.

Detter, D., Fölster, S., and Ryan-Collins, J. (2020). *Public wealth funds: Supporting economic recovery and sustainable growth*. UCL Institute for Innovation and Public Purpose, IIPP Policy Report (IIPP 2020-16). Available at https://www.ucl.ac.uk/bartlett/public-purpose/wp2020-16.

Dierksmeier, C. (2016). *Reframing Economic Ethics: The Philosophical Foundations of Humanistic Management*. Palgrave Macmillan.

Dodd, E. M. (1932). 'For whom are corporate managers trustees?', *Harvard Law Review*, 45(7), pp. 1145–63. Available at https://doi.org/10.2307/1331697.

Dolderer, J., Felber, C., and Teitscheid, P. (2021). 'From Neoclassical Economics to Common Good Economics', *Sustainability*, 13(4). Available at http://dx.doi.org/10.3390/su13042093.

Dosi, G., Marengo, L., Staccioli, J., and Virgillito, M. E. (2023a). 'Big Pharma and monopoly capitalism: A long-term view', *Structural Change and Economic Dynamics*, 65, pp. 15–35. Available at https://doi.org/10.1016/j.strueco.2023.01.004.

Dosi, G., Palagi, E., Roventini, A., and Russo, E. (2023b). 'Do patents really foster innovation in the pharmaceutical sector? Results from an evolutionary, agent-based model', *Journal of Economic Behavior and Organization*, 212, pp. 564–89. Available at https://doi.org/10.1016/j.jebo.2023.05.039.

Druedahl, L. C., Minssen, T., and Price, W. N. (2021). 'Collaboration in times of crisis: A study on COVID-19 vaccine R&D partnerships', *Vaccine*, 39(42), pp. 6291–5. Available at https://doi.org/10.1016/j.vaccine.2021.08.101.

Dryzek, J. S. (2000). *Deliberative Democracy and Beyond: Liberals, Critics, Contestations*. Oxford University Press.

Dunz, N., Hrast Essenfelder, A., Mazzocchetti, A., Monasterolo, I., and Raberto, M. (2023). 'Compounding COVID-19 and climate risks: The interplay of banks' lending and government's policy in the shock recovery', *Journal of Banking & Finance*, 152, p. 106306. Available at https://doi.org/10.1016/j.jbankfin.2021.106306.

Dupré, L. (1993). 'The Common Good and the Open Society', *Review of Politics*, 55(4), pp. 687–712. Available at https://doi.org/10.1017/S0034670500018052.

Dutt, D., Mazzucato, M., and Torreele, E. (2024). 'An mRNA technology transfer programme and economic sustainability in health care', *Bulletin of the World Health Organization*. Available at https://cdn.who.int/media/docs/default-source/bulletin/online-first/blt.24.291388.pdf?sfvrsn=c55ad77e_3.

Eccles, R. G., and Klimenko, S. (2019). 'The investor revolution', *Harvard Business Review*, 97(3), pp. 106–16. Available at https://www.scirp.org/reference/referencespapers?referenceid=2755951.

Eliasson, G. (2017). *Visible Costs and Invisible Benefits: Military Procurement as Innovation Policy*. Springer.

Enke, S. (1967). 'Government–industry development of a commercial supersonic transport', *American Economic Review*, 57(2), pp. 71–9. Available at https://www.jstor.org/stable/1821609.

Etzioni, A. (2004). *Common Good*. Polity.

Evans, P. (1995). *Embedded Autonomy: States and Industrial Transformation*. Princeton University Press.

Fancourt, D., and Finn, S. (2019). *What is the evidence on the role of the arts in improving health and well-being? A scoping review*. WHO. Regional Office for Europe. Available at https://iris.who.int/handle/10665/329834.

Fehr, E., and Gächter, S. (2000). 'Cooperation and Punishment in Public Goods Experiments', *American Economic Review*, 90(4), pp. 980–94. Available at https://www.jstor.org/stable/117319.

Financial Stability Board. (2024). *Total assets of financial institutions worldwide from 2002 to 2023 (in trillion U.S. dollars)*. Available at https://www.statista.com/statistics/421060/global-financial-institutions-assets/.

Finch, D., Gazzillo, A., and Vriend, M. (2025). *Investing in the public health grant: What it is and why greater investment is needed.* Health Foundation. Available at https://www.health.org.uk/reports-and-analysis/analysis/investing-in-the-public-health-grant.

Finn, D. K. (ed.). (2017). *Empirical Foundations of the Common Good: What Theology Can Learn from Social Science.* Oxford University Press.

Fishkin, J. S. (2009). *When the People Speak: Deliberative Democracy and Public Consultation.* Oxford University Press.

Fleurbaey, M. (2009). 'Beyond GDP: The Quest for a Measure of Social Welfare', *Journal of Economic Literature*, 47(4), pp. 1029–75. Available at https://www.jstor.org/stable/40651532.

Food and Agriculture Organization of the United Nations (FAO). (2001). *International Treaty on Plant Genetic Resources for Food and Agriculture.* Available at https://treaties.un.org/pages/showDetails.aspx?objid=080000028006554e.

Forbes. (2025). 'World's Billionaires List – The Richest in 2025', *Forbes.* Available at https://www.forbes.com/billionaires/.

Forbes. (2026). 'The top ten richest people in the world', *Forbes.* Available at https://www.forbes.com/sites/forbeswealthteam/article/the-top-ten-richest-people-in-the-world/.

Fossil Free Sweden. (2021). *Becoming the First Fossil Free Welfare Nation in the World.* Fossilfritt Sverige. Available at https://fossilfrittsverige.se/wp-content/uploads/2021/04/Fossilfritt_folder_ENG_TGA.pdf.

Fossil Free Sweden. (2024). *The journey to a fossil-free Sweden.* Fossilfritt Sverige. Available at https://fossilfrittsverige.se/en/the-journey/chapter-1/.

Fowler, R. (2025). 'Inside America's Quiet Safety Revolution: How Local Leaders Are Cutting Crime Without More Cops', *Forbes.* Available at https://www.forbes.com/sites/richardfowler/2025/07/17/inside-americas-quiet-safety-revolution-how-local-leaders-are-cutting-crime-without-more-cops/.

Freeman, R. E. ([1984, 2010]). *Strategic Management: A Stakeholder Approach.* Cambridge University Press.

Freeman, R. E., Harrison, J. S., and Zyglidopoulos, S. (2018). *Stakeholder Theory: Concepts and Strategies.* Cambridge University Press.

Freetown City Council. (2023). *Transform Freetown: Four Year Report January 2022–January 2023*. Available at https://fcc.gov.sl/transform-freetown-4th-year-report/.

Freire, P. (1970). *Pedagogy of the Oppressed*. Continuum Books.

Fressoz, J. B. (2024). *More and More and More: An All-Consuming History of Energy*. Penguin Allen Lane.

Friedman, M. (1970). 'A Friedman doctrine – The Social Responsibility of Business Is to Increase Its Profits'. *The New York Times*, 13 September. Available at https://www.nytimes.com/1970/09/13/archives/a-friedman-doctrine-the-social-responsibility-of-business-is-to.html.

Friends of Wandsworth Common, The. (n.d.). *History of Wandsworth Common*. Available at https://www.wandsworthcommon.org/history.

Frischmann, B., and Lemley, M. (2007). 'Spillovers', *Columbia Law Review*, 107, pp. 257–301.

Fulton, L. (2020). *Codetermination in Germany: A Beginner's Guide*. Institute for Codetermination and Corporate Governance (IMU) of the Hans-Böckler-Stiftung.

Furtado, C. (1984). *Cultura e desenvolvimento em época de crise*. Paz e Terra.

Furtado, C. (2012). *Ensaios sobre cultura e o Ministério da Cultura*. Contraponto.

GHIAA. (2021). *Supply agreement for AZD1222*. Global Health Innovation Alliance Accelerator. Available at https://ghiaa.org/wp-content/uploads/2021/05/AZD1222-Supply-Agreement-REDACTED.pdf.

Giglio, E. M., Silva, 2., and Cruz, L. G. (2020). *As Escolas de Samba do Brasil como espaço social de educação e inclusão social*. Universidade Paulista.

Gillard, R. (2016). 'Revisiting "Streets in the Sky": The social meaning of Robin Hood Gardens and collective housing', *Journal of Urban Design*, 21(2), pp. 176–92. Available at https://doi.org/10.1080/13574809.2015.1101611.

Global Commission on the Economics of Water (GCEW). (2024). *The Economics of Water: Valuing the Hydrological Cycle as a Global Common Good*. Co-chaired by M. Mazzucato, N. Okonjo-Iweala, J. Rockström and T. Shanmugaratnam. Paris. Available at https://economicsofwater.watercommission.org/.

Global SWF. (2025). *Sovereign Wealth Funds and Public Pension Funds Data Platform*. Available at https://globalswf.com/.

Gmeinder, M., Morgan, D., and Mueller, M. (2017). *How much do OECD countries spend on prevention?* OECD Health Working Papers No. 101. Available at https://dx.doi.org/10.1787/f19e803c-en.

Gobierno de Chile. (2023). *Estrategia Nacional del Litio: Por Chile y su Gente*. Available at https://s3.amazonaws.com/gobcl-prod/public_files/Campa%C3%B1as/Litio-por-Chile/Estrategia-Nacional-del-litio-ES_14062023_2003.pdf.

Goldin, K. D. (1977). 'Equal Access vs. Selective Access: A critique of Public Goods Theory', *Public Choice*, 29(1), pp. 53–71. Available at https://doi.org/10.1007/BF01718562.

Gomez-Alvarez, R., and Morales-Sánchez, R. (2021). 'How does collaborative economy contribute to common good?' *Business Ethics, the Environment & Responsibility*, 32(S2), pp. 68–83. Available at https://doi.org/10.1111/beer.12348.

Gómez Garcia, J. J., van der Ree, M., Villas Boas, R., and Gramkow, C. (2019). *Mid-term evaluation report on the effectiveness of the Amazon Fund 2008–2018*. Available at https://www.researchgate.net/publication/340950257_MID-TERM_EVALUATION_REPORT_ON_THE_EFFECTIVENESS_OF_THE_AMAZON_FUND.

Gov.UK (2025). *Capital Gains Tax: what you pay it on, rates and allowances*. Available at https://www.gov.uk/capital-gains-tax/rates.

Government of Brazil. (2024). 'Creative economy moves billions of dollars around the world and is highlighted in the discussions at the G20 side event'. Available at https://www.gov.br/g20/en/news/creative-economy-moves-billions-of-dollars-around-the-world-and-is-highlighted-in-the-discussions-at-the-g20-side-event.

Governo da Bahia (2010). *Infocultura*, no. 06. *Carnaval 2010 – Comportamento dos Residentes de Salvador na Festa e suas Práticas Culturais*. Available at http://sniic.cultura.gov.br/publicacoes/infocultura-no-06-carnaval-2010-comportamento-dos-residentes-de-salvador-na-festa-e-suas-praticas-culturais/.

Gowdy, J. M., and Ferrer-i-Carbonell, A. (1999). 'Toward consilience between biology and economics: the contribution of Ecological Economics', *Ecological Economics*, 29(3), pp. 337–48. Available at https://doi.org/10.1016/S0921-8009(99)00035-X.

Gramsci, A. (1947, 1973). *Letters From Prison*. Harper & Row.

Green, J., and Laffont, J.-J. (1977). 'Characterization of satisfactory mechanisms for the revelation of preferences for public goods', *Econometrica*, 45(2), pp. 427–38. Available at https://doi.org/10.2307/1911219.

Greenly. (2025). *The Environmental Impact of Artificial Intelligence.* Available at https://greenly.earth/en-gb/leaf-media/data-stories/the-environmental-impact-of-artificial-intelligence.

Greenwald, B. C., and Stiglitz, J. E. (1986). 'Externalities in Economies with Imperfect Information and Incomplete Markets', *Quarterly Journal of Economics*, 101(2), pp. 229–64. Available at https://doi.org/10.2307/1891114.

Greer, A. (2012). 'Commons and Enclosure in the Colonization of North America', *American Historical Review*, 117(2), pp. 365–86. Available at https://doi.org/10.1086/ahr.117.2.365.

Grumbach, K. (2023). 'Forging a Social Movement to Dismantle Entrenched Power and Liberate Primary Care as a Common Good', *Annals of Family Medicine*, 21(2), pp. 180–84. Available at https://www.annfammed.org/content/21/2/180.

Gudynas, E. (2011). 'Buen vivir: Germinando alternativas al desarrollo', *America Latina en Movimiento*, 462, pp. 1–20. Available at https://gudynas.com/publicaciones/articulos/GudynasBuenVivirGerminandoALAI11.pdf.

Gurstein, P., Patten, K., and Rao, P. (2015). *The future of public housing: trends in public housing internationally.* School of Community and Regional Planning (SCARP) at University of British Columbia. Available at https://scarp-futureofpublichousing.sites.olt.ubc.ca/files/2016/07/The-Future-of-Public-Housing-Report-05-11-15.pdf.

Habermas, J. (1984). *The Theory of Communicative Action: Reason and the Rationalization of Society*, vol. 1. Beacon Press.

Hacker, J. S. (2011). *Winner-Take-All Politics: How Washington Made the Rich Richer – and Turned Its Back on the Middle Class*. Simon & Schuster.

Haldane, A. G. (2016). *Whose recovery?* Speech given by the Chief Economist of the Bank of England in Port Talbot, Wales, 30 June 2016.

Hall, J., and Preston, I. (1998). *Public and Private Choice in UK Health Insurance* (WP98/19). The Institute for Fiscal Studies. Available at https://discovery.ucl.ac.uk/id/eprint/14965/1/14965.pdf.

Hall, P., and Soskice, D. (2001). 'An Introduction to Varieties of Capitalism'. In P. Hall and D. Soskice (eds.), *Varieties of Capitalism: The Institutional Foundations of Comparative Advantage*. Oxford University Press, pp. 1–70. Available at http://dx.doi.org/10.1093/0199247757.003.0001.

Hanley, L. (2022). 'From Thatcher to Johnson: how right to buy has fuelled a 40-year housing crisis'. *Guardian*. Available at https://www.theguardian.com/society/2022/jun/29/how-right-to-buy-ruined-british-housing#:~:text=In%201979%2C%20there%20were%206.5,many%20as%2015%20years%20ago.

Hardin, G. (1968). 'The Tragedy of the Commons', *Science*, 162(3859), pp. 1243–8. Available at https://www.jstor.org/stable/1724745.

Hardin, R. (1982). *Collective Action*. Johns Hopkins University Press.

Harrison, T. M., and Sayogo, D. S. (2014). 'Transparency, participation, and accountability practices in open government: A comparative study', *Government Information Quarterly*, 31(4), pp. 513–25. Available at https://doi.org/10.1016/j.giq.2014.08.002.

Hattenstone, S. (2024). 'The good hacker: can Taiwanese activist turned politician Audrey Tang detoxify the internet?', *Guardian*. Available at https://www.theguardian.com/world/article/2024/aug/17/audrey-tang-toxic-social-media-fake-news-taiwan-trans-government-internet.

Hausmann, R., and Rodrik, D. (2003). 'Economic Development as Self-Discovery', *Journal of Development Economics*, 72(2), 603–33.

Hayek, F. (1945). 'The Use of Knowledge in Society', *American Economic Review*, 35(4), pp. 519–30.

Hayek, F. A. (1968[, 2002]). 'Competition as a discovery procedure', *Quarterly Journal of Austrian Economics*, 5(3), pp. 9–23.

Hazelkorn, E., and Gibson, A. (2018). 'Public goods and public policy: what is public good, and who and what decides?', *Higher Education*, 78, pp. 257–71.

Heath, J. (2024). 'Methodological individualism'. In E. N. Zalta and U. Nodelman (eds.), *The Stanford Encyclopedia of Philosophy*. Available at https://plato.stanford.edu/archives/sum2024/entries/methodological-individualism/.

Hebous, S., Prihardini, D., and Vernon, N. (2022). *Excess Profit Taxes: Historical Perspective and Contemporary Relevance.* International Monetary Fund (WP/22/187). Available at https://www.imf.org/en/Publications/WP/Issues/2022/09/16/Excess-Profit-Taxes-Historical-Perspective-and-Contemporary-Relevance-523550.

Hegel, G. W. F. (1991). *Hegel: Elements of the Philosophy of Right*. Translated by H. B. Nisbet. Cambridge University Press.

Heikkila, T. (2004). 'Institutional boundaries and common-pool resource management: A comparative analysis of water management programs in California', *Journal of Policy Analysis and Management*, 23(1), pp. 97–117.

Henrich, J. (2004). 'Cultural group selection, coevolutionary processes and large-scale cooperation', *Journal of Economic Behavior & Organization*, 53(1), pp. 3–35. Available at https://doi.org/10.1016/S0167-2681(03)00094-5.

Henry, C., and Stiglitz, J. (2010). 'Intellectual Property, Dissemination of Innovation and Sustainable Development', *Global Policy*, 1(3), pp. 237–51. Available at https://doi.org/10.1111/j.1758-5899.2010.00048.x.

Hess, C., and Ostrom, E. (2003). 'Ideas, Artifacts, and Facilities: Information as a Common-Pool Resource', *Law and contemporary Problems*, 66(1), pp. 111–46. Available at https://scholarship.law.duke.edu/lcp/vol66/iss1/5.

Hill, D. (2016). 'The pool as piazza: The public pool as Australia's public space', *Medium*. Available at https://medium.com/iamacamera/the-pool-as-piazza-e58057781of7.

Hill, D., Eno, B., Glaser, P., Halloran, A., Isaksson, D., Melander, A., Mazzucato, M., Steinberg, M., Trollbäck, J., and Wood, A. (2022). 'Mission-oriented innovation in Sweden – A practice guide by Vinnova', *Designing Missions*. Available at https://www.vinnova.se/en/publikationer/mission-oriented-innovation---a-handbook-from-vinnova/.

Hockett, R. (2020). 'The US must take equity stakes in the companies it rescues', *Financial Times*, 28 March. Available at https://www.ft.com/content/86a333d0-6dc3-11ea-89df-41bea055720b.

Holcombe, R. G. (2000). 'Public Goods Theory and Public Policy', *Journal of Value Inquiry*, 34, pp. 273–86.

Holder, C. L., and Corntassel, J. (2002). 'Indigenous Peoples and Multicultural Citizenship: Bridging Collective and Individual Rights', *Human*

Rights Quarterly, 24(1), pp. 126–51. Available at https://doi.org/10.1353/hrq.2002.0012.

Hollenbach, D. (2002). *The Common Good and Christian Ethics*. Cambridge University Press. Available at https://doi.org/10.1017/CBO9780511606380.

Hopman, L., Kishimoto, S., Russell, B., and Valentin, L. (2021). *Democratic and collective ownership of public goods and services: Exploring public–community collaborations*. Transnational Institute. Available at https://www.tni.org/files/publication-downloads/public_community_collaborations_report_web_19_aug_2021.pdf.

Hourani, D., and Perret, S. (2025). *Taxing capital gains: Country experiences and challenges*. OECD Taxation Working Papers No. 72. Available at https://www.oecd.org/content/dam/oecd/en/publications/reports/2025/02/taxing-capital-gains_76a32327/9e33bd2b-en.pdf.

Hurwicz, L. (1972). 'On informationally decentralized systems'. In R. Radner and C. B. McGuire (eds.), *Decision and Organization: A Volume in Honor of Jacob Marschak*. North-Holland.

Hussain, W. (2018). 'The Common Good'. In E. N. Zalta and U. Nodelman (eds.), *The Stanford Encyclopedia of Philosophy*. Available at https://plato.stanford.edu/entries/common-good/.

Independent Report of the G20 TFCLIMA Group of Experts co-chaired by M. Mazzucato and V. Songwe (2024). *A Green and Just Planet*. Available at https://www.g20.org/en/tracks/sherpa-track/climate-change/the-g20-taskforce-on-a-global-mobilization-against-climate-change-tf-clima.

International Energy Agency (IEA). (2022). *Africa Energy Outlook 2022*. Available at https://www.iea.org/reports/africa-energy-outlook-2022.

International Labour Organization (ILO). (2024). *Global Wage Report 2024–25*. Available at https://www.ilo.org/sites/default/files/2025-02/GWR-2024_Layout_E_RGB_Web.pdf.

International Labour Organization (ILO). (2025). *2024 Labour Overview Latin America and the Caribbean*. Available at https://www.ilo.org/publications/2024-labour-overview-latin-america-and-caribbean.

International Monetary Fund (IMF). (2024). *G-20 Note on Alternative Options for Revenue Mobilization* (June 2024). International Monetary Fund. Available at https://www.imf.org/en/Publications/WP/

Issues/2024/06/24/G-20-Note-on-Alternative-Options-for-Revenue-Mobilization.

International Monetary Fund (IMF). (2025). *World Economic Outlook: GDP, current prices, April 2025*. Washington, DC: International Monetary Fund. https://www.imf.org/external/datamapper/NGDPD@WEO/OEMDC/ADVEC/WEOWORLD.

Jaede, M. (2017). *The Concept of the Common Good (PSRP Working Paper No. 8)*. University of Edinburgh. Available at https://www.thebritishacademy.ac.uk/documents/1851/Jaede.pdf.

Jäger, S., Noy, S., and Schoefer, B. (2022). 'What Does Codetermination Do?', *ILR Review*, 75(4), 857–90. Available at https://doi.org/10.1177/00197939211065727.

Jamali, D. (2008). 'A Stakeholder Approach to Corporate Social Responsibility: A Fresh Perspective into Theory and Practice', *Journal of Business Ethics*, 82, pp. 213–31. Available at https://doi.org/10.1007/s10551-007-9572-4.

Jayanetti, C. (2025). 'Councils and NHS could face millions in extra costs due to disability benefit cuts', *Guardian*, 22 March. Available at https://www.theguardian.com/society/2025/mar/22/government-plans-to-cut-pip-benefits-could-pile-more-pressure-on-councils.

Jehiel, P., and Moldovanu, B. (2001). 'Efficient design with interdependent valuations', *Econometrica*, 69(5), pp. 1237–59. Available at http://www.jstor.org/stable/2692220.

Jensen, M. C. (1986). 'Agency costs of free cash flow, corporate finance, and takeovers', *American Economic Review*, 76(2), pp. 323–9.

Jensen, M. C., and Meckling, W. H. (1976). 'Theory of the firm: Managerial behavior, agency costs and ownership structure', *Journal of Financial Economics*, 3(4), pp. 305–60.

Jongh, M. de (2020). 'Public Goods and the Commons: Opposites or Complements?', *Political Theory*, 49(5), pp. 774–800. Doi: https://doi.org/10.1177/0090591720979916.

JUMEME Rural Power Supply. (2018). *About us*. JUMEME. Available at https://www.jumeme.com/.

Just, R., Hueth, D. L., and Schmitz, A. (2008). *Applied Welfare Economics*. Edward Elgar Publishing.

Kahneman, D. (2011). *Thinking, Fast and Slow*. Farrar, Straus and Giroux.

Kattel, R., and Mazzucato, M. (2018). 'Mission-oriented innovation policy and dynamic capabilities in the public sector', *Industrial and Corporate Change*, 27(5), pp. 787–801. Available at https://doi.org/10.1093/icc/dty032.

Kattel, R., and Mazzucato, M. (2023). *Mission-oriented innovation policies in Europe: From normative to epistemic turn?* UCL Institute for Innovation and Public Purpose, Working Paper Series (IIPP WP 2023-09). Available at https://www.ucl.ac.uk/bartlett/public-purpose/wp2023-09.

Kattel, R., Mazzucato, M., Baafi, K., Monge, F., Goulden, A., Gronchi, I., Kalema, N., and Puttick, R. (2025a). *Dynamic Capabilities for Transformative Change in City Governments*. UCL Institute for Innovation and Public Purpose, Working Paper Series (IIPP WP 2025-03). Available at http://www.ucl.ac.uk/bartlett/public-purpose/publications/2025/feb/dynamic-capabilities-transformative-change-city-governments.

Kattel, R., Mazzucato, M., Puttick, R., Baafi, K., Chau, B., Dhamija, A., Goulden, A., Gronchi, I., Kalema, N., Fernandez-Monge, F., and Tarp, M. (2025b). *Assessing City Government Dynamic Capabilities: Interim report of the Public Sector Capabilities Index project*. UCL Institute for Innovation and Public Purpose. IIPP Policy Report 2025/01. Available at https://www.ucl.ac.uk/bartlett/public-purpose/publications/2025/feb/assessing-city-government-dynamic-capabilities.

Katz, B., and Noring, L. (2017). *The Copenhagen City and Port Development Corporation: A Model for Regenerating Cities*. Centennial Scholar Initiative at Brookings. Available at https://www.brookings.edu/wp-content/uploads/2017/05/csi_20170601_copenhagen_port_paper.pdf.

Katz, B., and Nowak, J. (2018). 'How a dying city transformed into one of the wealthiest in the world', *The New Localism*. Available at https://www.thenewlocalism.com/research/how-a-dying-city-transformed-into-one-of-the-wealthiest-in-the-world/.

Kaul, I. (2016). *Global Public Goods*. The International Library of Critical Writings in Economics series.

Kaul, I., Grunberg, I., and Stern, M. (eds.). (1999). *Global Public Goods: International Cooperation in the 21st Century*. Oxford University Press. Available at https://doi.org/10.1093/0195130529.001.0001.

Kay, J. (2012). *The Kay review of UK equity markets and long-term decision making*, final report. Available at https://www.gov.uk/government/publications/the-kay-review-of-uk-equity-markets-and-long-term-decisionmaking-final-report.

Kedward, K., and Poupard, A. (2024). *The economic and financial risks of implementing the '30x30' Global Biodiversity Framework targets.* UCL Institute for Innovation and Public Purpose Working Paper Series (IIPP WP 2024-13). Available at https://www.ucl.ac.uk/bartlett/public-purpose/wp2024-13.

Kempf, R. (1995). 'Exploitation of rights from the US space program by NASA (presented by B. Gimeno)', in G. Lafferranderie (ed.), *Proceedings of the Workshop on Intellectual Property Rights and Space Activities: A World-Wide Perspective*, ESA SP-378. European Space Agency, 27.

Keynes, J. M. (1926). *The End of Laissez-Faire*. Hogarth Press.

Keynes, J. M. (1936, 1973). *The General Theory of Employment, Interest and Money.* Macmillan and the Royal Economic Society.

Kim, T. (2013). 'Social Rights as a Global Public Good: Development, Human Rights, and Accountability', *Journal of International and Area Studies*, 20(2), pp. 21–37.

Kimmerer, R. W. (2013). *Braiding Sweetgrass: Indigenous Wisdom, Scientific Knowledge, and the Teachings of Plants.* Milkweed Editions.

King & Spalding. (2023). *The Administration Takes Aim At Drug Prices Again – This Time Through A Controversial Framework for Exercising March-In Rights*. Available at https://www.kslaw.com/news-and-insights/the-administration-takes-aim-at-drug-prices-again-this-time-through-a-controversial-framework-for-exercising-march-in-rights.

Klein, E., and Thompson, D. (2025). *Abundance*. Avid Reader press / Simon & Schuster.

Klinenberg, E. (2002). *Heat Wave: A Social Autopsy of Disaster in Chicago*. University of Chicago Press.

Klinenberg, E. (2018). *Palaces for the People: How to Build a More Equal and United Society*. The Bodley Head.

Korn, D., and Heinig, S. (2004). 'Recoupment Efforts Threaten Federal Research', *Issues in Science and Technology*, 20(4), pp. 26–30.

Kosack, S., and Fung, A. (2014). 'Does Transparency Improve Governance?', *Annual Review of Political Science*, 17, pp. 65–87. Available at https://doi.org/10.1146/annurev-polisci-032210-144356.

Kruse, D. L. (1996). 'Why Do Firms Adopt Profit-Sharing and Employee Ownership Plans?', *British Journal of Industrial Relations*, 34(4), pp. 515–38. Available at https://doi.org/10.1111/j.1467-8543.1996.tb00488.x.

Laplane, A., and Mazzucato, M. (2020). 'Socializing the risks and rewards of public investments: Economic, policy, and legal issues', *Research Policy*, 49 (Supplement). Available at https://doi.org/10.1016/j.repolx.2020.100008.

Łaszewska-Hellriegel, M. (2022). 'Environmental Personhood as a Tool to Protect Nature', *Philosophia*, 51, pp. 1369–84. Available at https://doi.org/10.1007/s11406-022-00583-z.

Layton, J., and Latham, A. (2021). 'Social infrastructure and public life – notes on Finsbury Park, London', *Urban Geography*, 43(5), pp. 755–76. Available at https://doi.org/10.1080/02723638.2021.1934631.

Lazonick, W. 2014. 'Profits Without Prosperity', *Harvard Business Review*. Available at https://hbr.org/2014/09/profits-without-prosperity.

Lazonick, W., and Mazzucato, M. (2013). 'The risk–reward nexus in the innovation–inequality relationship: who takes the risks? Who gets the rewards?' *Industrial and Corporate Change*, 22(4), pp. 1093–1128. Available at https://doi.org/10.1093/icc/dtt019.

Lazonick, W., and Tulum, Ö. (2023). 'Sick with "shareholder value": US pharma's financialized business model during the pandemic', *Competition & Change*, 28(2), pp. 251–73. Available at https://doi.org/10.1177/10245294231210975.

Ledyard, J. O. (1995). 'Public Goods: A Survey of Experimental Research'. In J. H. Hagel and A. E. Roth (eds.), *The Handbook of Experimental Economics*. Princeton University Press, pp. 111–84.

Lekkas, N. (2025). *GAFAM: The Big Five Tech Companies Facts (FAAMG)*. GrowthRocks. Available at https://growthrocks.com/blog/big-five-tech-companies-acquisitions/.

Levaggi, R. (2010). 'From local to global public good: How should externalities be represented?', *Economic Modelling*, 27(5), pp. 1040–42. Available at https://doi.org/10.1016/j.econmod.2010.04.006.

Lipsky, M. (1980). *Street-Level Bureaucracy: Dilemmas of the Individual in Public Services*. Russell Sage Foundation.

Livsmedelsverket (2023a). *Procurement and purchase of sustainable food, products and services*. Available at https://www.livsmedelsverket.se/matvanor-halsa--miljo/maltider-i-vard-skola-och-omsorg/sa-kan-skolmaltidssystemet-bidra-till-ett-hallbarare-samhalle/arbete-for-att-forandra-skolmaltidssystemet/upphandling-och-inkop-av-hallbara-livsmedel-produkter-och-tjanster.

Livsmedelsverket (2023b). *The involvement of students and school staff in the design of the school meal system*. Available at https://www.livsmedelsverket.se/matvanor-halsa--miljo/maltider-i-vard-skola-och-omsorg/sa-kan-skolmaltidssystemet-bidra-till-ett-hallbarare-samhalle/arbete-for-att-forandra-skolmaltidssystemet/elevernas-och-skolpersonalens-involvering-i-utformningen-av-skolmaltidssystemet-.

Lo, P. C., and Solomon, D. (2014). 'The Common Good'. In D. Solomon and P. C. Lo (eds.), *The Common Good: Chinese and American Perspectives*. Springer, pp. 3–18.

Locke, J. (1988). *Locke: Two Treatises of Government*. Cambridge University Press.

Lourenço, R. P. (2015). 'An analysis of open government portals: A perspective of transparency for accountability', *Government Information Quarterly*, 32(3), pp. 323–32. Available at https://doi.org/10.1016/j.giq.2015.05.006.

Lutz, M. A. (1999). *Economics for the Common Good: Two Centuries of Social Economic Thought and the Humanistic Tradition*. Routledge.

Lutz, M. A. (2002). 'Social economics, justice and the common good', *International Journal of Social Economics*, 29(1/2), pp. 26–44. Available at http://dx.doi.org/10.1108/03068290210412967.

Macfarlane, R. (2025). *Is a River Alive?* Hamish Hamilton.

Machlup, F. (1958). *An Economic Review of the Patent System (No. 15)*. United States Government Printing Office.

MacInnes, T., Tinson, A., Hughes, C., Born, T. B., and Aldrige, H. (2015). *Monitoring poverty and social exclusion 2015*. Joseph Rowntree Foundation. Available at https://www.jrf.org.uk/monitoring-poverty-and-social-exclusion-2015.

MacIntyre, A. (1981). *After Virtue: A Study in Moral Theory*. University of Notre Dame Press.

Madden, M. (2022). 'Crop Over forecast to contribute to further economic growth in 2022', *Barbados Today*. Available at https://barbadostoday.bb/2022/07/28/crop-over-forecast-to-contribute-to-further-economic-growth-in-2022/.

Maine, L. L. (2020). 'An Unparalleled Spirit of Collaboration Amid the COVID-19 Pandemic', *American Journal of Pharmaceutical Education*, 84(6). Available at https://doi.org/10.5688/ajpe8155.

Maire, J., Mazarei, A., and Truman, E. M. (2021). *21-3 Sovereign Wealth Funds Are Growing More Slowly, and Governance Issues Remain*. Peterson Institute for International Economics. Available at https://www.piie.com/sites/default/files/documents/pb21-3.pdf.

Malone, T. W., and Bernstein, M. S. (2015). *Handbook of Collective Intelligence*. Massachusetts Institute of Technology.

Mancuso, S. (2021). *The Nation of Plants*. Translated by G. Conti. Profile Books.

Mannix, E., and Neale, M. A. (2005). 'What Differences Make a Difference? The Promise and Reality of Diverse Teams in Organizations', *Psychological Science in the Public Interest*, 6(2), pp. 31–55. Available at https://doi.org/10.1111/j.1529-1006.2005.00022.x.

Marmot, M. G. (1999). *Social Determinants of Health*. Oxford University Press.

Marsden, L. (2024). *Response to EIOPA Consultation paper on the Report on biodiversity risk management by insurers*. University College London Institute for Innovation and Public Purpose. Available at https://www.ucl.ac.uk/bartlett/sites/bartlett/files/iipp_eiopa_biodiversity_response.pdf.

Martin, M., and Perez, A. (2025). 'Baltimore Mayor Brandon Scott discusses how the city has brought violent crime down' (interview), *NPR Morning Edition*, 20 August. Available at https://www.npr.org/2025/08/19/nx-s1-5503390/baltimore-mayor-brandon-scott-low-crime-rates.

Marx, K. (1887). *Capital: A Critical Analysis of Capitalist Production*, vol. I. Swan Sonnenschein, Lowry & Co.

Mas-Colell, A., Whinston, M. D., and Green, J. R. (1995). *Microeconomic Theory*, vol. 1. Oxford University Press.

Maskin, E., and Tirole, J. (2001). 'Markov Perfect Equilibrium: I. Observable Actions', *Journal of Economic Theory*, 100(2), pp. 191–219. Available at https://doi.org/10.1006/jeth.2000.2785.

Mastromatteo, G., and Solari, S. (2014). 'The idea of "common good" and the role of the state in present day social economics', *Rivista Internazionale di Scienze Sociali*, 1, pp. 85–102. Available at https://www.jstor.org/stable/43830201.

Matschoss, K., Mikkonen, I., Gynther, L., Koukoufikis, G., Uihlein, A., and Murauskaite-Bull, I. (2022). 'Drawing policy insights from social innovation cases in the energy field', *Energy Policy*, 161. Available at https://doi.org/10.1016/j.enpol.2021.112728.

Mattern, S. (2014). 'Library as Infrastructure'. *Places*. Available at https://doi.org/10.22269/140609.

Mattessich, P. W., and Johnson, K. M. (2018). *Collaboration: What Makes It Work*. 3rd edn. Fieldstone Alliance.

Mauro, F., and Hardison, P. D. (2000). 'Traditional knowledge of indigenous and Local communities: International debate and policy initiatives'. *Ecological Applications*, 10(5), 1263–94. Available at https://doi.org/10.2307/2641281.

Mayor of London (2023). Free School Meals. London.gov.uk. Available at https://www.london.gov.uk/who-we-are/what-mayor-does/priorities-london/free-school-meals#:~:text=Primary%20school%20children%20in%20state,in%20urgent%20need%20of%20support.

Mazepus, H. (2018). 'Does Political Legitimacy Matter for Policy Capacity?' In X. Wu, M. Howlett, and M. Ramesh (eds.), *Policy Capacity and Governance: Assessing Governmental Competences and Capabilities in Theory and Practice*. Springer International Publishing, pp. 229–42.

Mazzoleni, R., and Nelson, R. R. (1998). 'Economic Theories about the Benefits and Costs of Patents', *Journal of Economic Issues*, 32(4), pp. 1031–52. Available at https://www.jstor.org/stable/4227385.

Mazzonetto, M. (2025). *Mutual learning exercise on public engagement in R&I: Final report*. European Commission Publications Office of the European Union. Available at https://data.europa.eu/doi/10.2777/0673481.

Mazzucato, M. (2000). *Firm Size, Innovation and Market Structure: The Evolution of Market Concentration and Instability*, Edward Elgar Publishing.

Mazzucato, M. (2013). *The Entrepreneurial State: Debunking Public vs. Private Sector Myths*. Anthem Press.

Mazzucato, M. (2016). 'From market fixing to market creating: a new framework for innovation policy', *Industry and Innovation*, 23(2), pp. 140–56. Available at https://doi.org/10.1080/13662716.2016.1146124.

Mazzucato, M. (2018a). 'Mission-oriented innovation policy: challenges and opportunities', *Industrial and Corporate Change*, 27(5), pp. 803–15. Available at https://doi.org/10.1093/icc/dty034.

Mazzucato, M. (2018b). *Mission-oriented research & innovation in the European Union: A problem-solving approach to fuel innovation-led growth*. Report for the European Commission. Available at https://www.horizon-europe.gouv.fr/sites/default/files/2022-11/mazzucato-report-2018-pdf-7474.pdf.

Mazzucato, M. (2018c). *The Value of Everything: Making and Taking in the Global Economy*. Allen Lane.

Mazzucato, M. (2019a). *Governing Missions in the European Union*. European Commission Report. Available at https://research-and-innovation.ec.europa.eu/knowledge-publications-tools-and-data/publications/all-publications/governing-missions-european-union_en.

Mazzucato, M. (2019b). *Preventing Digital Feudalism*. Project Syndicate. Available at https://www.project-syndicate.org/commentary/platform-economy-digital-feudalism-by-mariana-mazzucato-2019-10.

Mazzucato, M. (2021). *Mission Economy: A Moonshot Guide to Changing Capitalism*. Allen Lane.

Mazzucato, M. (2022a). 'Collective value creation: a new approach to stakeholder value', *International Review of Applied Economics*, 38(1–2), pp. 43–57. Available at https://doi.org/10.1080/02692171.2022.2144149.

Mazzucato, M. (2022b). *Rethinking the social contract between the state and business: A new approach to industrial strategy with conditionalities*. UCL Institute for Innovation and Public Purpose Working Paper Series (IIPP WP 2022-18). Available at https://www.ucl.ac.uk/bartlett/publications/2022/nov/rethinking-social-contract-between-state-and-business.

Mazzucato, M. (2022c). 'What Role Should Business Play in Society?', *Harvard Business Review*. Available at https://hbr.org/2022/09/what-role-should-business-play-in-society.

Mazzucato, M. (2023a). *Financing the Sustainable Development Goals through mission-oriented development banks*. UN Department of Economic and Social Affairs Policy Brief Special Issue. Available at https://www.un.org/development/desa/dpad/publication/un-desa-policy-brief-special-issue-financing-the-sustainable-development-goals-through-mission-oriented-development-banks/.

Mazzucato, M. (2023b). 'Governing the economics of the common good: from correcting market failures to shaping collective goals', *Journal of Economic Policy Reform*, 27(1), pp. 1–24. Available at https://doi.org/10.1080/17487870.2023.2280969.

Mazzucato, M. (2023c). *Transformational change in Latin America and the Caribbean: A mission oriented approach*. (LC/TS.2022/150/Rev.1). Economic Commission for Latin America and the Caribbean (ECLAC). Available at https://www.ucl.ac.uk/bartlett/publications/2022/oct/transformational-change-latin-america-and-caribbean-mission-oriented-approach.

Mazzucato, M. (ed.). (2024a). *State Transformation in Brazil: Designing public procurement, state-owned enterprises and digital public infrastructure to advance sustainable and inclusive growth*. UCL Institute for Innovation and Public Purpose. IIPP Policy Report 2024/15. Available at https://www.ucl.ac.uk/bartlett/public-purpose/policyreport-2024-15.

Mazzucato, M. (2024b). 'The ugly truth behind ChatGPT: AI is guzzling resources at planet-eating rates'. Project Syndicate, 30 May. Available at https://www.theguardian.com/commentisfree/article/2024/may/30/ugly-truth-ai-chatgpt-guzzling-resources-environment.

Mazzucato, M. (2025a). *Principles for an Inclusive and Sustainable Global Economy: A discussion paper for the G20*. UCL Institute for Innovation and Public Purpose. Available at https://www.ucl.ac.uk/bartlett/ucl-institute-innovation-and-public-purpose/

principles-inclusive-and-sustainable-global-economy-discussion-paper-g20.

Mazzucato, M. (2025b). *Reimagining financing for the SDGs – from filling gaps to shaping finance*. UNDESA Policy Brief, No. 170, Special Issue. UN Department of Economic and Social Affairs; UN High-level Advisory Board on Economic and Social Affairs; University College London Institute for Innovation and Public Purpose. Available at https://desapublications.un.org/policy-briefs/un-desa-policy-brief-no-170-special-issue-reimagining-financing-sdgs-filling-gaps.

Mazzucato, M. (2025c). *Resisting Digital Feudalism*. Project Syndicate, 7 February. Available at https://www.project-syndicate.org/commentary/ai-digital-feudalism-inevitable-unless-policymakers-step-in-to-shape-markets-by-mariana-mazzucato-2025-02.

Mazzucato, M. (2025d). 'The Broken Economic Order: How to Rewire the International System in the Age of Trump', *Foreign Affairs*, 25 February. Available at https://www.foreignaffairs.com/south-africa/broken-economic-order-mariana-mazzucato.

Mazzucato, M. (2025e). *The Public Value of Arts and Culture: Investing in Arts and Culture to Reimagine Economic Growth in the 21st Century*. UCL Institute for Innovation and Public Purpose. Available at https://www.ucl.ac.uk/bartlett/publications/2025/sep/public-value-arts-and-culture.

Mazzucato, M., and Barrington, A. (2024). *Carnival Economics*. Project Syndicate, 22 August. Available at https://www.project-syndicate.org/commentary/arts-and-culture-immense-public-value-often-unappreciated-or-extracted-by-private-interests-by-mariana-mazzucato-and-alvaro-barrington-2024-08.

Mazzucato, M., and Collington, R. (2023). *The Big Con: How the Consulting Industry Weakens Our Businesses, Infantilizes Our Governments, and Warps Our Economies*. Allen Lane.

Mazzucato, M., and Doyle, S. (2025). *A Mission-Oriented Approach to School Meals. An opportunity for cross-departmental and multi-sector industrial strategy*. UCL Institute for Innovation and Public Purpose. IIPP Policy Report 2025/04. Available at https://www.vcl.ac.uk/bartlett/publication/2025/sep/mission-oriented-approach-school-meals.

Mazzucato, M., and Farha, L. (2023). *The Right to Housing: A mission-oriented and human rights-based approach*. Council on Urban Initiatives. (CUI WP 2023-01). UCL Institute for Innovation and Public Purpose, Working Paper Series. (IIPP WP 2023-07). Available at https://www.ucl.ac.uk/bartlett/public-purpose/publications/2023/may/right-housing-mission-oriented-and-human-rights-based-approach.

Mazzucato, M., and Gernone, F. (2025). *AI Should Help Fund Creative Labor*. Project Syndicate (25 July). Available at https://www.project-syndicate.org/onpoint/how-ai-profits-can-help-fund-cultural-production-by-mariana-mazzucato-and-fausto-gernone-2025-07.

Mazzucato, M., and Kattel, R. (2020). 'Covid-19 and public-sector capacity', *Oxford Review of Economic Policy*, 36(1), pp. S256–S269. Available at https://doi.org/10.1093/oxrep/graa031.

Mazzucato, M., and Kühn von Burgsdorff, L. (2025). *A Mission-Oriented Approach to Governing Our Global Water Challenges and Opportunities*. UCL Institute for Innovation and Public Purpose Policy Brief 31. Available at https://www.ucl.ac.uk/bartlett/public-purpose/PB-31.

Mazzucato, M., and Li, H. L. (2021). 'A Market Shaping Approach for the Biopharmaceutical Industry: Governing Innovation towards the Public Interest', *Journal of Law, Medicine & Ethics*, 49(1), pp. 39–49. Available at https://doi.org/10.1017/jme.2021.8.

Mazzucato, M., and Macfarlane, L. (2025). 'The Role of Mission-Oriented Development Banks in Greening', in John. A. Mathews and Arkebe Oqubay (eds.), *The Oxford Handbook on the Greening of Economic Development*. Oxford University Press.

Mazzucato, M., and Penna, C. C. R. (2016). 'Beyond market failures: the market creating and shaping roles of state investment banks', *Journal of Economic Policy Reform*, 19(4), pp. 305–26. Available at https://doi.org/10.1080/17487870.2016.1216416.

Mazzucato, M., and Rodrik, D. (2023). *Industrial Policy with Conditionalities: A Taxonomy and Sample Cases*. UCL Institute for Innovation and Public Purpose, Working Paper Series (IIPP WP 2023-07). Available at https://www.ucl.ac.uk/bartlett/public-purpose/publications/2023/oct/industrial-policy-conditionalities-taxonomy-and-sample-cases.

Mazzucato, M., and Ryan-Collins, J. (2022). 'Putting value creation back into "public value": from market-fixing to market-shaping', *Journal of Economic Policy Reform*, 25(4), pp. 345–60. Available at https://doi.org/10.1080/17487870.2022.2053537.

Mazzucato, M., and Silvers, D. (2023). 'Auto Strikes and Climate Change', Project Syndicate, 23 September. Available at https://www.project-syndicate.org/commentary/uaw-strike-worker-empowerment-means-political-support-for-green-transition-by-mariana-mazzucato-and-damon-silvers-2023-09.

Mazzucato, M., and Wainwright, D. (2024). *Mission-led procurement and market-shaping: Lessons from Camden Council.* UCL Institute for Innovation and Public Purpose Policy Report No. 2024/06. Available at https://www.ucl.ac.uk/bartlett/public-purpose/policy-report-2024-06.

Mazzucato, M., Conway, R., Mazzoli, E. M., Knoll, E., and Albala, S. (2020). *Creating and measuring dynamic public value at the BBC. A scoping report.* UCL Institute for Innovation and Public Purpose, Policy Report, (IIPP 2020-19). Available at https://www.ucl.ac.uk/bartlett/publications/2020/dec/creating-and-measuring-dynamic-public-value-bbc.

Mazzucato, M., Eaves, D., and Vasconcellos, B. (2024). *Digital Public Infrastructure and Public Value: What is 'public' about DPI?* UCL Institute for Innovation and Public Purpose Working Paper 2024-05. Available at https://www.ucl.ac.uk/bartlett/publications/2024/mar/digital-public-infrastructure-and-public-value-what-public-about-dpi.

Mazzucato, M., Entsminger, J., and Kattel, R. (2020). *Public value and platform governance.* UCL Institute for Innovation and Public Purpose Working Paper Series (IIPP WP 2020-11). Available at https://www.ucl.ac.uk/bartlett/public-purpose/wp2020-11.

Mazzucato, M., Kattel, R., Begovic, M., and Quaggiotto, G. (2021). *COVID-19 and the Need for Dynamic State Capabilities: An International Comparison.* United Nations Development Programme and UCL Institute for Innovation and Public Purpose. Available at https://www.ucl.ac.uk/bartlett/public-purpose/sites/public-purpose/files/54241_-_undp_wp-covid-19_state_ressilience-v51.pdf.

Mazzucato, M., Macfarlane, L., Mikheeva, O., and Bellinson, R. (2022a). *A mission-oriented community wealth fund for Camden: Governing finance with public purpose*. UCL Institute for Innovation and Public Purpose, IIPP Policy Report No.2022/03. Available at https://www.ucl.ac.uk/bartlett/publications/2022/nov/mission-oriented-community-wealth-fund-camden-governing-finance-public-purpose.

Mazzucato, M., Schaake, M., Krier, S., and Entsminger, J. (2022b). *Governing artificial intelligence in the public interest*. UCL Institute for Innovation and Public Purpose Working Paper Series (IIPP WP 2022-12). Available at https://www.ucl.ac.uk/bartlett/publications/2022/jul/governing-artificial-intelligence-public-interest.

Mazzucato, M., Stratton, T., and Williams-Eliyesil, S. (2025). *Mission-Oriented Public–Private Partnerships: Lessons from the Oxford–AstraZeneca COVID-19 vaccine*. UCL Institute for Innovation and Public Purpose, Working Paper Series (IIPP WP 2025-18). Available at https://www.ucl.ac.uk/bartlett/publications/2025/sep/mission-oriented-public-private-partnerships-lessons-oxford-astrazeneca-covid-19-vaccine.

McGinnis, M. D., and Ostrom, E. (2014). 'Social-ecological system framework: initial changes and continuing challenges', *Ecology and Society*, 19(2). Available at https://www.jstor.org/stable/26269580.

McNeil, D., Jr (2001). 'A nation challenged: the drug, a rush for Cipro and the global ripples', *The New York Times*, 17 October. Available at http://www.nytimes.com/2001/10/17/world/a-nation-challenged-the-drug-a-rush-for-cipro-and-the-global-ripples.html.

McNutt, P. (1999). 'Public Goods and Club Goods', *Encyclopedia of Law and Economics*, 1, pp. 927–51.

McQueen, H. (2011). *We Built this Country: Builders' Labourers and their Unions 1787 to the Future*. Ginninderra Press.

McShane, I., and Coffey, B. (2022). 'Rethinking community hubs: community facilities as critical infrastructure', *Current Opinion on Environmental Sustainability*, 54. Available at https://doi.org/10.1016/j.cosust.2022.101149.

Médecins Sans Frontières (MSF). (2021). *COVID-19 Vaccine Distribution to Save Lives Now: Why high-income countries must immediately redistribute excess COVID-19 vaccines to address global vaccine inequity*. MSF

Technical Brief, October 2021. Available at https://msfaccess.org/covid-19-vaccine-redistribution-save-lives-now.

Melendez, S. (2024). *Taiwan's digital revolution: Healing polarization and strengthening democracy*. Harvard Business School – Institute for Business in Global Society. Available at https://www.hbs.edu/bigs/taiwans-digital-revolution-audrey-tang.

Merson, J. (2000). 'Bio-prospecting or bio-piracy: intellectual property rights and biodiversity in a colonial and postcolonial context', *Osiris*, 15, pp. 282–96. Available at https://pubmed.ncbi.nlm.nih.gov/11973830/.

Mill, J. ([1859,] 2003]). *On Liberty*. Yale University Press.

Ministério da Gestão e da Inovação em Serviços Públicos (MGI) (2023). *Conheça a estrutura do Ministério da Gestão e da Inovação em Serviços Públicos*. Available at https://www.gov.br/gestao/pt-br/assuntos/noticias/2023/janeiro/conheca-a-estrutura-do-ministerio-da-gestao-e-da-inovacao-em-servicos-publicos.

Monge, F., Barns, S., Kattel, R., and Bria, F. (2022). *A new data deal: the case of Barcelona*. UCL Institute for Innovation and Public Purpose, Working Paper Series (No. WP 2022/02). Available at https://www.ucl.ac.uk/bartlett/public-purpose/wp2022-02.

Moore, M. H. (1995). *Creating Public Value: Strategic Management in Government*. Harvard University Press.

Moore, M. H. (2014). 'Public Value Accounting: Establishing the Philosophical Basis', *Public Administration Review*, 74(4). Available at https://doi.org/10.1111/puar.12198.

Moore, T., and McKee, K. (2012). 'Empowering Local Communities? An International Review of Community Land Trusts', *Housing Studies*, 27(2), pp. 280–90. Available at https://doi.org/10.1080/02673037.2012.647306.

Morgera, E., Tsioumani, E., and Buck, M. (2024). *Unraveling the Nagoya Protocol*. Brill. Available at https://doi.org/10.1163/9789004217188.

Morozov, E., and Bria, F. (2018). *Rethinking the Smart City: Democratizing Urban Technology*. Rosa Luxemburg Stiftung. Available at https://rosalux.nyc/rethinking-the-smart-city/.

Motta, M. (2004). *Competition Policy: Theory and Practice*. Cambridge University Press.

Motune, V. (2024). 'EXCLUSIVE: Carnival generates £396 million for London's economy', *The Voice* (2 Aug.). Available at https://www.voice-online.co.uk/news/uk-news/2024/08/02/carnival-generates-396-million-for-londons-economy/.

Mpanga, G. (2021). 'Songs Make Jobs', *Have You Heard George's Podcast?* (Podcast). Available at https://www.bbc.co.uk/programmes/p09w1xd4#:~:text=28.-,Songs%20Make%20Jobs,24:57%20%2D%2029:04.

Mpanga, G. (2024). *Track Record: Me, Music, and the War on Blackness*. Hodder & Stoughton.

Mueller, D. C. (2003). *Public Choice III*. Cambridge University Press.

Mullenbach, A. (2007). 'L'apport de la théorie des parties prenantes à la modélisation de la responsabilité sociétale des entreprises', *La Revue des Sciences de Gestion*, 223(1), pp. 109–20. Available at https://doi.org/10.3917/rsg.223.0109.

Murphy, T., and Parkey, J. (2016). 'An economic analysis of the philosophical common good', *International Journal of Social Economics*, 43(8), pp. 823–40. Available at https://doi.org/10.1108/IJSE-08-2014-0168.

Mustonen, M. (2003). 'Copyleft – the economics of Linux and other open source software', *Information Economics and Policy*, 15(1), pp. 99–121. Available at https://doi.org/10.1016/S0167-6245(02)00090-2.

Myerson, R. B. (1981). 'Optimal auction design', *Mathematics of Operations Research*, 6(1), pp. 58–73. Available at https://www.jstor.org/stable/3689266.

National Health Service (NHS). (2014). *Five Year Forward View*. Available at https://www.england.nhs.uk/wp-content/uploads/2014/10/5yfv-web.pdf.

National Youth Agency (NYA). (2023). *Youth centre closures linked to greater risk of young people entering criminal justice system*. Available at https://nya.org.uk/youth-centre-closures-linked-to-greater-risk-of-young-people-entering-criminal-justice-system/.

Neeson, J. M. (1993). *Commoners: Common Right, Enclosure and Social Change in England, 1700–1820*. Cambridge University Press.

Nega, B., and Schneider, G. (2014). 'NGOs, the State, and Development in Africa', *Review of Social Economy*, 72(4), pp. 485–503. Available at https://doi.org/10.1080/00346764.2014.958901.

Nelson, R. R. (1987). 'Roles of Government in a Mixed Economy', *Journal of Policy Analysis and Management*, 6(4), pp. 541–57. Available at https://doi.org/10.2307/3323507.

Nelson, R. R. (2022). 'The economic system question revisited', *Industrial and Corporate Change*, 31, pp. 591–609. Available at https://doi.org/10.1093/icc/dtac012.

Nelson, R. R., and Winter, S. (1982). *An Evolutionary Theory of Economic Change*. Harvard University Press.

Newell, P., and Phillips, J. (2016). 'Neoliberal energy transitions in the South: Kenyan experiences', *Geoforum*, 74, pp. 39–48. Available at https://doi.org/10.1016/j.geoforum.2016.05.009.

Newell, P., Srivastava, S., Naess, L. O., Torres Contreras, G. A., and Price, R. (2021). 'Toward transformative climate justice: An emerging research agenda', *WIREs Climate Change*, 12(6). Available at https://doi.org/10.1002/wcc.733.

Nitsch, T. O. (2005). 'Economics, social justice and the common good: Roman-Catholic perspectives', *International Journal of Social Economics*, 32(6), pp. 554–69. Available at https://doi.org/10.1108/03068290510597023.

North, D. C. (1991). 'Institutions, Ideology, and Economic Performance', *Cato Journal*, 11, pp. 477–88. Available at https://www.cato.org/sites/cato.org/files/serials/files/cato-journal/1992/1/cj11n3-11.pdf.

Nowak, M. A. (2006). 'Five rules for the evolution of cooperation', *Science*, 314 (5805), pp. 1560–63. Available at https://www.ncbi.nlm.nih.gov/pmc/articles/PMC3279745/.

Nozick, R. (1974). *Anarchy, State and Utopia*, Basic Books.

Nugent, C. (2023). 'How an Artificial Island in Denmark Became One of Europe's Most Controversial Climate Projects', *TIME* (22 March). Available at https://time.com/6264861/copenhagen-lynetteholm-artificial-island-climate-change/.

Nuru (2023). *About us*. Nuru. Available at https://www.nuru.cd/.

Nussbaum, M. C. (1997). *The Feminist Critique of Liberalism*. University of Kansas. Available at https://hdl.handle.net/1808/12410.

Nussbaum, M. C. (2000). *Women and Human Development: The Capabilities Approach*. Cambridge University Press.

O'Connor, J. (2024). *Culture is Not an Industry: Reclaiming Art and Culture for the Common Good*. Manchester University Press.

Ola, M. H. (2024). 'Taxonomy of wealth taxation literature: A study of implementation, effects, responses and regulatory policy context'. *Journal of Governance and Regulation*, 13(4), pp. 117–31. Available at https://doi.org/10.22495.jgrv 13i4art12.

O'Reilly, T., Strauss, I., and Mazzucato, M. (2024). 'Algorithmic Attention Rents: A theory of digital platform market power', *Data & Policy*, 6(e6). Available at https://doi.org/10.1017/dap.2024.1.

Organization for Economic Cooperation and Development (OECD). (2023). *OECD/G20 Inclusive Framework releases new multilateral convention to address tax challenges of globalisation and digitalisation*. Available at https://www.oecd.org/en/about/news/press-releases/2023/10/inclusive-framework-releases-new-multilateral-convention-to-address-tax-challenges-of-globalisation-and-digitalisation-.html.

Organization for Economic Cooperation and Development (OECD). (2024a). *Base erosion and profit shifting (BEPS)*. Available at https://www.oecd.org/en/topics/policy-issues/base-erosion-and-profit-shifting-beps.html.

Organization for Economic Cooperation and Development (OECD). (2024b). *Corporate Tax Statistics*. Available at https://www.oecd.org/content/dam/oecd/en/publications/reports/2024/07/corporate-tax-statistics-2024_ce7e5701/9c27d6e8-en.pdf.

Organization for Economic Cooperation and Development (OECD). (2024c). *Society at a Glance 2024: OECD Social Indicators*. Available at https://www.oecd.org/en/publications/society-at-a-glance-2024_918d8db3-en/full-report/life-expectancy_37a61588.html.

Organization for Economic Cooperation and Development (OECD). (2024d). *OECD Affordable Housing Database – indicator PH4.2. Social rental housing stock*. Available at https://www.oecd.org/content/dam/oecd/en/data/datasets/affordable-housing-database/ph4-2-social-rental-housing-stock.pdf.

Organisation for Economic Cooperation and Development (OECD). (2025). *Taxing wages 2025: Decomposition of personal income taxes*. Available at https://www.oecd.org/content/dam/oecd/en/topics/policy-issues/tax-policy/taxing-wages-brochure.pdf.

Organization for Economic Cooperation and Development (OECD) and UN Capital Development Fund (UNCDF). (2020). *Blended Finance in the Least Developed Countries 2020: Supporting a Resilient COVID-19 Recovery*. OECD Publishing. Available at https://doi.org/10.1787/57620d04-en.

Ostrom, E. (1990). *Governing the Commons: The Evolution of Institutions for Collective Action*. Cambridge University Press.

Ostrom, E. (2005). *Understanding Institutional Diversity*. Princeton University Press.

Ostrom, E. (2010). 'Beyond Markets and States: Polycentric Governance of Complex Economic Systems', *American Economic Review*, 100(3), pp. 641–72. Available at https://doi.org/10.1257/aer.100.3.641.

Page, S. E. (2007). *The Difference: How the Power of Diversity Creates Better Groups, Firms, Schools, and Societies*. Princeton University Press.

Palma, J. G. (2019). Behind the Seven Veils of Inequality. What if it's all about the Struggle within just One Half of the Population over just One Half of the National Income?, *Development and Change*, Distinguished Lecture 2018, 50(5), 1133–1213. Available at https://doi.org/10.1111/dech.12505.

Parvez Butt, A., Berkhout, E., Chawkat Zaghubour, M., Bush, A., Liepollo Pheko, L., and Verma, R. (2023). *Radical Pathways beyond GDP: Why and How We Need to Pursue Feminist and Decolonial Alternatives Urgently*. Oxfam.

Pekanov, A., and Schratzenstaller, M. (2019). 'A Global Financial Transaction Tax – Theory, Practice and Potential Revenues', *SSRN*. Available at https://dx.doi.org/10.2139/ssrn.3407855.

Pelle-Culpin C. I. (1998). *Du paradoxe de la diffusion d'informations environnementales par les entreprises européennes*, Thèse de Doctorat, Université de Paris IX Dauphine.

Perez, C. (2002). *Technological Revolutions and Financial Capital: The Dynamics of Bubbles and Golden Ages*. Edward Elgar Publishing.

Peters, A. (2021). 'Copenhagen is building a huge island in its harbor to protect against sea level rise', *Fast Company* (9 June). Available at https://www.fastcompany.com/90645186/

copenhagen-is-building-a-huge-island-in-its-harbor-to-protect-against-sea-level-rise.

Peters, M. A., and Mika, C. T. (2017). 'Aborigine, Indian, indigenous or first nations?', *Educational Philosophy and Theory*, 49(13), pp. 1229–34. Available at https://doi.org/10.1080/00131857.2017.1279879.

Phillips, K. W. (2014). 'How Diversity Makes Us Smarter', *Scientific American* (1 Oct.). Available at https://www.scientificamerican.com/article/how-diversity-makes-us-smarter/.

Phillips, R., Freeman, E., and Wicks, A. C. (2003). 'What Stakeholder Theory Is Not', *Business Ethics Quarterly*, 13(4), pp. 479–502. Available at https://www.jstor.org/stable/3857968.

Pigou, A. C. (1951). 'Some aspects of welfare economics', *American Economic Review*, 41(3), pp. 287–302. Available at https://www.jstor.org/stable/1802103.

Piketty, T. (2014). *Capital in the Twenty-First Century*. Harvard University Press.

Piketty, T. (2022). *A Brief History of Equality*. Harvard University Press.

Piketty, T., Saez, E., and Zucman, G. (2023). 'Rethinking capital and wealth taxation', *Oxford Review of Economic Policy*, 39, pp. 575–91. Available at https://doi.org/10.1093/oxrep/grad026.

Pistor, K. (2019). *The Code of Capital: How the Law Creates Wealth and Inequality*. Princeton University Press.

Planas, M., and Martínez, J. (2020). *Water should be a public good, not a commodity. Catalonia is showing how*. openDemocracy. Available at https://www.opendemocracy.net/en/oureconomy/water-should-be-public-good-not-commodity-catalonia-showing-how/.

Plato (1991). *The Republic of Plato*. Translated by A. Bloom. 2nd edn. Basic Books.

Poggi, A. (2025). *The Digital Divide: A Barrier to Social, Economic and Political Equity*. Italian Institute for International Political Studies. Available at https://www.ispionline.it/en/publication/the-digital-divide-a-barrier-to-social-economic-and-political-equity-204564.

Polanyi, K. (1944, 2024). *The Great Transformation: The Political and Economic Origins of Our Time*. Penguin Classics.

Pontifical Academy of Social Sciences (PASS) and the Initiative for Policy Dialogue (IPD). (2025). *The Jubilee Report: A Blueprint for*

Tackling the Debt and Development Crises and Creating the Financial Foundations for a Sustainable People-Centered Global Economy. Available at https://ipdcolumbia.org/wp-content/uploads/2025/06/Jubilee-report_veryfinal.pdf .

Pope Francis. (2015). *Encyclical Letter Laudato si' of the Holy Father Francis on Care for Our Common Home.* The Holy See. Available at https://www.vatican.va/content/dam/francesco/pdf/encyclicals/documents/papa-francesco_20150524_enciclica-laudato-si_en.pdf.

Pope Leo XIII. (1891). *Rerum Novarum: Encyclical of Pope Leo XIII on Capital and Labor.* The Holy See. Available at https://www.vatican.va/content/leo-xiii/en/encyclicals/documents/hf_l-xiii_enc_15051891_rerum-novarum.html.

Pope Pius XI. (1931). *Quadragesimo Anno: Encyclical of Pope Pius XI on Reconstruction of the Social Order.* The Holy See. Available at https://www.vatican.va/content/pius-xi/en/encyclicals/documents/hf_p-xi_enc_19310515_quadragesimo-anno.html.

Potts, J., and Cunningham, S. (2008). 'Four models of the creative industries', *International Journal of Cultural Policy*, 14(3), 233–47. Available at https://doi.org/10.1080/10286630802281780.

PowerGen. (2023). *What we do*. PowerGen Renewable Energy. Available at https://www.powergen-re.com/.

Prahalad, C. K., and Ramaswamy, V. (2004). 'Co-creation experiences: The next practice in value creation', *Journal of Interactive Marketing,* 18(3), pp. 5–14. Available at https://doi.org/10.1002/dir.20015.

Pritchett, L., Woolcock, M., and Andrews, M. (2013). 'Looking Like a State: Techniques of Persistent Failure in State Capability for Implementation', *Journal of Development Studies*, 49(1), pp. 1–18. Available at https://doi.org/10.1080/00220388.2012.709614.

Putnam, R. D. (2000). *Bowling Alone: The Collapse and Revival of American Community*. Simon & Schuster.

Quesnay, F. (1776). *Tableau Economique*.

Quilligan, J. B. (2012). 'Why Distinguish Common Goods from Public Goods'. In D. Bollier and S. Helfrich (eds.), *The Wealth of the Commons: A World beyond Market and State*. Levellers Press.

Rabin, M. (1993). 'Incorporating Fairness into Game Theory and Economics', *American Economic Review*, 83(5), pp. 1281–1302. Available at https://www.jstor.org/stable/2117561.

Rahman, M. M., Khanam, R., and Rahman, M. (2018). 'Health care expenditure and health outcome nexus: new evidence from the SAARC-ASEAN region', *Global Health*, 14(113). Available at: https://doi.org/10.1186/s12992-018-0430-1.

Rahmatian, A. (2009). 'Neo-Colonial Aspects of Global Intellectual Property Protection', *Journal of World Intellectual Property*, 12(1), pp. 40–74. Available at https://papers.ssrn.com/sol3/papers.cfm?abstract_id=1629228.

Rajamäe-Soosaar, K., and Nikiforova, A. (2024). *Exploring Estonia's Open Government Data Development as a Journey towards Excellence: Unveiling the Progress of Local Governments in Open Data Provision*. Proceedings of the 25th Annual International Conference on Digital Government Research. Available at https://arxiv.org/abs/2403.11952.

Ranger, N., Mahul, O., and Monasterolo, I. (2021). 'Managing the financial risks of climate change and pandemics: What we know (and don't know)', *One Earth*, 4(10), pp. 1375–85. Available at https://doi.org/10.1016/j.oneear.2021.09.017.

Rawls, J. (1971). *A Theory of Justice*. Harvard University Press.

Rawls, J. (1993). 'The Law of Peoples', *Critical Inquiry*, 20(1), pp. 36–68. Available at https://www.jstor.org/stable/1343947.

Raworth, K. (2017). *Doughnut Economics: Seven Ways to Think Like a 21st-Century Economist*. Random House.

Reeves, J.-A., and Peters, T. D. (2022). 'Responding to anthropocentrism with anthropocentrism: the biopolitics of environmental personhood', *Griffith Law Review*, 30(3), pp. 474–504. Available at https://doi.org/10.1080/10383441.2022.2037882.

Regulator of Social Housing (RSH). (2025). *RSH publishes annual statistics on stocks and rents in the social housing sector*. Gov.uk. Available at https://www.gov.uk/government/news/rsh-publishes-annual-statistics-on-stocks-and-rents-in-the-social-housing-sector#:~:text=Of%20the%20c.%204.5%20million,2024%20and%202025%20was%207.7%25.

Reich, R. B. (1991). 'Secession of the Successful', *The New York Times Magazine*. Available at https://go.gale.com/ps/i.do?id=GALE%7CA175088963&sid=googleScholar&v=2.1&it=r&linkaccess=abs&issn=00287822&p=LitRC&sw=w&userGroupName=nclivemtoc&aty=ip.

Reich, R. B. (2018). *The Common Good*. Pisces Books.

Reichman, J. (2009). 'Compulsory Licensing of Patented Pharmaceutical Inventions: Evaluating the Options', *Journal of Law, Medicine & Ethics*, 37(2), pp. 247–63. https://www.cambridge.org/core/journals/journal-of-law-medicine-and-ethics/article/abs/comment-compulsory-licensing-of-patented-pharmaceutical-inventions-evaluating-the-options/549F58F3506E892E49EAFD44C3399AA3.

Ricardo, D. (1817). *On the Principles of Political Economy and Taxation*. John Murray.

Rikap, C., and Lundvall, B. A. (2021). *The Digital Innovation Race: Conceptualizing the Emerging New World Order*. Springer.

Rittel, H., and Webber, M. (1973). 'Dilemmas in a general theory of planning', *Policy Sciences*, 4(2), pp. 155–69. Available at https://doi.org/10.1007/BF01405730.

Rodrik, D. (2007). *One Economics, Many Recipes: Globalization, Institutions and Economic Growth*. Princeton University Press.

Rosa Neto, C., and Alves, E. A. (2024). *Perfil socio econômico e produtivs dos cafeicultores da região das Matas de Rondônia*. Embrapa Rondônia. (Série Documentos, 170.)

Rosini, A. M., Gomes, S. C., Palmisano, A., et al. (2024). 'Volunteer social work: A case study in a school of samba in Brazil'. *RISUS: Journal on Innovation and Sustainability*, 12(4), pp. 69–76.

Russell, B. (2019). *This small German town took back the power – and went fully renewable. The Conversation*. Available at https://theconversation.com/this-small-german-town-took-back-the-power-and-went-fully-renewable-126294.

Russell, B., and Milburn, K. (2018). 'What Can an Institution Do? Towards Public–Common Partnerships and a New Common-Sense.' *Renewal*, 26(4), pp. 45–55. Available at https://renewal.org.uk/wp-content/uploads/2020/09/milburn_russell_what_can_an_institution_do-1.pdf.

Ryan-Collins, J., Greenham, T., Werner, R., and Jackson, A. (2012). *Where Does Money Come From? A Guide to the UK Monetary and Banking System*. New Economics Foundation.

S&P Global. (2025). *S&P 500 Q4 2024 Buybacks Increase 7.4% and 2024 Expenditure Sets New Record by Increasing 18.5%; Earnings Per Share Increases from Buybacks Decline for the Quarter, as Q1 2025's Impact is Expected to Increase* (19 March). Available at https://press.spglobal.com/2025-03-19-S-P-500-Q4-2024-Buybacks-Increase-7-4-and-2024-Expenditure-Sets-New-Record-by-Increasing-18-5-Earnings-Per-Share-Increases-from-Buybacks-Decline-for-the-Quarter,-as-Q1-2025s-Impact-is-Expected-to-Increase.

S&P Global Sustainable1 and Capital Coalition (2024). *Unpriced Environmental Costs: The Top Externalities of the Global Market*. Available at https://capitalscoalition.org/wp-content/uploads/2024/07/Unpriced-Environmental-Costs-The-Top-Externalities-of-the-Global-Market-Report.pdf.

Sachs, J. D., Lafortune, G., Fuller, G., and Iablonovski, G. (2025). *Financing Sustainable Development to 2030 and Mid-Century*. Sustainable Development Report 2025. SDSN; Dublin University Press. Available at https://doi.org/10.25546/111909.

Saez, E., and Zucman, G. (2019a). 'Progressive Wealth Taxation', *Brookings Papers on Economic Activity*, pp. 437–511. Available at https://www.jstor.org/stable/26996616.

Saez, E., and Zucman, G. (2019b). *The Triumph of Injustice: How the Rich Dodge Taxes and How to Make Them Pay*. W. W. Norton & Company.

Saez, E., and Zucman, G. (2022). 'Wealth Taxation: Lessons from History and Recent Developments', *AEA Papers and Proceedings*, 112, pp. 58–62. Available at https://doi.org/10.1257/pandp.20221055.

Sainato, M. (2025). 'A bargaining breakdown and strikes: the bitter union fight at Starbucks', *Guardian*. Available at https://www.theguardian.com/business/2025/jan/14/starbucks-union-fight.

Sampat, B., and Lichtenberg, F. (2011). 'What Are The Respective Roles Of The Public And Private Sectors In Pharmaceutical Innovation?', *Health Affairs*, 30, pp. 332–9. Available at https://doi.org/10.1377/hlthaff.2009.0917.

Samuelson, P. A. (1947). *Foundations of Economic Analysis*. Harvard Economic Studies No. 80. Harvard University Press.

Samuelson, P. A. (1954). 'The Pure Theory of Public Expenditure', *Review of Economics and Statistics*, 36(4), pp. 387–9. Available at https://www.jstor.org/stable/1925895.

Sandel, M. J. (1982, 1998). *Liberalism and the Limits of Justice*. 2nd edn. Cambridge University Press. Available at https://doi.org/10.1017/CBO9780511810152.

Sandel, M. J. (2012). *What Money Can't Buy: The Moral Limits of Markets*. Allen Lane.

Sandel, M. J. (2020). *The Tyranny of Merit: What's Become of the Common Good?* Farrar, Straus and Giroux.

Sanders, L. M. (1997). 'Against deliberation', *Political Theory*, 25(3), pp. 347–76. Available at https://doi.org/10.1177/0090591797025003002.

Sandmo, A. (2007). 'Global public economics: Public goods and externalities', *Public Economics*, pp. 18–19. Available at https://doi.org/10.4000/economiepublique.4282.

Santos, B. de Sousa. (1998). 'Participatory Budgeting in Porto Alegre: Toward a Redistributive Democracy', *Politics & Society*, 26(4), pp. 461–510. Available at https://doi.org/10.1177/0032329298026004003.

Saunders, F. (2014). 'The promise of common pool resource theory and the reality of commons projects', *International Journal of the Commons*, 8(2), 636. Available at https://doi.org/10.18352/ijc.477.

Scherer, F. M., and Ross, D. R. (1990). *Industrial Market Structure and Economic Performance*. 3rd edn. Houghton Mifflin.

Schick, A. (2001). 'Reflections on the New Zealand Model', lecture at the New Zealand Treasury. Available at https://treasury.govt.nz/sites/default/files/2008-02/schick-rnzm01.pdf.

Schneider, E. C., Shah, A., Doty, M. M., Tikkanen, R., Fields, K., and Williams, R. D. (2021). *Mirror, Mirror 2021 – Reflecting Poorly: Health Care in the U.S. Compared to Other High-Income Countries*. Commonwealth Fund. Available at https://doi.org/10.26099/01dv-h208.

Schroders. (2019). *SustainEx: Examining the social value of corporate activities*. Available at https://mybrand.schroders.com/m/6cf6703eeb5bc0e7/original/SustainEx-short.pdf.

Schumpeter, J. A. (1942). *Capitalism, Socialism and Democracy*. Routledge.

Secretaría de la Mujer. (2023). *Respuesta derecho de petición* (Radicado No. 1-2023-006927). Gobierno de Colombia.

Self-Determination Fund. (n.d.). Available at https://www.selfdeterminationfund.org.au/.

Sen, A. (1979). Equality of What? Stanford University: Tanner Lectures on Human Values.

Sen, A. (2009). *The Idea of Justice*. Harvard University Press.

Sennett, R. (2018). *Building and Dwelling: Ethics for the City*. Allen Lane.

Serres, M. (1995). *The Natural Contract*. Translated by E. MacArthur and W. Paulson. University of Michigan Press.

Shelter. (n.d.). *Loss of social housing*. Available at https://england.shelter.org.uk/support_us/campaigns/social_housing/loss_of_social_housing.

Shelter (n.d.). *The story of social housing*. Available at https://england.shelter.org.uk/support_us/campaigns/social_housing/story_of_social_housing#:~:text=At%20the%20start%20of%20the,service%2C%20relying%20on%20ageing%20infrastructure.

Sieker, F. (2024). *Bridge-building instead of polarization: How algorithms can improve digital discourse*. Bertelsmann Stiftung. Available at https://www.bertelsmann-stiftung.de/en/our-projects/reframetech-algorithmen-fuers-gemeinwohl/project-news/bridge-building-instead-of-polarization-how-algorithms-can-improve-digital-discourse.

Simard, S. (2022). *Finding the Mother Tree: Uncovering the Wisdom and Intelligence of the Forest*. Penguin Books.

Simon, H. A., Egidi, M., Viale, R., and Marris, R. (2008). *Economics, Bounded Rationality and the Cognitive Revolution*. Edward Elgar Publishing.

Sismondi, J. C. L. S. de. (1819, 1990). *New Principles of Political Economy*. 2nd edn. Routledge.

Smith, A. (1759, 1761). *The Theory of Moral Sentiments*. 2nd edn. A. Millar, A. Kincaid and J. Bell.

Smith, A. (1776, 2005). *The Wealth of Nations*. W. Strahan; Hazelton, PA: Electronic Classic Series.

Smith, G. (2009). *Democratic Innovations: Designing Institutions for Citizen Participation*. Cambridge University Press.

Sobhani, S. (2019). 'From privatization to health system strengthening: how different International Monetary Fund (IMF) and World Bank policies impact health in developing countries', *Journal of the Egyptian Public Health Association*, 94. Available at https://doi.org/10.1186/s42506-019-0013-x.

Sommers, S. R. (2006). 'On racial diversity and group decision making: Identifying multiple effects of racial composition on jury deliberations', *Journal of Personality and Social Psychology*, 90(4), pp. 597–612. Available at https://psycnet.apa.org/doi/10.1037/0022-3514.90.4.597.

Stahel, W. R. (2013). 'Policy for material efficiency – sustainable taxation as a departure from the throwaway society', *Philosophical Transactions of the Royal Society A: Mathematical, Physical and Engineering Sciences*, 371(1986). Available at https://doi.org/10.1098/rsta.2011.0567.

Standing, A. (2011). *Making Transparency Work in Africa's Marine Fisheries*. Chr. Michelsen Institute.

Standing, G. (2011). *The Precariat: The New Dangerous Class*. Bloomsbury Academic.

Starik, M. (1995). 'Should trees have managerial standing? Toward stakeholder status for non-human nature', *Journal of Business Ethics*, 14, pp. 207–17. Available at https://doi.org/10.1007/BF00881435.

Stavins, R. N. (2010). *The Problem of the Commons: Still Unsettled After 100 Years*. NBER Working Paper Series, Working Paper 16403.

Stiglitz, J. E. (2000). 'The Contributions of the Economics of Information to Twentieth Century Economics', *Quarterly Journal of Economics*, 115(4), pp. 1441–78. Available at https://doi.org/10.1162/003355300555015.

Stiglitz, J. E. (2002). *Globalization and Its Discontents*. Penguin Books.

Stiglitz, J. E. (2010). *Freefall: America, Free Markets, and the Sinking of the World Economy*. W. W. Norton.

Stiglitz, J. E. (2012). *The Price of Inequality: How Today's Divided Society Endangers Our Future*. W. W. Norton.

Stiglitz, J. (2017). 'America Has a Monopoly Problem – and It's Huge', *The Nation*. Available at https://www.thenation.com/article/archive/america-has-a-monopoly-problem-and-its-huge.

Stiglitz, J. E., Sen, A., and Fitoussi, J. P. (2009). *Report by the Commission on the Measurement of Economic Performance and Social Progress*. European

Commission. Available at https://ec.europa.eu/eurostat/documents/8131721/8131772/Stiglitz-Sen-Fitoussi-Commission-report.pdf.

Studio Other Spaces (SOS). (2021). *Future Assembly.* Available at https://studiootherspaces.net/futureassembly/index.html.

Subsidy Tracker. (n.d.). *Discover Where Corporations are Getting Taxpayer Assistance Across the United States.* Available at https://subsidytracker.goodjobsfirst.org/.

Suresh, N., Ghaw, R., Obeng-Osei, R., and Wickstead, T. (2024). *Discussion paper no. 5: public investment and potential output.* Office for Budget Responsibility (OBR), August 2024. Available at https://obr.uk/public-investment-and-potential-output/.

Sustainable Energy for All (SEforALL). (2021). *Energizing Finance: Understanding the Landscape 2021.* Sustainable Energy for All and Climate Policy Initiative. Available at https://www.seforall.org/system/files/2021-10/EF-2021-UL-SEforALL.pdf.

Tang, A. (2024). 'Democracy in the age of AI', *RSA Journal*, 2. Available at https://www.thersa.org/rsa-journal/democracy-in-the-age-of-ai/.

Tax Justice Network. (2024). *State of Tax Justice 2024.* Available at https://taxjustice.net/reports/the-state-of-tax-justice-2024/.

Taylor, C. (1989). *Sources of the Self.* Harvard University Press.

Thaler, R. H., and Sunstein, C. R. (2008). *Nudge: Improving Decisions About Health, Wealth, and Happiness.* Yale University Press.

Thrall, P., Hochberg, M.E., Burdon, J. J., and Bever, J. D. (2007). 'Coevolution of symbiotic mutualists and parasites in a community context', *Trends in Ecology & Evolution*, 22(3), pp. 120–26. Available at: https://doi.org/10.1016/j.tree.2006.11.007.

Throsby, D. (2001). *Economics and Culture.* Cambridge University Press.

Tibbitt, A., and Edwards, R. (2021). 'Windfall: one third of Scotland's biggest wind farms linked to tax havens', *The Ferret*, 13 July. Available at https://theferret.scot/wind-farms-linked-to-tax-havens/.

Tirole, J. (2017). *Economics for the Common Good.* Princeton University Press.

Torkington, S. (2024). *What does the OECD global minimum tax mean for global cooperation?* World Economic Forum. Available at https://www.weforum.org/stories/2024/02/oecd-minimum-tax-rate/.

Torslov, T., Wier, L., and Zucman, G. (2023). 'The missing profits of nations', *Review of Economic Studies*, 90(3), pp. 1499–1534. Available at https://doi.org/10.1093/restud/rdac049.

Transnational Institute, The. (2018). *Financialisation: A Primer.* Available at https://www.tni.org/en/publication/financialisation-a-primer.

Trust for America's Health (TFAH). (2024). *The Impact of Chronic Underfunding on America's Public Health System 2024: Trends, Risks, and Recommendations*, 21 August. Available at https://www.tfah.org/wp-content/uploads/2024/08/2024-PublicHealthFunding-FINAL.pdf.

Tung, I., and Milani, K. (2018). *Curbing Stock Buybacks: A Crucial Step to Raising Worker Pay and Reducing Inequality.* Available at https://rooseveltinstitute.org/publications/curbing-stock-buybacks-crucial-step-raising-worker-pay-reduce-inequality/.

Tversky, A., and Kahneman, D. (1992). 'Advances in prospect theory: Cumulative representation of uncertainty', *Journal of Risk and Uncertainty*, 5, pp. 297–323. Available at https://doi.org/10.1007/BF00122574.

Unison. (2024). 'Closure of more than a thousand youth centres could have lasting impact on society', *Unison*, 15 June. Available at https://www.unison.org.uk/news/2024/06/closure-of-more-than-a-thousand-youth-centres-could-have-lasting-impact-on-society/.

United Nations (UN). (2023a). *Our Common Agenda: Report of the Secretary-General.* United Nations Publications.

United Nations (UN). (2023b). United Nations Secretary-General's SDG Stimulus to Deliver Agenda 2030. United Nations Publications.

United Nations Conference on Trade and Development (UNCTAD). (2024). 'Chapter IV: Rise, retreat and repositioning: Lessons from the global South'. In UNCTAD *2024 Trade and Development Report*. Available at https://unctad.org/system/files/official-document/tdr2024_en.pdf.

United Nations Conference on Trade and Development (UNCTAD). (2025). *Financing for development: Reforming global systems to drive progress.* Available at https://unctad.org/news/financing-development-reforming-global-systems-drive-progress.

United Nations Department of Economic and Social Affairs (UNDESA). (2025). *The Sustainable Development Goals Report 2025* (revision August 2025). Available at https://unstats.un.org/sdgs/report/2025/The-Sustainable-Development-Goals-Report-2025.pdf.

United Nations Educational, Scientific and Cultural Organization (UNESCO). (2022). *Re|Shaping Policies for Creativity: Addressing culture as a global public good*. Available at https://www.unesco.org/reports/reshaping-creativity/2022/en.

United Nations General Assembly (UNGA). (2025). *Terms of reference for a United Nations Framework Convention on International Tax Cooperation*. Available at https://financing.desa.un.org/sites/default/files/2025-01/n2501014_E.pdf.

Varian, H. R. (2010). *Intermediate Microeconomics: A Modern Approach*. 8th edn. W. W. Norton & Company.

Veblen, T. (1908). 'On the Nature of Capital: Investment, Intangible Assets, and the Pecuniary Magnate', *Quarterly Journal of Economics*, 23(1), pp. 104–36. Available at https://doi.org/10.2307/1883967.

Vestager, M. (2024). *Remarks by Executive Vice-President Vestager following the Court of Justice rulings on the Apple tax State aid and Google Shopping anti-trust cases*. European Commission. Available at https://ec.europa.eu/commission/presscorner/detail/cs/speech_24_4624.

Villa, C. (2024). *How cuts to clubs affected teen crime and education*. Institute for Fiscal Studies (IFS), 13 November. Available at https://ifs.org.uk/articles/how-cuts-youth-clubs-affected-teen-crime-and-education.

Vinnova. (2021). *School meals should speed up the transition to a sustainable food system*. Available at https://www.vinnova.se/en/m/sustainable-food-systems/the-public-meals-of-the-future/school-meals-should-speed-up-the-transition-to-a-sustainable-food-system/.

Vogl, V., Åhman, M. and Nilsson, L. J. (2021). 'The making of green steel in the EU: a policy evaluation for the early commercialization phase', *Climate Policy*, 21, pp. 78–92. Available at https://doi.org/10.1080/14693062.2020.1803040.

Voorberg, W. H., Bekkers, V. J. J. M., and Tummers, L. G. (2014). 'A Systematic Review of Co-Creation and Co-Production: Embarking on the social innovation journey', *Public Management Review*, 17(9), pp. 1333–57. Available at https://doi.org/10.1080/14719037.2014.930505.

Wandsworth Heritage Services. (1870a). Preservation of Wandsworth Common. Available at https://www.olbc.co.uk/wp-content/uploads/2023/10/IMG_2382-scaled.jpeg.

Wandsworth Heritage Services. (1870b). Preservation of Wandsworth Common. Available at https://www.olbc.co.uk/wp-content/uploads/2023/10/Amicable-Resolution-22nd-October-1870.pdf.

Wang, Q. S., Hua, Y. F., Tao, R., and Moldovan, N. C. (2021). 'Can health human capital help the Sub-Saharan Africa out of the poverty trap? An ARDL model approach', *Frontiers in Public Health*, 9. https://doi.org/10.3389/fpubh.2021.697826.

Weaver, H. N. (2001). 'Indigenous Identity: What Is It, and Who Really Has It?' *American Indian Quarterly*, 25(2), pp. 240–55. Available at https://www.jstor.org/stable/1185952.

Welch, J., and Gunther, M. (2009). 'Welch condemns share price focus', *Financial Times*, 12 March. Available at https://www.ft.com/content/294ff1f2-0f27-11de-ba10-0000779fd2ac.

Whitehouse, M., and Wasson, E. (2022). 'All About Stock Buybacks, a $1 Trillion Market Force', *Bloomberg* (18 Aug.). Available at https://www.bloomberg.com/news/articles/2022-08-18/all-about-stock-buybacks-a-1-trillion-market-force-quicktake.

Whyte, W. F., and Whyte, K. K. (1991). *Making Mondragón: The Growth and Dynamics of the Worker Cooperative Complex*. Cornell University Press.

Wilber, C. (1987). 'Economic theory and the common good'. In Oliver F. Williams and John W. Houck (eds.), *The Common Good and US Capitalism*, University Press of America.

Wilkinson, R., and Pickett, K. (2010). *The Spirit Level: Why Equality is Better for Everyone*. Penguin Books.

Williams, F. (2018). *Finding the beauty in bureaucracy: public service and planning*. Lendlease. Available at https://www.lendlease.com/au/insights/20180823-finding-the-beauty-in-bureaucracy/.

Williamson, O. E. (1981). *The Modern Corporation: Origins, Evolution, Attributes*. University of Chicago Press.

Wiltse, J. (2007). *Contested Waters: A Social History of Swimming Pools in America*. University of North Carolina Press.

Woodhouse, J., Samuel, H., and Zayed, Y. (2025). *Research Briefing: Future of public libraries.* House of Commons Library. Available at https://commonslibrary.parliament.uk/research-briefings/cdp-2025-0097/.

World Bank. (2013). *From Transparent Budgets to Shared Prosperity*. World Bank Group. Available at https://www.worldbank.org/en/news/feature/2013/12/03/from-transparent-budgets-shared-prosperity.

World Bank Group. (n.d.). *Mission 300 is Powering Africa: Connecting 300 million People to Electricity*. Available at https://www.worldbank.org/en/programs/energizing-africa.

World Economic Forum (WEF). (2021). *Closing the Loop on Energy Access in Africa.* World Economic Forum White Paper Series. Available at https://www.weforum.org/publications/closing-the-loop-on-energy-access-in-africa.

World Health Organization (WHO). (2020). 'COVID-19 Technology Access Pool'. Available at https://www.who.int/initiatives/covid-19-technology-access-pool.

World Health Organization (WHO). (2023). *Health for All: Transforming economies to deliver what matters. Final Report*. Available at https://cdn.who.int/media/docs/default-source/council-on-the-economics-of-health-for-all/council-eh4a_finalreport_web.pdf?sfvrsn=a6505c22_5&download=true.

World Health Organization (WHO). (2025). *Universal health coverage* (UHC). Available at https://www.who.int/news-room/fact-sheets/detail/universal-health-coverage-(uhc).

Xenophon (1994). *Oeconomicus*. Clarendon Press.

Xu, J., Marodon, R., Ru, X., Ren, X., and Wu, X. (2021). 'What are public development banks and development financing institutions? – qualification criteria, stylized facts and development trends', *China Economic Quarterly International*, 1(4), pp. 271–94. Available at https://doi.org/10.1016/j.ceqi.2021.10.001.

Xu, J., Marodon, R., Ru, X., Ren, X., and Wu, X. (2023). *The PBD and DFI Database July 2023*. Peking University and Agence Française de

Développement. Available at https://www.nse.pku.edu.cn/dfidatabase/datadownloading/index.htm.

Yuengert, A. M. (2001). 'The Common Good for Economists', *Faith & Economics*, 38 (Fall), pp. 1–9.

Zadek, S., Forstater, M., and Polacow, F. (2010). *The Amazon Fund: Radical simplicity and old ambition (Working Paper)*. Available at https://oxfordclimatepolicy.org/sites/default/files/Amazon_Fund_working_paper.pdf.

Zanotti, L. (2010). 'Cacophonies of Aid, Failed State Building and NGOs in Haiti: setting the stage for disaster, envisioning the future', *Third World Quarterly*, 31(5), pp. 755–71. Available at https://doi.org/10.1080/01436597.2010.503567.

Zucman, G. (2024). *A blueprint for a coordinated minimum effective taxation standard for ultra-high-net-worth individuals. Commissioned by the Brazilian G20 presidency*. Available at https://gabriel-zucman.eu/files/report-g20.pdf.

Index